MONETARY POLICY IMPLEMENTATION

Monetary Policy Implementation

THEORY—PAST—PRESENT

Ulrich Bindseil

OXFORD
UNIVERSITY PRESS

OXFORD
UNIVERSITY PRESS

Great Clarendon Street, Oxford OX2 6DP

Oxford University Press is a department of the University of Oxford.
It furthers the University's objective of excellence in research, scholarship,
and education by publishing worldwide in

Oxford New York

Auckland Bangkok Buenos Aires Cape Town Chennai
Dar es Salaam Delhi Hong Kong Istanbul Karachi Kolkata
Kuala Lumpur Madrid Melbourne Mexico City Mumbai Nairobi
São Paulo Shanghai Taipei Tokyo Toronto

Oxford is a registered trade mark of Oxford University Press
in the UK and in certain other countries

Published in the United States
by Oxford University Press Inc., New York

British Library Cataloguing in Publication Data

Data available

Library of Congress Cataloging in Publication Data

Data available

ISBN 0-19-927454-1 (hbk.)

1 3 5 7 9 10 8 6 4 2

Typeset by Newgen Imaging Systems (P) Ltd., Chennai, India
Printed in Great Britain
on acid-free paper by
Biddles Ltd., King's Lynn, Norfolk

Acknowledgements

I need to thank colleagues from the Deutsche Bundesbank and the European Central Bank who were so kind as to read earlier versions of the manuscript and to provide detailed comments: Henner Asche, Denis Blenck, Steen Ejerskov, Vitor Gaspar, Philipp Hartmann, Paul Mercier, Francesco Papadia, Mika Pösö, Franz Seitz, Leopold von Thadden, and Flemming Würtz. I am especially indebted to Ann-Marie Meulendyke, who pointed out various issues that needed further clarification. In addition, two anonymous referees provided very useful comments. Of course, the remaining mistakes go exclusively on to my account. I also wish to thank Sirkka Hämäläinen, Gertrude Tumpel-Gugerell and the management in the Directorate General Operations for encouragement. Opinions expressed in this book are not related to views of the European Central Bank.

Ulrich Bindseil
March 2004

Contents

List of Figures

List of Tables

Notation

j_t $= i_t - E(\pi_{t+1} | I_t)$, the expected real rate of interest in period t

π Inflation rate

OTHER

$P(X)$	Probability of event X
f_X	Density function of random variable X
$X \mid I_t$	Random variable X conditional on information available to relevant economic agent at time t
p	Price index
Y	Real GDP
v	Velocity of money
M	Monetary aggregate (but also: outstanding volume of open market operations)
CD	Customer deposits, that is, deposits of non-banks with banks
c	Cash holding ratio of non-banks, $= K/(K+CD)$
r	Reserve requirement ratio (also: natural rate of interest)
q	Individual reserve holdings of a bank
ω	Frequency of open market operations (per day)
W	Amount of collateral available to the banking system

SHOCKS (RANDOM VARIABLES)

$u, v, \mu, \varepsilon, \eta, \zeta$	are all identically independently distributed random variables with expected value zero.
$\tilde{x}$	a specific realization of the random variable x.

Introduction

AIMS AND SCOPE

Why is the committee responsible for defining US monetary policy called the 'Federal Open Market Committee' (FOMC) and not 'Federal Interest Rate Committee' (FIRC), even though it undisputedly sets and announces a target for the overnight interest rate? Why did the Fed for around eighty years offer a borrowing facility to banks, the 'discount window', at an interest rate *below* market rates, thus creating an arbitrage opportunity that needed to be restricted through moral suasion and by attaching to it some costly administrative procedures? Why has the Bank of England always conducted its open market operations as fixed interest rate tenders, while the Fed has always applied variable rate tenders? Why, in contrast, have the Bundesbank and the European Central Bank (ECB) tended to switch from time to time from one tender method to the other?

Besides addressing such questions, this book generally aims at clarifying today's perception of monetary policy implementation and how opinion in that field evolved in the course of the twentieth century. Monetary policy *implementation* is understood as the choice of an operational target of monetary policy and as the way this target is achieved from day to day with the help of monetary policy instruments. A book on this topic may be justified on two grounds. First, no comprehensive treatment of monetary policy implementation yet exists. Textbooks on monetary theory and policy often treat implementation only as a side issue, and today's central bankers would probably also find that books like Mishkin (2004) or Walsh (2003), for instance, do not really answer all the major questions arising from monetary policy implementation. Woodford (2003) contains a short theoretical treatment on monetary policy instruments which is in line with the approach presented here, but he does not go into the details of alternative operations techniques. Studies of monetary policy implementation are either of a technical nature (for example, Borio 1997) or treat only one country (for example, Board of Governors 1994) (see the short literature survey at the end of this Introduction). It is hence not easy to rapidly obtain a general understanding of the topic. Second, there appear to be a number of chronic misunderstandings in the domain of monetary policy implementation that deserve a treatment in the light of the views that have emerged among central banks in the past two decades. It will indeed be argued that some of the twentieth-century literature on the topic needs to be reassessed, and that a series of dubious conclusions were reached that have not only persisted in academic circles and infiltrated textbooks but also, at least temporarily, influenced central banks.

Two findings of the book should be mentioned at the outset. First, we will find Keynes and Friedman united in praising what will be called in this book the quantity oriented view on monetary policy implementation and in disliking the short-term interest rate as an operational target of monetary policy. One of the main aims of this book is to try to show that their position was wrong. Second, it will be argued that another author, William Poole, contributed two influential papers to the field, one of which (Poole 1968) appears most useful and which will provide the basis for almost all of the modelling in this book, while the other, published just two years later (Poole 1970), helped to perpetuate existing confusion. Both papers address the fundamental question of the relationship between interest rates and quantities in monetary policy implementation. While the former adopts a microeconomic approach and the latter a macroeconomic approach, there is no obvious link between the two. The main problem with some of the monetary policy implementation literature since 1970 is that it starts from the 1970 paper, not the 1968 one. For instance Walsh (2003) does not refer to the 1968 paper at all, while dedicating many pages to the literature based on the 1970 paper.

While recognizing the benefits of comparing the evolution of monetary policy implementation not only over time but also across different central banks, the focus of this text is, for the sake of brevity, limited to just three central banks. The choice fell on the US Federal Reserve System ('the Fed'), the Bank of England, and the Reichsbank/Deutsche Bundesbank. The last of these became, just before the end of the twentieth century, an integral part of the Eurosystem, which is therefore also included. The selection may be justified to some extent as follows. The *Fed* followed a remarkable policy of transparency since its first days. It is therefore relatively easy to follow what the Fed has done, or at least claimed to do, over time. Also, no central bank has been as open to new ideas from the academic world as the Fed. Finally, the dominance of American research in economics and the focus of US academic monetary economists on the Fed make it necessary to look at the Fed's practice in order to understand much of the literature. The *Bank of England*, by contrast, has not had the best traditions of transparency but may be seen as the world's front runner in central banking and central bank operations until at least the first decade of the twentieth century. Finally, the *German central banks* may be seen to represent one continental European central banking tradition. Also, in terms of monetary policy implementation, the Deutsche Bundesbank seems to have largely inspired the Eurosystem, which might suggest that its monetary policy implementation in the 1990s was particularly convincing to its fellow central banks when the framework for the euro was being prepared. Anecdotal evidence from other central banks will be mentioned only exceptionally. Of course, this focus on only three central banks will leave us ignorant about many interesting ideas and details from other central banks, which were probably often more effective and more elegant in their monetary policy implementation than the three examined here.

The text avoids more complicated mathematical models in order to remain accessible. However, on some occasions it was necessary to provide exact representations to the arguments. Only elementary stochastic calculus appeared to be necessary.

OUTLINE

Chapter 1 situates 'monetary policy implementation within the theory of monetary policy' by defining key concepts like the operational target and the instruments of monetary policy, the monetary policy strategy, intermediate and final targets of monetary policy, and so forth. Furthermore, it provides an overview of academic doctrine on monetary policy implementation, which constitutes the background to the actual approaches of central banks described in Chapters 4–7. This book generally contains as little as possible on the appropriate monetary policy *strategy*; that is, it says nothing about whether a central bank should consider monetary aggregates as an intermediate target, or target inflation directly, or follow any other kind of macroeconomic approach. Instead, it argues (see Chapter 8) that monetary policy strategy is not of key relevance to choosing an appropriate approach to monetary policy implementation, i.e. monetary policy is implemented through the control of short-term interest rates, irrespective of the strategy.

Chapter 2, the 'central bank balance sheet and the quantity side of monetary policy implementation', introduces monetary policy implementation as taking place in the framework of the central bank balance sheet. In principle, all changes of balance sheet items affect the reserve holdings of banks with the central bank and hence the scarcity of these reserves. The price of reserves, that is, the overnight interest rate, is, as the starting point of the yield curve, also the starting point of monetary policy transmission. Monetary policy operations (open market operations and standing facilities), being themselves items of the central bank balance sheet, are discussed in detail in Chapters 4, 5, and 6. In addition, however, the central bank balance sheet contains various 'autonomous' balance sheet items, which are not, or only partially, controlled by the central bank (that is, items not representing monetary policy instruments, such as banknotes, net foreign assets, or the net position towards the Treasury). Therefore, to neutralize the effects of changes of these factors on the scarcity of reserves, the central bank normally needs to adjust correspondingly its open market operations. Indeed, most if not practically all of the changes of outstanding open market operations are (and should be) reactions to changes of autonomous liquidity factors, and do not reflect changes of the monetary policy stance.

Chapter 3, 'the control of short-term interest rates—a simple model', explains how the central bank can actually steer short-term interest rates, and what implications this has for its monetary policy balance sheet items such as open market operations and recourse to standing facilities. The simple model, which is based on Poole (1968), is supposed to be general enough to be applicable in principle to all circumstances of monetary policy implementation. It is used on various occasions throughout the book to understand different tools and approaches.

Chapters 4 to 6 each treat one of the three main instruments of monetary policy in more detail and with some focus on their historical evolution. Chapter 4 starts with 'standing facilities', since these were the first, if not the only, monetary policy instruments until the beginning of the twentieth century. Standing facilities are used at the discretion of individual commercial banks: that is, the central bank defines only the conditions but its commercial counterparts decide on the actual use. The different types of standing facilities are explained and the evolution of their specification is reviewed. In particular, the previous US view on standing facilities, leading to the discount window rate being set below market rates until the end of 2002, is discussed.

Chapter 5 turns to 'open market operations', probably the instrument considered key to monetary policy implementation during most of the twentieth century. In contrast to standing facilities, each open market operation is conducted at the initiative of the central bank. Open market operations were originally understood as outright purchases or sales of securities, normally government paper, in the 'open market', that is, the inter-bank market. In contrast, today they mainly or exclusively consist in repurchase operations or collateralized credit operations with limited maturity (for example, two weeks) conducted in the form of specific auctions, that is, not really in the 'open market'. Today's open market operations are therefore, especially if conducted regularly at a high frequency with predictable interest rates and allotment amounts, not as different from standing facilities as they originally were. Alternative specifications of open market operations and their use by the three selected central banks are discussed.

Chapter 6 reviews the instrument of 'reserve requirements'. Originating in the US in the nineteenth century and hence from pre-Fed regulations, which were supposed to address the problem of bank runs, they spread over many countries after the Second World War. While monetary policy motivations and specifications of reserve requirements changed dramatically over time, it is plausible that central banks' preference for this instrument is partially explained by the income it generates as long as required reserves remain unremunerated. In recent years, one of the motivations of reserve requirements has persisted, namely, to contribute to stabilizing short-term interest rates.

Chapter 7 reviews the evolution of 'central banks' practice of monetary policy implementation in the twentieth century', that is, how the three selected central banks actually used their instruments to achieve their operational targets in the twentieth century. Special attention is devoted to the various US approaches, which focused temporarily on quantitative targets such as 'borrowed', 'free', and 'non-borrowed' reserves.

Chapter 8 summarizes the contemporaneous views of the selected central banks and argues that an astonishingly homogeneous 'new view on monetary policy implementation' has emerged in the last ten or twenty years. The key proposition of the new view is that the appropriate operational target of monetary policy implementation is the short-term interest rate, and that this is the case independently of the characteristics of financial markets and independently of the monetary policy strategy. Furthermore, the new view considers that the operational framework and the day-to-day steering of short-term interest rates should aim primarily at transparency, simplicity, and efficiency.

GENERAL LITERATURE ON MONETARY POLICY IMPLEMENTATION

Detailed comparative studies of the approaches to monetary policy implementation by different central banks include, for instance, Palgrave (1903), Amatayakul (1942), Fousek (1957), Tamagna (1963), Batten et al.

(1989), Kasman (1993), Bisignano (1996), Borio (1997), Balino and Zamalloa (1997), and Blenck et al. (2001). BIS (1997) includes, in addition to the paper by Borio, detailed descriptions of operational procedures of thirteen central banks written by staff members of these respective central banks. Kneeshaw and Van den Bergh (1989) adopt simultaneously cross-country and evolutionary perspectives, limited however to the 1980s. Some textbooks on monetary economics devote space to what they call monetary policy implementation, but do not really go beyond a discussion of monetary policy strategy (for example, Walsh 2003). Mishkin (2004) goes into more detail than other textbooks, but seems to support a quantity-oriented approach to monetary policy implementation, which has played a more limited role in the practice of central banks during the last two decades (although the 2004 edition of his book is more differentiated in this respect than previous ones). Bofinger (2001) and Görgens et al. (forthcoming) describe well the Eurosystem's monetary policy implementation. Woodford (2001*b*, 2003) contain short theoretical treatments of monetary policy implementation as practised by, for example, Australia, Canada, and New Zealand. There are also older books focusing on monetary policy implementation, such as, for instance, Woodworth (1972), Young (1973), and Jarchow (1974), who, however, limit their analysis to their respective countries. Another good introduction to monetary policy implementation are central bank booklets on the topic, such as, for instance, the publications of the Board of Governors of the Federal Reserve System (1954, 1974, 1994), Deutsche Bundesbank (1995), Reichsbank (1900, 1925*a*), and ECB (2001*c*). However, they are necessarily uncritical and also each focuses only on one case. Regular central bank publications such as monthly or quarterly bulletins and annual reports usually also describe monetary policy implementation. ECB (2002*a*) is a detailed description of the framework for monetary policy implementation of the Eurosystem. For the US, there is also a tradition of semi-official descriptions of monetary policy implementation by central bank staff, such as Goldenweiser (1925), Burgess (1927), and Meulendyke (1998). Another possible source of insights into monetary policy implementation is histories of central banks with details on central bank operations, although they do not cover the more recent past: King (1936), Wood (1939), Clapham (1944), and Sayers (1976) for the Bank of England; Friedman and Schwartz (1963) and Meltzer (2003) for the US Fed.

1

Monetary Policy Implementation within the Theory of Monetary Policy

This chapter provides some key definitions and gives a first broad overview of the evolution of 'academic' thinking on monetary policy implementation.

1.1 SOME TERMINOLOGY

A series of misunderstandings have arisen in the domain of monetary policy implementation due to ambiguous or varying definitions of a few key concepts. The following definitions, which will be used throughout this book, reflect as much as possible the mainstream use of the terminology in recent years. The terms are divided into two groups, on 'implementation' and 'monetary macroeconomics'. This book is obviously about the former, but it is worth defining the latter to allow for a clear distinction.

1.1.1 *Implementation*

Monetary policy implementation consists of three elements. The first is the selection of an operational target of monetary policy (for example, the overnight market interest rate). The second is the establishment of an operational framework that permits the central bank to control the selected operational target (for example, setting up the instruments, selecting counterparts, defining a list of eligible collateral). The third is to use the instruments on a daily basis in order to achieve the operational target.

An *operational target* is an economic variable that the central bank wants to control and indeed can control to a very large extent on a daily basis through the use of its monetary policy instruments. It is the variable whose level the monetary policy decision-making committee of the central bank actually decides upon in each of its meetings. The operational target thus (*a*) gives guidance to the implementation officers in the central bank on what to do on a day-by-day basis in the inter-meeting period, and (b) serves to communicate the stance of monetary policy to the public. Today, there is consensus among central banks to the effect that the short-term inter-bank interest rate is the appropriate operational target. In the past, however—and some textbooks still support this view—it was argued that quantitative concepts, such as the monetary base, or some reserves concept would be preferable. Also, some central banks applied a quantitative operational target, at least in theory. The Fed, for instance, experimented with 'free reserves', 'money market conditions', 'borrowed reserves', and 'non-borrowed reserves' as operational targets (see Chapter 2 for definitions of these concepts).

A *monetary policy instrument* is a tool available to the central bank that it can use to reach its operational target. Today, central banks use three such tools, namely standing facilities, open market operations, and reserve requirements. In the past (mainly from the 1930s to the early 1980s), a further category of instruments was the so-called direct methods of monetary control, like retail interest rate ceilings or margin requirements (see, for instance, M. Friedman, 1960, for a critique of these instruments). 'Direct methods' are not treated in this book since their inappropriateness, at least in a modern market environment, has long been recognized. Unfortunately, the term 'instrument' was used in an ambiguous way in, for instance, the influential article of Poole (1970) to designate both operational and intermediate targets (short-term interest rates and monetary aggregates).

1.1.2   *Monetary macroeconomics*

The *monetary policy strategy* of the central bank may be conceived as being composed of two elements. The first is the macroeconomic model of the transmission mechanism the central bank has in mind, that is, how it thinks that the operational target, indicator variables, intermediate targets, and random shocks are linked to its final targets. The second element is the way the central bank, within this model, adjusts its operational target on the basis of new information and communicates it to the public in order to exert influence on its intermediate and/or final targets. This book does not at all look at issues relating to the monetary policy strategy. As will repeatedly be argued, it is indeed possible to analyse monetary policy implementation without considering the macroeconomic strategy.

The *monetary policy stance* at a certain moment in time consists of the prevailing value of the operational target and the expected changes thereof that result from the central bank's communication. Whether a certain level of the operational target variable reflects a tight or loose stance cannot be determined independently of the circumstances. For instance, a target short-term interest rate of 5 per cent would be very tight in a deflationary environment (for example, Japan in 2002) but would be loose in a highly inflationary one (for example, Turkey in 2002). Thus, the tightness of the stance is reflected in the difference between the operational target and a 'neutral' level, that is, one that does not create pressure on the final target variables to change.

The *final target* of monetary policy is the economic variable that the central bank eventually aims at. Thus, operational and intermediate targets are nothing more than means towards reaching the final target without a specific value of their own. The final target of a central bank is often enshrined in its statutes. The ECB, for instance, according to Article 105(1) of the EU Treaty, has the primary objective of maintaining price stability. The Fed's final targets are less clear-cut: they include economic growth in line with the economy's potential, a high level of employment, stable prices, and moderate long-term interest rates (Board of Governors 1994: 2). Under the Bank Act of 1998, the Bank of England's objective in relation to monetary policy is 'to maintain price stability and subject to that, to support the economic policy of Her Majesty's Government, including its objectives for growth and employment'.

An *intermediate target* is an economic variable that (*a*) the central bank can control with a reasonable time lag and with a reasonable degree of precision, and (*b*) which is in a relatively stable or at least predictable relationship with the final target of monetary policy, of which the intermediate target is a leading indicator. The typical intermediate target is a monetary aggregate like M1 or M3,[1] an exchange rate, or some medium or longer-term interest rate. It is assumed that, via its operational target, the intermediate target can be controlled or at least influenced in a significant way. The popularity of the intermediate target concept has decreased considerably over the last two decades.

An *indicator variable* is an economic variable that at the moment when it can be observed contains valuable information (that is, information not available at the same time from other variables) on how the central bank may need to adjust the level of its operational target variable in order to achieve its final target as precisely as possible. Indicator variables contain fully exogenous variables such as the oil price, the likelihood of the outbreak of a war, or major technological innovations, but also more

---

[1] M1 is defined as the sum of currency in circulation and sight deposits of non-banks with banks. M3 is normally defined as M1 plus time deposits of up to four years and savings deposits with up to three months' notice.

endogenous variables like monetary aggregates. Whereas for an intermediate target the central bank may reason 'information from the intermediate target variable suggests that the level of the operational target
variable needs to be changed to keep the intermediate target on track',
for a more endogenous indicator variable it would reason: 'information
from the indicator variable suggests that the level of the operational target needs to be changed to keep the final target on track'. In practice,
there is a continuum between the extremes of pure indicator variables
and pure intermediate targets. Today, when intermediate targets have lost
their popularity, one would tend to prefer to classify most if not all variables that were once considered to be intermediate targets as indicator
variables.

The rest of this chapter deals mainly with the choice of the operational
target, and how views on that issue have evolved. Today's views and
practice on monetary policy implementation and in particular on the
choice of the operational target have returned to what economists considered adequate 100 years ago, namely, to target short-term interest
rates; and much twentieth-century thinking, which regarded quantities
as suitable operational targets, is today nearly unanimously rejected by
the central banking community. A comprehensive discussion of why
short-term interest rates are the appropriate operational target of monetary policy may be found in Chapter 8.

1.2   BEFORE 1914

Before reviewing the main contributions to the theory of monetary policy in the twentieth century, one should briefly look at their origins in
the pre-1914 world, that is, normally the world of metal convertibility.[2]
There was little doubt especially towards the end of this period that central bank policy meant in practice 'Bank rate' policy, meaning that short-
term interest rates were the operational target of monetary policy. The
Bank rate was the rate at which the Bank of England was discounting on
demand first-class bills of exchange; that is, it was the rate it charged on
the borrowing facility it offered to the market. All central banks on the
European continent set similar discount rates. In the following, five

---

[2] Meltzer (2003: 19–64) provides a more detailed survey of the pre-Fed and hence pre-1914 history of thought on central banking, though with a different focus. He also describes classical debates
like the bouillonist controversy or the banking vs. currency school debate, which we leave aside for
brevity's sake. A detailed survey on Bank of England policy (and relating theories) in the first half
of the nineteenth century is provided by Wood (1939).

major contributions of the nineteenth-century authors will be high-lighted which still have a key importance today.[3]

1.2.1 Central bank policy is 'Bank rate' policy

Already Henry Thornton, who is today praised as the most advanced monetary policy theorist before the twentieth century (see, for example, Meltzer 2003),[4] views central bank policy as 'Bank rate' policy, and analyses how Bank rate policy should be conducted. The idea, further elaborated by Wicksell, that Bank rate needs to follow the real rate of capital in order to allow the expansion of money and hence inflation to be controlled was probably first spelled out by him:

In order to ascertain how far the desire of obtaining loans at the bank [the Bank of England] may be expected at any time to be carried, we must enquire into the subject of the quantum of profit likely to be derived from borrowing there under the existing circumstances. This is to be judged by considering two points: the amount, first, of interest to be paid on the sum borrowed; and secondly, of the mercantile or other gain to be obtained by the employment of the borrowed capital . . . We may, therefore, consider this question as turning principally on a comparison of the rate of interest taken at the bank with the current rate of mercantile profit.

The bank is prohibited, by the state of [usury] law, from demanding, even in time of war, an interest of more than five per cent, which is the same rate at which it discounts in a period of profound peace. It might, undoubtedly, at all seasons, sufficiently limit its paper by means of the price at which it lends, if the legislature did not interpose an obstacle to the constant adoption of this principle of restriction. (H. Thornton 1802: 254)

The idea that the central bank should 'limit its paper by means of the price at which it lends' seems to anticipate precisely monetary control techniques applied for instance during the 1970s in the US. A key point of Thornton is that the Bank rate is *always* an adequate and sufficient tool of central bank policy to prevent over-issuance of money and hence inflation, and that, in the case of the Bank of England, only the usury laws applicable until 1833 prevented the Bank from systematically using this tool. The right way to set the interest rate seems to be to follow the 'rate of mercantile profit', although Thornton is careful enough to not argue that the two rates must necessarily be equivalent.

---

[3] For a detailed treatment of theories of monetary policy implementation before 1858, see Wood (1939). Apart from H. Thornton (1802), the focus here is on post-1858 theories.

[4] He had the advantage, from today's perspective, of having written during a period of a paper standard in the UK (1797–1821). Therefore, in contrast to other authors, his thinking did not mainly focus on the protection of the central banks' gold reserves through Bank rate policy.

Thornton's concept of a 'rate of mercantile profit' looks in fact much like the better-known concept of the 'natural rate' described in 1898 by Wicksell (1936: 102) as follows:

There is a certain rate of interest on loans which is neutral in respect to commodity prices, and tends neither to raise nor to lower them. This is necessarily the same as the rate of interest which would be determined by supply and demand if no use were made of money and all lending were effected in the form of real capital goods. It comes to much the same thing to describe it as the current value of the natural rate of interest on capital.

That, under stable prices, the rate of interest on money has to correspond to the real rate of interest, which can be thought of as independent of the 'monetary sphere' of the economy, is indeed implied by simple arbitrage logic. Consider the arbitrage diagram (Fig. 1.1) by Richter (1990: 55), which represents a very basic economy with two periods ('today' and 'tomorrow') and two good types ('wheat' and 'money'), such that there are practically four distinct goods and three independent relative prices. The diagram needs to be read as follows: the relative prices between the four goods W1, W2, \$1, \$2 are indicated on each of the arrows, whereby the price is understood as the units of the good at the origin of the arrow that are needed to obtain one unit of the good at the end of the arrow. For instance, one needs P1 units of money today (\$1) to obtain one unit of wheat today (W1). All prices refer to contracts made today. The real rate of interest is r, since one will obtain $1 + r$ units of W2 for one unit of W1. The price P2 is the amount of money today (\$1) one needs to pay today to obtain a unit of wheat tomorrow (W2). The price P2* is the amount of money tomorrow (\$2) that is needed to obtain a unit of wheat tomorrow (the future price of wheat).

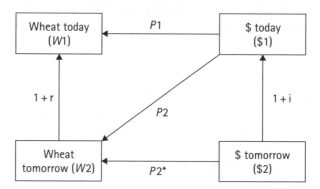

Figure 1.1   *Simple arbitrage diagram illustrating the idea of the natural rate of interest*

Source: Richter (1990).

The arbitrage logic allows establishing some basic relationships between relative prices by moving within the diagram from one good to the other via different paths. There are three ways to trade wheat tomorrow against wheat today, that should all in an arbitrage equilibrium be equivalent:

$W2 \Rightarrow W1$:	$(1 + r)W1 = W2$
$W2 \Rightarrow \$1 \Rightarrow W1$:	$(P1/P2)W1 = W2$
$W2 \Rightarrow \$1 \Rightarrow \$1 \Rightarrow W1$:	$(P1(1 + i)/P2^*)W1 = W2$

This allows establishing the following two arbitrage relationships:

$$1 + r = P1/P2 = P1(1 + i)/P2^* \tag{1.1}$$

Defining the inflation rate π according to $(1 + \pi) = P2^*/P1$, equation (1.1) also includes the so-called *Fisher equation*:

$$1 + r = (1 + i)/(1 + \pi) \tag{1.2}$$

which is normally more known under its linear simplified form $i = r + \pi$. From the arbitrage diagram and equation (1.2) it is obvious that, if in equilibrium the interest on money (the 'Bank rate') corresponds to the 'real rate of capital', then there will be no inflation. Wicksell was, of course, aware that the real rate of interest was not stable, and concluded, like Thornton, that the rate of interest on money needed to be adjusted accordingly over time to maintain price stability. Wicksell (1936: 102) was also well aware that the dynamics of money, interest rates and prices outside equilibrium were much more complex to describe and indeed admitted to not having a clear solution to this problem:

But whether this result is achieved with sufficient rapidity to prevent a continual rise in prices at times when the capital rate is rising (so that the money rate is left below the natural rate), or to obviate a gradual fall in prices at times when the capital rate is falling (and consequently the money rate is left higher than the natural rate), seems a priori very doubtful. This question involves a survey of various complications which unfortunately requires a far more intimate insight into the secrets of banking technique than is at my disposal.

Although indeed simple arbitrage logic does not allow dynamic issues to be addressed, basic intuition on the transmission mechanism can still be formulated within the framework of the arbitrage diagram. When, for example, the central bank does not pay attention to an increase of the real rate of capital and the money interest rate therefore is too cheap for a given expected inflation rate, then arbitrageurs will borrow more money to invest in real goods today and to sell real goods tomorrow. This will increase the quantity of money and eventually prices today to levels above those originally prevailing. If, in contrast, the central bank does not note a decrease in the rate of return of real capital (or if the central bank perceives inflation to be excessive and it takes the initiative to increase money rates), then it becomes a loss-making activity to borrow money to invest in real capital, the demand for money will thus decrease, the demand for goods today will decrease, and inflation rates will tend to fall. Still, the arbitrage diagram itself does not provide a framework for really capturing this logic. Section 1.5 will review how macroeconomic modelling in the 1990s made for a better understanding of the disequilibrium case.

This intuitive idea of a transmission mechanism based on the comparison of the interest rates on money and on capital goods was explored in various ways by monetary economists around 1900 and in the following decades. Cassel (1928: 517), who was one of the last academic authors for more than 50 years to advocate unambiguously that central bank policy should be Bank rate policy, described the core issue of monetary policy as follows:

By what principles shall the central bank be guided in fixing its rate? The answer is easy enough as soon as we have perceived that there exists a definitive equilibrium rate of interest. If the bank rate is lower than this equilibrium rate, people will go to the bank for covering their needs for capital, and the bank will have to issue notes in order to meet such needs. This leads to an unnecessarily large issue of notes, and fresh purchasing power is created without any more goods having been produced, and this increase of nominal purchasing power is bound to force up prices. Thus the result is simply an inflation of the currency . . .

The conclusion from this is clear. Stability of prices is possible only when the bank rate is kept equal to the equilibrium rate of interest. When this is done, the bank does not interfere with the capital market, which is therefore left to find its natural equilibrium. We have here arrived at the exact solution of the central problem of money, and we shall see that this solution immediately clears up the whole series of difficult questions connected with this central problem. There can be no other solution, and other formulas that have been represented as being solutions of the problem of monetary stabilization are theoretically defective.

The cogency of this passage may reflect the fact that it was written when the quantitative approach to monetary policy implementation was rapidly gaining ground in the US, that is, when many observers were becoming convinced that monetary policy implementation was about controlling the monetary base or another narrow monetary quantity (see Section 1.3).

1.2.2 *Can the central bank control the money market interest rate?*

King (1936) reports about various debates in the London financial market during the entire nineteenth and even eighteenth century on whether (*a*) the Bank of England was able to set Bank rate as it wished and whether (*b*) there was a well-defined relationship between Bank rate and the market rate (again, see also Wood 1939). If both questions are answered affirmatively, then the central bank can indeed be responsible for short-term market interest rates. The Bank of England often tended to deny such responsibility, while the market tended to take the opposite view. Denying full responsibility for short-term interest rates has two key implications for central banks. First, it allows central banks to deny responsibility for all effects of short-term interest rate developments, such as the direct financial impact on groups of economic agents ('borrowers' and 'lenders') and the economic imbalances that may arise from an inadequate level of interest rates. Second, it leads the central bank, which needs to admit to control something, to focus more on quantities. Control of quantities through means other than the price was typically exercised in nineteenth-century central banking by loosening or tightening eligibility criteria for bills accepted for discounting. Other means, like restrictions of the counterparts admitted to discount, or moral suasion, were also used at some time. The US Fed in particular would return to such techniques in the twentieth century.

A detailed nineteenth-century treatment of the question whether the Bank of England was able to set Bank rate as it wished stems from Bagehot (1873: 56). Of course, the question at that time was linked to the gold standard. Bagehot argues that the Bank of England is such a large player in the inter-bank market that it always clears it, such that the price it sets is always the marginal price, which becomes the market price:

Many persons believe that the Bank of England has some peculiar power of fixing the value of money. They see that the Bank of England varies its minimum rate of discount from time to time, and that, more or less, all other banks follow its lead, and charge much as it charges. The Bank of England used to be a predominant, and is still a most important dealer in money. It lays down the least price at which alone it will dispose of its stock, and this, for the most part, enables other dealers to obtain that price, or something near it.

However, Bagehot (1873: 59) also warns that the Bank of England has no power to fix the value of money (under the gold standard) *in the long run*, since the value of money is determined in the same way as the value of any commodity. He derives from that a responsibility on the part of the Bank of England to steer interest rates in the short term so as to preserve the stability of the system, that is, by avoiding uncontrollable dynamics of gold reserves, interest rates, growth, and prices. Thus he outlines how Bank rate policy should be conducted:

These considerations enable us to estimate the responsibility which is thrown on the Bank of England by our system, and by every system on the bank or banks who by it keep the reserve of bullion or of legal tender exchangeable for bullion. These banks can in no degree control the permanent value of money, but they can completely control its momentary value . . . If the dominant banks manage ill, the rate of interest will at one time be excessively high, and at another time excessively low: there will be first a pernicious excitement, and next a fatal collapse. But if they manage well, the rate of interest will not deviate so much from the average rate, it will neither ascend so high nor descend so low. As far as anything can be steady the value of money will then be steady, and probably in consequence trade will be steady too— at least a principal cause of periodical disturbance will have been withdrawn from it.

Again, the idea of a 'natural' level of the money interest rate developed further by Wicksell (1936) is at least in principle anticipated.

As for the question whether there is a well-defined relationship between Bank rate and market rates, Chapter 4 will review in more detail the extensive nineteenth-century debates. Eventually, just before 1900, consensus emerged on a clear affirmative answer with the development of techniques for 'making Bank rate effective', that is, bringing market rates close to Bank rate. The modelling of the relationship between market rates and central bank rates in Chapter 3 will summarize today's view of the question.

1.2.3   *The inherent instability of the money market when left alone by the central bank*

The inherent instability of the money market when left alone by the central bank was first described by Bagehot (1873: 58). It results from the combination of the volatility of the inelastic supply of central bank reserves with the extremely low short-term interest rate elasticity of the demand for reserves in the money market. It is one of the key arguments for choosing rates, and not quantities, as operational targets. According to Bagehot:

But though the value of money is not settled in an exceptional way, there is nevertheless a peculiarity about it, as there is about many articles. It is a commodity subject to great fluctuations of value and those fluctuations are easily produced by a slight excess or a slight deficiency of quantity. Up to a certain point money is a necessity. If a merchant has acceptances to meet tomorrow, money he must and will find today at some price or other. And it is this urgent need of the whole body of merchants which runs up the value of money so wildly and to such a height in a great panic. On the other hand, money easily becomes a 'drug', as the phrase is, and there is soon too much of it.

The extremely low interest-rate elasticity of demand and supply in the money market (unless supply is made elastic by the central bank) did not hold only in Bagehot's time, but actually throughout central bank history. Take as one further illustration the Macmillan Committee hearings in 1929 (Sayers 1976: iii. 148):

Governor Ernest Musgrave Harvey: After all, you must remember that it takes very little, really, to swing over from a shortage [should be 'excess'] of cash in the market to a tightness of cash. One man in the market with 250,000 Pound Sterling to lend when everybody has got what they want can go around, as we know has been done, and try to lend it here and there all round in the market, and nobody will take it, and we are then told 'money is unlendable' . . . But another day you may have one man who wants 100,000 Pound Sterling and who goes to one lender after another and says, 'Please can you give me 100,000?' And in every case receives the same reply, 'Impossible'. The story soon gets round, and people say 'Money seems tight today'.

The relationship described by Bagehot and Harvey implies that, if the central bank does not systematically neutralize exogenous money market shocks, short-term rates would regularly be either zero or be extremely high. This assessment is confirmed by modern central bank experience. Expectations of the likelihood of the two states in the future would determine longer-term interest rates, which would probably also fluctuate wildly and most of the time have rather extreme values. This obviously does not provide the best environment for a systematic and sensitive control of credit, money, and prices. The observation of Bagehot, together with the fact that the short-term supply and demand shocks that constantly hit the money market have nothing to do with macroeconomic textbook shocks (such as, for example, shifts of the IS and LM curves), will be key to understanding why the Poole (1970) approach is eventually misleading (see Section 1.4).

1.2.4 *Distinguishing between 'autonomous liquidity factors' and variables that have information content with regard to the optimal stance of monetary policy*

Another important point noted already by, for example, Thornton and Bagehot, and which is still most relevant to monetary policy implementation today, is the distinction between 'autonomous liquidity factors' and variables that reveal something of the optimal stance of monetary policy. Today (see Chapter 2), all central bank balance-sheet items other than reserve holdings and monetary policy instruments are 'autonomous liquidity factors', which normally tell the central bank very little about the appropriate stance of monetary policy (like for example banknotes or Treasury deposits with the central bank—see Chapter 2). Therefore, changes of autonomous factor balance-sheet items do not require changes in the policy stance as reflected in the short-term interest rate target. Instead, the central bank needs only to offset through open market operations the change in autonomous factors in order to avoid effects on short-term market rates, as described in Section 1.2.3.

Under the gold standard, in contrast, the development of the central bank balance-sheet item 'gold reserves' could indicate something about the appropriate stance, since the main ultimate goal of the central bank was to maintain the gold convertibility of the currency. It is in this context that one needs to see the classical distinction, also made by Thornton and Bagehot, between an *internal* and an *external* drain of gold. The former was considered in the way that today's central banks consider autonomous liquidity factors, and it was therefore proposed to let the implied change of gold reserves happen without adjusting Bank rate. It was felt that internal drains always reflected transitory developments, like seasonal demand for currency or financial unrest. An *external* drain, in contrast, was regarded as a potential threat to convertibility and hence possibly answered by a change in the monetary policy stance, that is, an increase in Bank rate, reflecting the insight that an external drain due to an international disequilibrium of prices was unlikely to be transitory so long as policy did not react.

1.2.5 *Monetary policy operations in crisis situations: (I) liquidity crisis*

During the first half of the nineteenth century, the Bank of England twice aggravated a banking crisis—in 1825 and in 1847—by refusing to lend any more in a situation of exceptional need for currency due to financial panic. In both cases, it recognized however after a while that not lending meant turning a bad situation into a catastrophe; eventually it lent freely, so bringing the crises to an end. The Bank of England's action in 1825, after having had this insight, was summarized in the famous words of Bank member Jeremiah Harman in the Lords' Committee in

1832 (quoted in King 1936: 36):

We lent . . . by every possible means, and in modes that we never had adopted before; we took in stock of security, we purchased Exchequer bills, we made advances on Exchequer bills, we not only discounted outright, but we made advances on deposits of bills to an immense amount; in short, by every possible means consistent with the safety of the Bank; . . . seeing the dreadful state in which the public were, we rendered every assistance in our power.

In the second half of the nineteenth century, the Bank of England did not repeat these mistakes, which ensured that liquidity problems of individual banks did not normally develop into an overall financial sector crisis. The US Federal Reserve System was set up in 1914 largely in order to solve the problem of recurring liquidity crises and bank runs.

Today, Walter Bagehot's *Lombard Street* (1873) is often cited as the origin of the insight that, in cases of an exceptional demand for central bank money due to a financial crises, the central bank should lend freely while accepting a broad range of collateral.[5] However, Bagehot was probably only popularizing an idea that was by this time already well established within the Bank of England. It is still to the credit of Bagehot that it became a universally known key principle of central banking. Recent examples of its application include the US stock market crash of 1987 and September 11, 2001. After the crash on Black Monday (19 October 1987), the Fed issued a press release with the following statement:

The Federal Reserve, consistent with the responsibilities as the nation's central bank, affirmed today its readiness to serve as a source of liquidity to support the economic and financial system.

A similar statement was issued on September 11, 2001, and the Fed indeed gave easy access to its discount window on that and following days. Even the ECB, less directly concerned, reacted to the attacks by publishing the following press release at around 9 p.m. on September 11:

After the unprecedented and tragic events in the United States today, the Eurosystem stands ready to support the normal functioning of the markets. In particular, the Eurosystem will provide liquidity to the markets, if need be.

---

[5] Of course, credit risks appear higher in a situation of financial crisis than under normal circumstances, which would suggest being even more prudent in respect of the collateral accepted. However, this kind of credit-risk consideration becomes secondary when lending by the central bank becomes crucial to the stability of the financial system in general. Even when the central bank considers only its own financial interests, it turns out to be preferable to lend new funds against a wider set of collateral than normal, instead of putting the entire asset side of the balance sheet at risk.

In the succeeding days it implemented exceptional liquidity-injecting open market operations, providing in total more than €100 billion to the market.

In sum, it will appear throughout this book that what one may call the 'Bank rate school' of central banking, being associated with names such as Thornton, Bagehot and Wicksell, developed various concepts that still appear valid today. Many of those were, however, temporarily buried under the influence of the quantity school of monetary policy implementation in the twentieth century, which is discussed in the following section.

1.3   THE QUANTITY-ORIENTED EPISODE (1920–1985)

1.3.1   *The foundations of a quantitative approach to monetary policy implementation: Irving Fisher and C. A. Phillips*

The quantity theory of money, whose origins can be traced back to the seventeenth century, was made popular mainly by Irving Fisher's *The Purchasing Power of Money* (1911). The quantity theory basically starts from the 'equation of exchange', namely, the equality of the total value of goods transacted to the total amount of money handed over in the transactions. Denoting by p the price of the basket of goods transacted, by Y the size of the basket of goods transacted in a certain period of time, by M the stock of money, and by v the number of times this stock of money is turned over in transactions during the specified period (the velocity), one obtains the equation of exchange.

$$p.Y = v.M \tag{1.3}$$

This equation is always verified *ex post*, and is thus more a description than a theory. It may form the foundation of a theory if assumptions are made about the behaviour of one or more of the variables involved. In particular, if v is assumed to be stable (or at least predictable), then any change of M will be reflected either in changes of p or of Y. Wherever it is reflected, this makes M a key policy variable. In practice, the crucial question is whether v is really stable or predictable and, related to that, which definition of M makes most sense because it implies a stable or predictable v.

The 'discovery' of the *money multiplier* by C. A. Phillips (1920) and work by other authors on the topic in the 1920s and 1930s were a key complement to the quantity equation since they made it possible to link the quantity equation to monetary policy *implementation* by building a bridge between broad monetary aggregates and the central bank balance sheet. Consider the following variables (for more details see Chapter 2): K is banknotes in circulation; R is the reserves held by commercial banks with the central bank and corresponds to required reserves (since banks are assumed not to hold any excess reserves); r is the reserve requirement ratio on non-banks' deposits, CD, with commercial banks (that is $R = rCD$); assume that a meaningful monetary aggregate according to (1–3) with stable v is $M = CD + K$. Assume furthermore that the non-banks have stable preferences to hold a part c of the money in their hands $(K + CD)$ in cash (K) and a part $1 - c$ in deposits with banks (CD), such that $K = cM$. On the basis of these assumptions, one may establish a multiplicative relationship between the 'monetary base' $K + R$ and the monetary aggregate M:

$$M = \frac{1}{c + r(1 - c)}(K + R) \qquad (1.4)$$

From there, quantity-oriented economists continued reasoning as follows: the central bank can influence via open market operations the reserves of commercial banks with the central bank R. On the assumption that if actual reserves are bigger than required reserves $(R > rCD)$ commercial banks will use excess reserves for further monetary expansion until excess reserves are again zero, the central bank appears able to control monetary aggregates directly via open market operations. For instance, if the central bank adds \$100 through an open market operation to reserves, banks can directly grant further credit of \$100 to non-banks and pay it out in cash. However, due to the preference of non-banks to hold only a share c of their additional money holdings in cash, they will again deposit a part $1 - c$ of it with banks, which can use $1 - r$ out of this deposited amount to grant further credit. Eventually, the \$100 will have created additional money M of $100/(c + r(1 - c))$. By controlling monetary aggregates, the central bank would eventually, via the quantity theory, also control prices and influence economic activity.[6] For at least seventy years, the money multiplier has provided the common denominator of almost all monetary economics textbooks. For instance, Mishkin (2004) still devotes forty pages to it. This is in marked contrast to central bank practice. At least since joining central banking in 1994, the author has never heard any reference to the money multiplier in internal discussions on policy decisions or in public announcements from central banks, in particular not with regard to open market operations.

---

[6] For example, Bomhoff (1977), Johannes and Rasche (1979) and Garfinkel and Thornton (1991) study the predictability of the money multiplier.

1.3.2 *Reserve position doctrine and the idiosyncratic effects of open market operations*

Along the lines of the work of Fisher and Phillips, and inspired by a certain interpretation of the experience of the early years of the Fed,[7] an extensive US literature developed that analysed quantitative monetary policy transmission from open market operations to macroeconomic aggregates, mostly with only a limited, if any, role for short-term interest rates. Recognizing that the monetary base was not itself suitable as an operational target, 'reserve position doctrine' considered many different concepts and sub-items of commercial banks' *reserves* with the central bank that could be chosen as an operational target of monetary policy implementation.

An early statement of reserve position doctrine was given by Paul M. Warburg, a Federal Reserve Board member from 1914 to 1918, in an interview in 1923 (Warburg 1930: ii. 851):[8]

Interviewer: As a check to unhealthy business developments, is a change in the discount rate more or less effective than open-market operations by the Reserve Banks?

Warburg: Changing the discount rate has the wider influence on sentiment, but its immediate actual effect may at times be slower and less definitive... Open market operations by the reserve banks, on the contrary, have more immediate and definitive effects. By increasing or decreasing its open-market investments, the Federal Reserve System can on its own initiative exercise a strong regulatory effect... When the Federal Reserve System increases or decreases its aggregate of investments, it thereby expands, contracts, or re-establishes the reserves of member banks. It therefore commands very far-reaching effects, because by its open market operations it may lengthen or shorten the reserve base which supports and controls the size of the inverted pyramid of bank loans that rests upon it.

J. M. Keynes provided from the other side of the Atlantic strong support for reserve position doctrine in his detailed discussion of monetary policy implementation in the second volume of his *Treatise on Money*. Keynes (1930: 224–5) explicitly attacks what he names the 'orthodox doctrine in England', which seems to correspond to the interest-rate focus of

---

[7] The US inflation of 1916–19, which was interpreted as following an excessive use of the discount window by banks (instead of being attributed to the failure by the Fed to raise interest rates) and a 'discovery' of open market operations in the early 1920s. These episodes will be reviewed in more detail in Chapters 4, 5, and 7.

[8] In a speech delivered in 1924, Warburg (1930: ii. 861) also speaks of 'the fallacy of the contention that it is practicable through discount rates to regulate the movement in prices'.

the Bank rate school:

Some authors have argued that the method of bank rate and the method of 'open market policy' really reduce theoretically to one, namely bank rate, the practical limitations of 'open market policy' unaccompanied by a change of bank rate being narrow. According to this argument, which—as we shall see—cannot be fully sustained, the central bank cannot vary the volume of its 'investments' without tending to produce an opposite and compensating variation in the volume of its 'advances', unless it accompanies its action with an appropriate change of bank rate . . . It is admitted that . . . the effect of 'open market policy', i.e. of varying the amount of its investments, can produce gradual and continuous movements within the range of more abrupt and discontinuous changes of bank rate. Nevertheless, according to this view, open market policy can only be employed by a central bank, not as a substitute for, to reinforce its bank rate policy by making the latter effective.

We will see below that the 'orthodox doctrine' of the Bank of England is actually not so different from today's predominant view of central bankers: that both types of monetary policy operations are only to be considered together, that is, that they eventually aim at one variable only, the inter-bank rate. Also, the 'orthodox doctrine' makes use, as central bankers do today, of the central bank balance-sheet identity (see Chapter 2). Keynes (1930: 225) goes on to argue that the two types of operations are suited for addressing either domestic or international disequilibrium, without, however, substantiating this claim:

. . . the kinds of effects produced by the two methods are materially different . . . whilst bank rate may be the most suitable weapon for use when the object of the central bank is to preserve international equilibrium, open market sales or purchases of securities may be more effective when the object is to influence the rate of investment.

As explained further in Chapter 6, it was also Keynes (1930) who first argued that *changes* of reserve requirements should be used as a monetary policy instrument, an idea that dominated the thinking of, for example, the Fed and the Bundesbank until the 1970s. It appears overall that Keynes was clearly influenced in his views by the Fisher-Phillips foundations of a quantity-oriented approach to monetary policy implementation, and it seems most likely that the popularity of Keynes contributed much to the dissemination of this doctrine.

The related literature of the first half of the twentieth century is summarized by Meigs (1962), who also coined the term 'reserve position doctrine'. While Riefler (1930) and Tinbergen (1939) assign some role to interest rates and hence to the money market,[9] Hardy (1932), Curie (1935), and Turner (1938) largely subscribe to a quantitative logic according to which open market operations, possibly mitigated by discount borrowing, directly affect, via some reserve quantity, credit and money expansion.[10] The basic idea was that, when free reserves or excess reserves are large, banks supposedly are eager to make loans to get rid of them. When they are small or negative, banks are supposedly under pressure to pay off their debts, and will restrict credit. The number of monographs published in the US during the 1930s on the topic shows how much US monetary economists were focusing on the quantity side in monetary policy implementation before the development of monetarism in the 1950s and 1960s. The substantial levels of excess reserves in the US Federal Reserve System during the Great Depression renewed the interest of monetary economists in the topic by raising the question of why banks did not make use of these excess reserves for monetary expansion.[11] The impact of reserve position doctrine on the Fed is confirmed by publications such as Board of Governors (1954), in which the transmission mechanism is indeed described as proceeding mainly from open market operations through reserves to credit expansion, with little mention of short-term interest rates. Work on the topic also continued to flourish after the Second World War, in, for example, Warburton (1948), Meigs (1962), Dewald (1963), Goldfeld and Kane (1966), and Modigliani, Rasche, and Cooper (1970)—the last of which, however, also models short-term interest rates. The lasting influence of reserve position doctrine in the US was revealed by the Fed turning to 'non-borrowed reserves targeting' in 1979 and to 'borrowed reserves targeting' in 1982 (see Chapter 7). These episodes gave further impetus to the literature; see,

---

[9] In fact, Riefler (1930) is still closer to the classical focus on interest rates. As is shown in Chapter 4, he also had rather clear ideas about the relationship between open market operations, the discount window, and the spread between market rates and the discount rate.

[10] A German contribution from the 1930s, which also seems close to reserve position doctrine, is Lutz (1936).

[11] Frost (1971) concludes that the large accumulation of excess reserves during the 1930s is explained by the fact that banks found it profitable to hold excess reserves at very low interest rates because the transaction costs of constantly adjusting reserve positions was greater than the interest that could be earned. Kaufman and Lombra (1980: 564) challenge the view of a macroeconomic relevance of excess reserves and argue that 'the central role of demand for excess reserves function in models of the money supply process is particularly suspect', and that it does not even make sense to talk about a 'demand' function for excess reserves since excess reserves are basically only the residual *ex post* result of payment shocks. Recent work on the topic tends to confirm this view. Dow (2001), starting from the microeconomic foundations laid by Orr and Mellon (1961), show that the demand for excess reserves in the US is indeed positively correlated to payment system activity and negatively correlated to interest rates. Bindseil et al. (2004) provide a model of excess reserves and calibrate it with Eurozone data in which transaction costs play a key role. A transaction cost model of excess reserves in the US has been proposed by Clouse and Dow (2002).

for example, Beek (1981), Axilrod and Lindsey (1981), Goodfriend (1983), Lindsey et al. (1984), Gilbert (1985), and Dotsey (1989). Still Walsh (2003) explains that 'in terms of an analysis of the reserve market and operating procedures, the most important . . . is the excess reserve ratio. Since reserves earn no interest, banks face an opportunity cost in holding excess reserves. As market rates rise, banks will tend to hold a lower average level of excess reserves. This drop in the excess reserves ratio will work to increase M1.'[12]

Overall, much of the reserve position doctrine literature appears from today's perspective to lack micro-foundations and especially a modelling of the banks' behaviour in the inter-bank market. Moreover, when turning empirical, it often seemed to mix macroeconomic and microeconomic time series and shocks of different significance and frequency. On the basis of the model presented in Chapter 3, it will be argued that reserve magnitudes are likely to be affected by various short-term factors with no information content about macroeconomic conditions, such that defining targets for them is of little interest and can, if taken seriously, lead only to unintended monetary impulses. One could argue that reserve position doctrine in fact ignored most of the key insights of the nineteenth century UK Bank rate school, which today are once again acknowledged.

1.3.3 *Monetarism on monetary policy implementation*

Views of monetarists on monetary policy implementation are generally in the tradition of reserve position doctrine, although they tended to be less keen in their analysis to split up further the monetary base into components such as reserves, 'non-borrowed reserves', and so on. For instance, Friedman (1960: 50–1) argues that open market operations alone are a sufficient tool for monetary policy implementation, and that standing facilities (such as the US discount facility) and reserve requirements could thus be abolished:

The elimination of discounting and of variable reserve requirements would leave open market operations as the instrument of monetary policy proper. This is by all odds the most efficient instrument and has few of the defects of the others . . . The amount of purchases and sales can be at the option of the Federal Reserve System and hence the amount of high-powered money to be created thereby determined precisely. Of course, the ultimate effect of the purchases or sales on the final stock

---

[12] Another body of literature that seems to be inspired by reserve position doctrine is the one on 'open market operations' as monetary quantities in macroeconomic models, such as, for example, in Blanchard and Fischer (1989: 181–8).

of money involves several additional links . . . But the difficulty of predicting these links would be much less . . . The suggested reforms would therefore render the connection between Federal Reserve action and the changes in the money supply more direct and more predictable and eliminate extraneous influences on reserve policy.

The basic components of Friedman's approach are the possibility of controlling the monetary base, the stability of the money multiplier, and the assumption that monetary targeting is the appropriate monetary policy strategy. What may be most striking in Friedman's (1960) analysis is his silence on the role of short-term interest rates and that his proposals would be likely to imply a high volatility of short- and medium-term rates. Very similarly, Friedman and Schwartz (1963), in their critique of the Fed policy in the 1930s, show little curiosity about interest rates, but argue in a strict multiplier framework. They follow the historical development of the monetary base and monetary aggregates, to argue within the multiplier model that open market operations could have increased the monetary base and hence the money stock, thus preventing or at least attenuating the crisis of the 1930s (1963: 393):[13]

If the deposit ratios had behaved as in fact they did, the change from a decline in high powered money of 2¹/₂ per cent to a rise of 6¹/₂ per cent . . . would have changed the monetary situation drastically, so drastically that such an operation was almost surely decidedly larger than was required to convert the decline in the stock of money into an appreciable rise.

The following passage suggests that Friedman and Schwartz do not see a relationship between reserve market conditions (including excess reserves) and the level of the market rate relative to the discount rate. In 1932, the Fed felt that the threat of massive gold drains, especially to France, obliged it to maintain a somewhat tight policy despite the sluggish economy. At the same time, the public was heavily withdrawing banknotes, endangering the gold coverage of banknotes. In this context, Friedman and Schwartz (1963: 398–9) suggest the following policy, similarly to Keynes (1930: 225):

Suppose the system had raised the discount rate when it did, adopting the 'classic' remedy for an external drain, but had accompanied the measure by purchases of government securities as called for by the 'classic' remedy for an internal drain and by its earlier sterilization policy . . . Reserve purchases of $1 billion of government securities would have meant an increase of $1,330 million in high powered money. That sum would have provided the whole $720 million in

---

[13] McCallum (1990) too argues in favour of this hypothesis.

currency withdrawn by the public and at the same time have enabled bank reserves to increase by $610 million. . . . The increase in bank reserves would have permitted a multiple expansion in deposits instead of the multiple contraction that actually took place.

Again, interest rates play no role in the argumentation, and the question, still at least *discussed* extensively by Keynes (1930), whether all instruments do not reduce essentially to one, which one would today affirm, is ignored. One would argue today that what matters in avoiding an external drain is the level of market rates: an increase of the discount rate is not relevant as long as it is not 'effective', that is, as long as it does not increase market rates, which is the case only if banks need to have effective recourse to the borrowing facility with some positive probability. Under the Friedman–Schwartz proposal, the discount rate would, however, certainly *not* have been effective, such that what they propose is simply a lowering of inter-bank rates through the injection of reserves. Perhaps this would have been the right policy measure overall, but it would not have addressed the Fed's fears about gold losses.

Friedman (1982) argues largely along the same lines as Friedman (1960) that interest rates as operational targets are neither possible nor desirable. In terms of operational target, he seems to suggest an 'open market operations volume target' (1982: 117):

Set a target path for several years ahead for a single aggregate—for example M2 or the base. . . . Estimate the change over an extended period, say three or six months, in the Fed's holdings of securities that would be necessary to approximate the target path over that period. Divide that estimate by 13 or 26. Let the Fed purchase precisely that amount every week in addition to the amount needed to replace maturing securities. Eliminate all repurchase agreements and similar short-term transactions.

The nineteenth-century Bank rate school and today's central banker would argue that this proposal would lead to extreme interest rate volatility and would make any systematic control of credit, money, prices, and business activity impossible.

How relevant a quantitative, Friedman-like view of monetary policy implementation still is today is revealed by, for instance, the popular textbook of Mishkin (2004), who is rather detailed on the specific topic. Regarding the US Fed approach to monetary policy implementation during the 1950s and 1960s, Mishkin (2004: 423) explains that interest rate control would have led to a 'pro-cyclical' monetary policy:

If the Fed saw interest rates rising as a result of a rise in income, it would pur- chase bonds to bid their price up and lower interest rates to their target level. The resulting increase in the monetary base caused the money supply to rise and the business cycle expansion to be accompanied by a faster rate of money growth.

Today's central bankers may argue that this reasoning contains two critical simplifications. The first consists of not distinguishing interest rates of different maturities, which leads to a confusing chain of causality. The Fed was targeting short-term market rates, and these *were* under the control of the Fed, such that the phrase 'if the Fed saw interest rates rising as a result of a rise of income' can refer only to medium- or long-term rates. Second, Mishkin's critique does not distinguish possible mistakes of the Fed with regard to its monetary policy stance with mistakes in the choice of the appropriate operational target variable. Obviously, when the economy is booming, a more restrictive policy in the form of a higher target short-term interest rate may be required. Therefore, the suggested pro-cyclical character of the Fed's policy had nothing to do with the choice of its target but with the way it mapped its information on the state of the economy into the level of its operational target variable.[14] Mishkin (2004: 424) similarly criticizes the use of the Fed funds rate (the US inter-bank overnight rate) as an operational target in the 1970s:

Using the federal funds rate as an operating target promoted a procyclical policy despite the Fed's lip service to monetary aggregate targets. If the Federal Reserve really intended to pursue monetary aggregate targets, it seems peculiar that it would have chosen an interest rate for an operating target rather than a reserve aggregate.

The claim by Mishkin that it is 'peculiar' to control monetary aggregates through short-term interest rates is not further explained. In fact, H. Thornton (1802) had already argued in favour of such an approach, and the fact that most central banks followed it during the 1970s and 1980s, some of them having been more successful in terms of controlling inflation rates than the Fed, also suggests that there is nothing wrong with it.[15]

Finally, to come to the most recent past, another prominent monetarist, Allan Meltzer (2003), in his book on the earlier part of the history of the Fed, also supports a Friedman-like view of monetary policy implementation. When reviewing the antecedents to the Fed, Meltzer criticizes in particular the poor level of the Bank of England's (and, for example, Bagehot's) nineteenth-century analysis of macroeconomic conditions and its focus on money markets and market rates. He also argues (2003: 22) that the main

---

[14] Mishkin (2004: 423) continues: 'A further problem with using interest rates as the primary operating target is that they may encourage an inflationary spiral to get out of control . . . When inflation and hence expected inflation rises, nominal interest rates rise via the Fisher effect. If the Fed attempted to prevent this increase by purchasing bonds, this would also lead to a rise in the monetary base and the money supply.'

[15] This point is also highlighted by Goodhart (2001). See also B. Friedman (1990).

mistake of the Fed in its early years was to focus too much on the Bank of England doctrine in the second half of the nineteenth century: 'Why did Thornton's rich and promising analysis degenerate first into a Bank of England policy of using bank rate mainly to protect the gold reserve and later into the Federal Reserve's concern for short-term market interest rates and money market conditions?'[16] The interpretation given here, especially in Chapters 4, 7, and 8, is quite different: the Fed embarked in its first years on some peculiar implementation techniques that determined its operations until the end of the twentieth century which could have been avoided if it *had* studied really sufficiently and copied the Bank of England's monetary policy implementation in the second half of the nineteenth century. Meltzer seems to insufficiently distinguish a critique of an inappropriate monetary policy *strategy* (too strong a focus on gold reserves) from a critique of the *implementation technique* (a focus on short-term interest rates). While the first critique may be legitimate (this is not discussed here), the second is less convincing in view of the experience of central banks. The obstinate insistence of the monetarist school on the quantity dimension also in monetary policy *implementation* and the refusal of a role for short-term interest rates, despite so much contrary evidence, is also illustrated by the following paragraph from Meltzer (2003: 62–3):

Every complete theory of the monetary system must provide answers to a number of related questions. What is the monetary standard, and what are the sources and components of the monetary base? Why do the source components expand or contract? Which items are included as uses of the monetary base? If the uses of the base consist of more than one item, what effect does the substitution of one item for another produce on the monetary system? By what means and to what end should the government of a central bank seek to control the base? What are the short- and longer-term consequences of a change in the base on the stock of means of payment? . . . What, if any, is the feedback from the changes in prices and real variables to the source components of the base?

Thus, according to Meltzer—and this summarizes well the monetarist tradition—monetary policy implementation requires studying all aspects of the monetary base and there is no need for a reference to interest rates when one outlines a 'complete theory of the monetary system'.

1.4   A SUPPOSED SOLUTION OF THE 'INSTRUMENTS CHOICE PROBLEM': POOLE (1970)

The Poole (1970) model was probably what academic economists had in mind in the 1970s and 1980s when thinking about the control of quantities

---

[16] See also Humphrey (2001) for a similar view.

versus the control of rates in monetary policy. As argued above, the question of controlling quantities versus rates had been present in central banking at least since the early nineteenth century and it was even the core question of debate in monetary economics in the 1950s and 1960s as exemplified by Friedman (1960) and Radcliffe et al. (1959). In this context, it is easy to understand that it appeared as a major breakthrough when Poole (1970) claimed to raise the debate on whether to use the interest rate or the money stock as the policy instrument to a higher level by arguing that both cases may be optimal, that everything depended on the stochastic structure of the economy, and that a combination policy was likely to be the best approach. On this question, Poole unfortunately mixed up three concepts clearly distinct in central bank practice (see the definitions in Section 1.1), namely, monetary policy instruments, the operational target, and the concept of intermediate target of monetary policy. Poole (1970: 198) defined an 'instrument' to be a 'policy variable which can be controlled without error' (which does not seem to apply to the 'money stock') and considered three possible approaches to its specification (1970: 199):

First, there are those who argue that monetary policy should set the money stock while letting the interest rate fluctuate as it will. The second major position in the debate is held by those who favor money market conditions as the monetary policy instrument. The more precise proponents of this general position would argue that the authorities should push interest rates up in times of boom and down in times of recession, while the money supply is allowed to fluctuate as it will. The third major position is taken by the fence sitters who argue that the monetary authorities should use both the money stock and the interest rate as instruments ... the idea seems to be to maintain some sort of relationship between the two instruments.

Consider briefly Poole's model to approach the (operational?) target selection problem. He starts from the following IS-LM model: $Y = a_0 + a_1 i$; $M = b_0 + b_1 Y + b_2 i$, whereby Y represents GDP, i is the interest rate, and M is the money stock, all variables being in real terms, and $a_0 > 0$, $a_1 < 0$, $b_0 > 0$, $b_1 > 0$, $b_2 < 0$. The model has two equations and three variables, Y, M, and i, and it is assumed that monetary policy can select one variable to become the exogenous policy variable, such as to make the system being exactly determined in the two endogenous variables. The purpose of policy is to achieve $Y = Y^*$, that is, GDP corresponding to its equilibrium level. This is obviously trivial in a deterministic model: any variable can be chosen as 'instrument' and be specified such that $Y = Y^*$ is achieved. Poole's idea consists of adding to the system of equations two non-correlated random terms, v and u, with zero mean and variances σ_v^2, σ_u^2, such that the model becomes:

$$Y = a_0 + a_1 i + v$$
$$M = b_0 + b_1 Y + b_2 i + i + u \tag{1.5}$$

It can be shown easily that the optimal instrument selection, that is, the one minimizing the variance of $(Y - Y^*)$, depends on the coefficients of the model and the variance of the two shocks. Furthermore, one can show that in most cases a combination policy of the type $M = c_1 + c_2 i$ is superior to any of the pure quantity or interest rate steering approaches. Indeed, one may, by substitution, obtain the following reduced form for Y:

$$Y = \frac{a_0(b_2 - c_2) + a_1 c_1}{b_2 + a_1 b_1 - c_2} + \frac{b_2 - c_2}{b_2 + a_1 b_1 - c_2} v + \frac{a_1}{b_2 + a_1 b_1 - c_2} u \tag{1.6}$$

One calculates the optimal value of c_2 by minimizing the variance of this expression. Then, in a second step, one chooses c_1 such that $E(Y) = Y^*$.

Poole's idea of 1970 is simple and elegant and contained a tempting analytical solution to an old alleged problem. It is therefore hardly surprising that Poole inspired many monetary economists during the following decades to develop sophisticated variants of his model and to view them as helping to understand the instrument-choice problem of monetary policy.

Unfortunately, it is not clear whether the approach of Poole (1970) was really appropriate to help finding a solution to the problem of choosing an operational target, and the unambiguous return of interest rates as operational targets in the 1990s in fact happened without reference to Poole's model. What could be wrong with the model? The main problem seems to be the mixing up of three distinct concepts (instruments and operational and intermediate targets), and the implied failure to distinguish between (*a*) short-term and long-term interest rates, (*b*) reserve market quantities and monetary aggregates, and (*c*) macroeconomic shocks and reserve market shocks. While clearly being in direct control of the short-term interest rate, the central bank does *not* control monetary aggregates and not even the monetary base, such that the choice presented by Poole does not exist in reality, at least not for day-to-day monetary policy implementation (see also Section 8.1). Although Poole briefly discussed the issue, he eventually swept it under the carpet. As the monetary-control experiment in the US in 1979–82 illustrates, the attempt to control monetary quantities in the short term implied extreme volatility not only of interest rates of all maturities but even of quantities themselves (see Chapter 7). If one really wanted to control monetary aggregates per se, one would do so through control of short-term interest rates: that is, one would map news regarding monetary quantities into changes of the short-term target rate (in the words of H. Thornton in 1802: 'limit its paper by means of the price at which it lends'). Even in the purest case of short-term monetary control, one would do so since there is simply no way to change monetary aggregates immediately. One may therefore argue that, by presenting money and the interest rate as alternative instruments, Poole's model is already mistaken, since money is a quantity that can be controlled only indirectly, reasonably using the interest rate as operational target. The real question from a macro-monetarist perspective, in fact, is: how strongly and how quickly should interest rate operational targets be adjusted to news on monetary quantities? Perhaps the answer is: 'very strongly and very directly'.[17] Still, a clear sequence remains: first the observation of news on the appropriate monetary policy stance (for example, news on monetary quantities), and then the decision to adjust the operational target, namely, the short-term interest rate, such as to bring the (intermediate) target variable back on track.

The lasting influence of the Poole (1970) approach is revealed, for instance, by the textbook by Walsh (2003).[18] Poole (1970) is presented as the key model of 'operating procedures' and some of its variants are discussed. Walsh, however, seems to be victim of the same imprecision as Poole by not following his own definition of an instrument: Walsh (2003: 430) defines instruments as the 'variables that are directly controlled by the central bank', which 'are usually manipulated to achieve a pre-specified value of an operating target, typically some measure of reserves, a very short term interest rate ... or a monetary conditions index that combines an interest rate and the exchange rate'. But then, in the next section, on 'The instrument choice problem', he starts by raising the question: 'If the monetary-policy authority can choose between employing an interest rate or a monetary aggregate as its policy tool, which should it choose?'

---

[17] It should be borne in mind that the monetary base, which is a balance sheet magnitude, can be observed with a daily frequency.

[18] There is also a body of literature one may call the 'macroeconomic liquidity effect literature', which can be regarded as a follow-up to Poole (1970) (for example, Christiano, Eichenbaum, and Evans 1996; Pagan and Robertson 1998). This literature models the monetary base or 'non-borrowed reserves' (see Chapter 2) as the central bank's operational target and claims to find a statistically significant 'liquidity effect', that is, an influence of innovations in this variable on nominal interest rates and various macroeconomic variables. D. Thornton (2001) argues that the evidence can be interpreted differently.

1.5 THE RETURN OF THE SHORT-TERM INTEREST RATE IN MONETARY ECONOMICS

After Cassel (1928), it is hard to find any academic work, including in the 1970s, that views monetary policy implementation as consisting in short-term interest rate targeting. This changes again in the 1980s (for example, McCallum 1981, 1986; Barro 1989; Judd and Motley 1992; Taylor 1993). In the late 1990s, the dominant approach of the younger generation of monetary economists is again to either model monetary policy implementation as a steering of interest rates (for example, Hamilton 1996; Bartolini, Bertola, and Prati 2002; Woodford 2001*a*; Ayuso and Repullo 2003), or to incorporate in macroeconomic models the assumption that the transmission mechanism starts with the central bank's steering of short-term interest rates (for example, Taylor 1993; Woodford 2003). For instance, Woodford (2003: ch. 1) starts his theory of monetary policy from the explicit observation that something is wrong in the way the issue has been treated for decades by academics (see also, for example, Goodhart 1989, 2001 or Moore 1988):

Monetary policy decision making almost everywhere means a decision about the operating target for an overnight interest rate, and the increased transparency about policy in recent years has almost meant greater explicitness about the central bank's interest-rate target and about the way in which its interest-rate decisions are made. . . . Nonetheless, theoretical analysis of monetary policy have until recently almost invariably characterised policy in terms of a path for the money supply, and discussions of policy rules in the theoretical literature have mainly considered money-growth rules of one type or another. This curious disjunction between theory and practice predates the enthusiasm of the 1970s for monetary targets.

Woodford (2001*b*, 2003) furthermore proposes a simple model of monetary policy implementation in the Poole (1968) tradition, which is also related to the basic model presented in Chapter 3 of the present book. In contrast to the old Bank rate literature, which failed to model convincingly the dynamics of short-term interest rates, economic activity, and the price level, the modern literature also addresses these issues with the help of new tools of economic analysis not available 100 years ago. Four elements of the literature are distinguished in the following. First, an example is provided of how the new approach models the role of interest rates as operational targets within a macroeconomic model. Second, the

Taylor rule, which describes and/or prescribes how the level of the short-term operational target rate is set, is reviewed. Third, the issue of yield curve control is briefly touched on. Finally, the choice of the operational target in case of a deflationary trap is discussed.

1.5.1   The role of interest rates in the new macroeconomic models

Although this book is not about monetary macroeconomics, it is worth examining briefly how the modern literature sees the relation between interest rates and prices, that is, between the operational and the main final target. The following is close to one example provided by Svensson (2003a: 6–10).[19] First, the central bank's final target(s) may be expressed in the form of an inter-temporal loss function, which consists in each period of the expected sum of discounted current and future losses:

$$E\left[(1 - \delta) \sum_{\tau = 1}^{\infty} \delta^{\tau} L_{t + \tau} | I_t\right] \tag{1.7}$$

The operator $E[\cdot|I_t]$ denotes rational expectations conditional on the central bank's information in period t about the state of the economy, the value of the operational target in period t, and the transmission mechanism of monetary policy. Furthermore, δ $(0 < \delta < 1)$ is a discount factor whereby the scaling $(1 - \delta)$ ensures that the scaled discount factors sum to unity, such that the expected inter-temporal loss is a weighted average of a magnitude corresponding to a one period loss. The one period loss function L_t can, for instance, be specified as a weighted sum of the squared inflation gap and the squared output gap:

$$L_t = (\pi_t - \pi^*)^2 + \lambda x_t^2 \tag{1.8}$$

where π_t is the inflation rate, $\pi^* \geq 0$ is an inflation rate target, $x = Y_t - Y_t^*$ is the output gap (with Y_t being output and Y_t^* being potential output which is assumed to be an exogenous stochastic process), and $\lambda > 0$ is the weight given to output-gap stabilization relative to inflation stabilization.

Suppose that the appropriate model of the macro-economy is as follows. First, inflation is determined by the following kind of Phillips curve:

$$\pi_{t + 1} = \pi_t + \alpha_x x_t + \alpha_z z_{t + 1} + \varepsilon_{t + 1} \tag{1.9}$$

---

[19] For other, more complex models, see in particular Woodford (2003) and, for example, Woodford (1995), and Alvarez, Lucas, and Weber (2001).

that is, inflation in period $t + 1$ is given by the previous period's inflation, the previous period's output gap ($\alpha_x > 0$), a vector of exogenous variables z_{t+1} in the same period (α_z being a corresponding row vector) and an i.i.d. shock ε_{t+1} with variance σ_ε^2. The exogenous variables in $t + 1$ may be anticipated to some extent by the central bank in period t. Finally, the output gap is assumed to be determined by:

$$x_{t+1} = \beta_x x_t + \beta_z z_{t+1} - \beta_r (j_t - r) + \eta_{t+1} \qquad (1.10)$$

that is, the output gap depends on the previous period's output gap ($\beta_x > 0$), a vector of exogenous variables (β_z being a corresponding row vector), and the deviation of the money interest rate net of expected inflation, $j_t = i_t - E(\pi_{t+1} | I_t)$, from the natural rate of interest r which is assumed to be constant, but that may as well be assumed to follow another exogenous stochastic process. Equation (1.10) thus takes up the Thornton-Wicksell idea of a natural rate of interest as reflected in the arbitrage diagram in Section 1.2.1 and integrates it in a dynamic model.[20]

Assume for a moment that the central bank is able to fully control the short-term (that is, one-period) money interest rate i_t such that, when it sets its operational target i_t^*, it always achieves $i_t = i_t^*$. Then, the monetary policy problem consists purely in the *macroeconomic* problem of choosing each period a value of the operational target i_t^*, together with a planned path of this variable for future periods, such that the expected discounted loss function is minimized. This can be done, for instance, by simulating the model under various assumptions regarding the exogenous variables and then choosing the path of the operational target variable that minimizes the expected discounted loss over all scenarios weighted with adequate probabilities.

The problem of monetary policy *implementation* focuses on the relationship between i_t^* and i_t, that is, to achieve through an adequate operational framework and day-to-day monetary policy operations that ideally $i_t = i_t^*$, for all t. The *choice* of the operational target is an issue of monetary policy *implementation* in so far as only a variable that *can* indeed be controlled to a sufficient extent qualifies to be an operational variable. However, the choice of the operational target is, of course, also a macroeconomic issue since it does not make sense to choose a variable which can well be controlled but does not have a meaningful and systematic impact in the macroeconomic model the central bank deems to be applicable. To that extent, the choice of the

---

[20] On this point, the interpretation by Svensson (2003a) of equation (1.10) is slightly different.

operational target is the point where *implementation* of monetary policy and the macroeconomic monetary policy strategy meet.

It is not easy to give a general formal representation to the problem of monetary policy implementation, since much depends on the setting of various institutional parameters (but see Chapter 3). Subject to a standard modern specification of the operational framework, a reasonable general representation of the relationship between the instruments, exogenous variables, and the actual interest rate may be

$$i_t = f(M_t - A_t, i_B, i_D) + v_t \tag{1.11}$$

where M_t is the amount of outstanding open market operations in period t, A_t are the 'autonomous liquidity factors', which follow some stochastic process which can be anticipated to some extent by the central bank, i_B, i_D are interest rates of standing facilities offered by the central bank, and v_t is an iid noise term with variance σ_v^2, which should, by definition of an operational target, be small (all this is better explained in Chapter 2 and Chapter 3). Two observations should be made. First, the instrument of reserve requirements is not explicitly reflected because, according to today's view, it corresponds more to an institutional parameter set once for a long period of time, and not to one which is manipulated on a day-by-day basis to achieve the target. Second, the central bank seems to have two instruments (open market operations and standing facilities) but only one target in its monetary policy implementation. The degree of freedom normally resulting from this fact plays a role throughout the rest of this book.

Furthermore, one may note that fitting an equation of type (1.11) into a full monetary policy model of the type (1.7)–(1.10) is not too helpful. First, the appropriate definition of a period for equation (1.11) is normally shorter than for the previous equations. For equation (1.11), the appropriate period corresponds to the reserve requirement averaging period, which is one day in the UK, two weeks in the US, and one month in the euro area. Of course, one may build averages for the variables in equation (1.11) to fit them into a macroeconomic model referring to longer periods of time, but this blurs the economic intuition behind that equation. Moreover, equation (1.11) is relevant to the rest of the model only in so far as it provides the actual money interest rate. The other explanatory variables in equation (1.11) do not appear in the other equations. Therefore, the two 'blocks' can easily be separated. Finally, the control of the operational target is normally so adequate and deviations so transitory that they are negligible in the macroeconomic equations with lower frequency.

1.5.2   *The Taylor rule*

Taylor (1993), assuming that the short-term interest rate is indeed the operational target of central banks, suggested that the following simple relationship fits US monetary policy in previous years remarkably well (notation as defined in the previous section):

$$i_t = 0.04 + 1.5(\pi_t - 0.02) + 0.5x_t \qquad (1.12)$$

In plain English: the Fed's interest rate target corresponds to a constant of 4 per cent plus the deviation of the inflation rate from a target of 2 per cent multiplied by 1.5, plus the output gap (in per cent) multiplied by one half. Clarida, Gali, and Gertler (1998) argue that the Taylor rule is also applicable to other countries with not too different coefficients. For Taylor, the rule may be considered both as an accurate description of actual Fed behaviour and as a normative rule, at least to give a first indication before further 'expert knowledge' is added to set the actual level of the operational target rate. To this extent, Taylor is not denying that one should go beyond the rule and that other variables and general knowledge available for decision-makers should be taken into account. Svensson (2003a) nevertheless criticizes the idea of what he calls an 'instrument rule' (what we would call an 'operational target rule') and promotes 'target rules' (that is, 'final target rules') which basically start from a model like the one expounded in Section 1.5.1 and through simulation tries to find out which path of the operational target allows for minimizing the loss function of the central bank. Another possible critique of the Taylor rule is that the specification of the output gap actually involves a series of issues that require judgement and allow for some discretion. As Woodford (2001: 236), furthermore, suggests, an optimal rule is likely to require that the intercept is adjusted in response to fluctuations in the Wicksellian natural rate of interest, which should vary in response to various real disturbances.

A key issue relating to the Taylor rule is whether it actually ensures determinacy of the price level. For example, Woodford (2001: 233) demonstrates within a model similar to the one presented in Section 1.5.1 that this is actually the case for all rules of the Taylor type in which the coefficient of the inflation rate term is at least one, which is intuitive. Sargent and Wallace (1975) had still argued that with interest rate targeting the price level is indeterminate, whereas their rule consisted of simply fixing the interest rate at some level, which is indeed not a good idea in an unstable world (see also Goodhart, 2001).

The widespread popularity that the Taylor rule has quickly gained is another illustration of how natural it again appears today to view short-term interest rates as the operational target of the central bank.

1.5.3   *The short-term interest rate and the yield curve*

The model, expounded in Section 1.5.1, of the transmission mechanism starting with an operational target interest rate does not distinguish between different maturities. However, it is generally recognized that central banks can control best the very short end of the yield curve,[21] say for instance the overnight rate, while longer-term rates are actually more relevant to the transmission mechanism. Therefore, the behaviour of the short-term yield curve, and specifically how medium- and longer-term rates react to a change in the operational target (overnight) rate, become a key issue.

Since the 1980s, various studies have investigated the time-series properties of the yield curve and in particular how medium- and longer-term interest rates react to changes in the short-term interest rate target of the central bank (for example, Mankiw and Miron 1986; McCallum 1994; Rudebusch 1995; Balduzzi et al. 1998; Kuttner 2001). The starting point of the analysis is usually the rational expectations theory of the term structure of interest rates, according to which long-term rates and expected short-term rates are bound to each other through an arbitrage relation. Indeed, with well-developed financial markets and absence of credit risk and liquidity considerations, the yield from investing money in T successive one-period deposits should be expected to be equal to the yield which would have been obtained through one long-term deposit of duration T. Let $i_{1,t}$, $i_{T,t}$ be the overnight and the T days interest rates on day t, respectively. The operator $E[\cdot|I_t]$ represents market expectations on the basis of the information available in period t. Then, according to the expectations theory:

$$1 + i_{T,t} = \left(\prod_{\tau=t}^{t+T-1} \left(1 + E[i_{1,\tau}|I_t] \right) \right)^{1/T} \tag{1.13}$$

In practice, there is normally a systematic term premium: that is, long-term rates appear empirically to be on average higher than short-term rates. Also, the equation above is often approximated in a linear form.

---

[21] See Section 3.1 on why the central bank should indeed target overnight interest rates and not longer maturities.

Empirical tests of the rational expectations hypothesis of the term structure are normally done by testing the predictive content of a two-period
(for example, six months) rate for the one-period rate one period ahead
(for example, the three months rate three months ahead). The tested
equation is then typically of the following format:

$$i_{1,t+1} - i_{1,t} = \alpha + \beta(i_{2,t} - i_{1,t}) + v_{t+1} \tag{1.14}$$

Under the hypothesis of validity of the expectations hypothesis, one
obtains $\beta = 2$. Furthermore, the error term v_{t+1} should then be orthog-
onal to the explanatory variables, such that ordinary least squares produce consistent estimates of the coefficients. Much of the literature until
the mid-1980s came to the conclusion that the expectations theory was
worthless for explaining the yield curve of up to one year, which would
have suggested serious problems for the transmission mechanism starting from a short-term interest rate target. The first ones to question this
view were Mankiw and Miron (1986), who argued that the lack of predictive power of very short-term rates for, for example, three or six
months rates is not sufficient for a rejection of the rational expectations
hypothesis since the coefficient β in equation (1.14) also depends on the
way the central bank sets its short-term interest rate targets. Mankiw and
Miron (1986) suggest that indeed the Fed would be setting its short-term
interest rate target such that short-term interest rates follow more or less
a random walk, implying there is no such thing as expected changes of
short-term rates. The following quotation from Goodhart (2000), a former member of the Bank of England's Monetary Policy Committee (MPC),
suggests that the policy of the Bank of England also would generate
something close to random walk behaviour of short-term rates:

When I was a member of the MPC I thought I was trying, at each forecast round,
to set the level of interest rates, on each occasion, so that without the need for
future rate changes, prospective (forecast) inflation would on average equal the
target at the policy horizon.

On the other side, Fig. 4.3, which shows the Fed funds target overnight
rate since 1971, suggests that there is definitely some serial correlation in
changes of interest rate targets. Apparently, the Fed in this period normally did move its target rate 'carefully' such that the likelihood of the
subsequent step having the same direction was above one half, and similar charts for other central banks and other periods seem to lead to similar conclusions. Rudebusch (1995) suggests that central bankers may
want to minimize the risk of overdoing it and the need to reverse an
interest rate step soon, or that they want to avoid unsettling financial

markets through sudden big steps. Whatever the strategy of the central bank is, it is probably key for the central bank control of medium-term rates (such as for example the one- or two-years rate) that it appears transparent and predictable, which requires a stability of its operational target rate-setting strategy over time. There is a trade-off at stake: a strategy of direct full adjustments of target rates as described by Goodhart (2000) inducing random walk-type behaviour of short-term rates is very transparent and ideally allows shifting the yield curve (at least for, say, six or twelve months) in parallel with the target rate. Its disadvantage could be the 'unsettling' of financial markets. A strategy of smoothed adjustments possibly avoids the latter, but is likely always to remain less transparent and hence to allow less precise control of the yield curve beyond its very short end.

In any case, more recent work on the topic, such as by Rudebusch (1995), Balduzzi et al. (1998) and Kuttner (2001), confirms that the rational expectations hypothesis of the term structure *has* explanatory power due to some tendency of the Fed to smooth short-term interest rates. But it needs to be repeated that it was already the result of Mankiw and Miron (1986), who had refuted the older literature's claim that the rational expectations hypothesis of the term structure of interest rates was invalid, which would have been a crucial counterargument to the choice of short-term interest rates as operational targets.

1.5.4   *Monetary policy operations in crisis situations (II): the operational target in the deflationary trap*

As seen in Section 1.2.5, a key principle of central banking developed during the nineteenth century is that, in financial crisis situations, the central bank should lend freely, that is, it should in this case not establish quantitative restrictions to lending due, for instance, to credit risk or monetary policy considerations.

After the experience of many countries during the 1930s, it was only in the last decade of the twentieth century that central banks would again be confronted with a different type of crisis situation, namely, the *deflationary trap*. Indeed, after the stock market bubble in Japan burst at the beginning of the 1990s, a successive reduction of the interest rate target did not help to revive the economy, and eventually the zero lower bound to the setting of the interest rate target prevented the implementation of a sufficiently loose monetary policy stance, while the price level started to fall year by year. Although this experience has not called into question short-term interest rates as the natural operational target of central banks, the Bank of Japan was forced to search for further operational targets to complement the zero interest rate target. A Bank of Japan press release on 19 March 2001 explained the solution chosen at that time as follows:

Japan's economic recovery has recently come to a pause after it slowed in late 2000 under the influence of a sharp downturn of the global economy. . . . In light of this, the Bank has come to a conclusion that the economic conditions warrant monetary easing as drastic as is unlikely to be taken under ordinary circumstances. Accordingly, the Bank decided at its Monetary Policy Meeting of today to take the following pol- icy actions: a) Change in the operating target for money market operations. The main operating target for money market operations be changed from the current uncollat- eralized overnight call rate to the outstanding balance of the current accounts at the Bank of Japan. Under the new procedures, the Bank provides ample liquidity . . . b) Duration of the new procedures: The new procedures for money market operations continue to be in place until the consumer price index (excluding perishables, on a nationwide statistics) registers stably a zero percent or an increase year on year. c) Increase in the current-account balance at the Bank of Japan and declines in inter- est rates. For the time being, the balance outstanding at the Bank's current accounts be increased to around 5 trillion yen, or 1 trillion yen increase from the average out- standing of 4 trillion yen in February 2001. As a consequence, it is anticipated that the uncollateralized overnight call rate will significantly decline from the current tar- get level of 0.15 percent and stay close to zero percent under normal circumstances.

Since March 2001, the Bank of Japan has several times raised its reserves target. For instance, in the one-month reserve maintenance period ending in May 2002, the actual current account of banks subject to reserve requirements amounted to ¥13.8 trillion against reserve requirements of ¥4.5 trillion, implying average excess reserves of ¥9.3 trillion. The last increase of the reserve target was decided in October 2003, when it reached ¥32 trillion (nearly US$300 billion).

Thus the Bank of Japan took recourse to an operational target concept that was 'unlikely to be taken under ordinary circumstances'. What might have persuaded the Bank of Japan to adopt quantitative operational targets again, at least as a complement to the zero interest rate policy? First, the key argument against quantitative operational targets–that they imply a loss of control and indeed huge volatility of short-term interest rates–is no longer valid under the assumption that the market is in any case left with an excess of reserves such that short-term rates will stay at zero. Second, although it may be unclear how exactly an excess reserves target is supposed to help a country escape from the deflationary trap, it at least seems unlikely to do any harm.

Also, the Bank of Japan may have felt that, even though most other quantity theory-oriented thoughts on monetary policy implementation are today rejected, there could, after all be a grain of truth in the reasoning by Friedman and Schwartz (1963) to the effect that the Great Recession would have been more moderate if the Fed had injected through open market operations more excess reserves into the market (see Section 1.3.3). Nevertheless, the counterargument to the Friedman–Schwartz reasoning—namely, that adding more and more of a free good should not in itself change the decisions of rational economic agents (and inter-bank interest rates of zero suggest that deposits are a free good)—still seems to apply. If a Japanese bank does not make use of its costless excess reserves to grant additional credit to, for example, corporate clients, then it seems unlikely that it will change behaviour if these excess reserves grow further.

Various researchers have proposed ways out of a Japan-style deflationary trap. A survey is provided by Svensson (2003b). A series of authors have recommended an expansion of the monetary base, which is probably in line with what the Bank of Japan has been doing in the last few years, although the authors might argue that the Bank's action was not strong enough. Other researchers have suggested that purchasing long-term bonds and thus reducing long-term interest rates would stimulate the economy. But, again, it appeared that the level of ten-year bonds was already so low (in summer 2003 below 0.5 per cent) that no substantial stimulus could be expected from this source. Other authors have proposed a currency tax so as to remove the lower, zero bound to nominal interest rates. This would, however, require some technical innovations. Other proposals focus on the foreign exchange side. The Bank of Japan could start expanding its foreign exchange assets until it depreciated its currency, which would stimulate demand through the trade balance and create inflation. In particular, the central bank could commit to implementing a depreciated exchange rate by offering to buy any amount of foreign currency offered at this rate. Svensson (2003b: 4) himself proposes a 'foolproof way' to escape from the deflationary trap, which consists of announcing and implementing (a) an upward-sloping price-level target path to be achieved, (b) a depreciation and a temporary crawling peg of the currency, and (c) an exit strategy in the form of the abandonment of the peg in favour of inflation targeting or price-level targeting when the price-level target path has been reached.

Eventually, the core idea of the most promising proposals seems to be that a central bank can always create a loss of purchasing power of its currency (that is, create inflation) by mounting a threat to eventually buy with its money *all the assets in the world*. If indeed the purchasing power of its currency could not fall, this threat would be credible: it could just buy everything. In practice, if the central bank starts with such a strategy, the world will hold very soon more yen, for example, than it wants, and people will start trying to get rid of their yen, which would eventually lower the value of yen relative to other goods (that is, the purchasing power of yen). Starting such a strategy, and threatening to continue with it until the yen has lost substantial purchasing power (and foreign exchange value), should therefore be a credible strategy to indeed engineer inflation and thus to escape the deflationary trap. Since it is credible, it should be successful, at least to some extent, not only through actual purchases but also through the threat alone.

Such quantitative operational targets to escape a deflationary trap are probably best expressed as central bank balance-sheet *asset* side-targets ('buy more and more assets'). Expressing those complementary targets, as some of the literature has, as excess reserves or monetary base targets (that is, central bank balance-sheet *liability* side targets) may be seen to be less intuitive since the escape from the deflationary trap will probably not be initiated through a money multiplier channel. Of course, purchasing assets (or threatening to purchase them) will normally mean expanding excess reserves (or threatening to) and hence the monetary base. Thus, in practice, the two strategies may be compatible with one another and may even be indistinguishable.

1.6 MICRO-MODELLING OF MONETARY POLICY INSTRUMENTS AND SHORT-TERM INTEREST RATES

Short-term interest rate targets refer to the interest rates in the inter-bank market of reserves with the central bank. Understanding the microeconomics of this market is therefore crucial to understanding modern day-to-day monetary policy implementation. Although Edgeworth (1888) had already addressed the topic, one refers today to Orr and Mellon (1961) and Poole (1968) as major contributions to the modelling of the demand for reserves by banks. Neither had much impact in the 1970s. A broader literature modelling the money market and the relationship between money market quantities and interest rates started to develop only later, with work such as by Laufenberg (1979) and Baltensperger (1980) and with many contributions in the 1990s such as Angeloni and Prati (1996), Hamilton (1996, 1997), Peres-Quiros and Rodriguez-Mendizábal (2001), and Bartolini Bertola, and Prati (2002) (see also the studies cited in Chapter 3). The first to study systematically time-series properties of central bank balance-sheet items as key factors driving the money market were Escriva and Fagan (1996) and Hamilton (1998). The basic model of monetary policy implementation presented in Chapter 3 is also a micro-economic model of the relationship between monetary policy instruments and short-term inter-bank interest rates.

This new microeconomic literature demystified the differences between the instruments of monetary policy implementation and made it clear that standing facilities and open market operations need to be seen from each other's perspective. Once they have been modelled correctly, little eventually remains that would justify viewing them as specific instruments on their own (as most monetary economists did in the decades before the 1980s). Therefore targeting, for instance, 'borrowed' reserves (those obtained through the discount window) or 'non-borrowed' reserves (those obtained through open market operations) means little in itself, or at least much less than targeting the short-term interest rate.

1.7   CONCLUSIONS

In this chapter, a series of key definitions relating to monetary policy implementation and to monetary policy in general were introduced. Although all terms are common in the literature of recent decades, the use of them has not always been consistent, and it was therefore deemed important to define them unambiguously for use throughout this book. Furthermore, the chapter reviewed the evolution of academic thinking on monetary policy implementation, which centred mainly on the question of whether to use 'rates' or 'quantities' as the operational target. It was demonstrated that today's view, which unambiguously supports short-term interest rates as the operational target, is not very different from the one that prevailed until the beginning of the twentieth century. According to this view, monetary quantities can represent only intermediate targets or indicator variables. Starting from the revival of the quantity theory of money by Fisher in 1911 and the money multiplier introduced by Phillips in 1920, and supportive thinking by, amongst others, Keynes (1930), Friedman (1960), and Poole (1970), a quantitative approach to monetary policy implementation dominated most of the twentieth century, at least among academics. How central banks tried to put these ideas into practice will be discussed in more detail mainly in Chapter 7, and Chapter 8 will again more systematically elaborate on the fallacies of this approach.

2

The Central Bank Balance Sheet

In Chapter 1 it was argued that monetary policy implementation normally means controlling short-term interest rates, not balance-sheet quantities like, for example, the monetary base. Still, as becomes clear in the present chapter, the best starting-point for understanding monetary policy implementation is the quantities in the central bank balance sheet. When a central bank transacts with the rest of the world—that is, when it issues currency, conducts foreign exchange operations, invests its own funds, engages in emergency liquidity assistance, and, last but not least, conducts monetary policy operations—all of these operations affect its balance sheet. As a central bank normally uses its own central bank money as the means of payment in all transactions, any of these transactions also potentially influences the *scarcity* of central bank money. This chapter sticks strictly with balance sheet *quantities* and avoids references to prices and interest rates, which are introduced in the subsequent chapter. Understanding the logic of quantities in the central bank balance sheet is the basis for understanding the key factors affecting short-term interest rates.

Central bank balance sheets are usually displayed in various central bank publications: annual reports (end-of-year balance sheets); statistical annexes to economic bulletins; press releases of, for example, weekly frequency. The format of, and the accounting practices underlying, central bank balance sheets are not homogeneous; which is to say that international standards are absent. To understand better the details of the different positions, it is therefore useful to consult the annual report of the central bank or any specific documentation the central bank may have issued. All central bank publications, including balance sheets, can normally be found on the websites of the central banks.[1]

---

[1] See the links provided by the Bank of International Settlements (BIS) at www.bis.org.

2.1 THE STRUCTURE OF THE CENTRAL BANK BALANCE SHEET

For an analysis of monetary policy implementation, the items in the central bank balance sheet need to be ordered into four distinct categories, the first three of which are represented both on the asset and the liability side.

1. *Autonomous liquidity factors* are all items in the balance sheet of the central bank that do not reflect monetary policy operations or the reserve holdings (that is, the 'deposits' or 'current accounts') of banks with the central bank. They therefore represent all other core or auxiliary functions of central banks. The most fundamental of these functions is probably issuing *banknotes*. Others include the holding and managing of *foreign exchange reserves* and their possible use for foreign exchange interventions; being the bank of the government and hence providing, for instance, a remunerated *current account to the government* which allows the government to avoid the credit risk it would have to bear if it held its liquid funds in the market; *investing funds in securities* in order to obtain income; being involved in the payment system and hence being affected by possible *float* which the system creates; conducting emergency liquidity assistance in case of need; and paying out profits to the government. It is crucial to note that all of these transactions *are not controlled by the monetary policy function* of the central bank, while at the same time all in principle include a leg in domestic currency, such that they affect the scarcity of reserves of banks with the central bank.

2. *Open market operations* are monetary policy operations *conducted at the initiative of the central bank* in order to achieve its operational target of monetary policy. They may consist of *reverse operations* (collateralized credit operations or repurchase operations) or of *outright purchases* or *sales* of securities (that is, securities bought or sold for good). Also, the central bank may issue its own debt certificates for monetary policy purposes.

3. *Standing facilities* are, in contrast to open market operations, monetary policy operations conducted *at the initiative of banks*. Historically, they were only liquidity-providing and consisted either of a discount facility or a lombard (advance) facility. In a discount, the counterpart sells short-term paper to the central bank but receives only a part of the nominal value of the asset at maturity, since the nominal value of the paper is 'discounted' at the prevailing discount rate. The maturity of a discount operation hence depends on the maturity of the

discounted paper. In a lombard loan, the counterpart in contrast obtains collateralized credit of a standardized maturity, which is today normally overnight. In this book, all liquidity-providing standing facilities will be called 'borrowing facility', taking the perspective of the central bank's counterpart. More recently, some central banks (for example, the ECB) have introduced a liquidity-absorbing facility ('deposit facility'). The deposit facility enables banks to place their end-of-day surplus liquidity with the central bank on a remunerated account. Today, rates of standing facilities are fixed by the central bank at a 'penalty level', such that the use of the facilities is normally not attractive. The interest rates on the two facilities then form the ceiling and the floor of a corridor within which short-term money market rates move. Such a corridor system is applied by the Bank of England and the Eurosystem, but also for instance by the central banks of Canada, Australia, and New Zealand.

4. *Commercial banks' reserves with the central bank* are perhaps the most crucial single item of the balance sheet for monetary policy implementation since they represent the good of which the short-term market interest rate is the price.

From the point of view of monetary policy implementation, the appropriate central bank balance sheet *format* is hence one in which: (*a*) the most important autonomous factors can be distinguished, that is, those which exhibit important volatility; (*b*) monetary policy operations are separated from other items; (*c*) the different types of monetary policy operations are precisely distinguished; (*d*) the reserves of banks are separated from other current accounts (for example, those of the government), especially if banks are subject to minimum reserves, in order to allow assessing the degree to which reserve requirements are fulfilled. Hence, an ideal balance sheet format would in principle be that shown in Table 2.1 The balance sheet identity, according to which the sum of assets and the sum of liabilities need to be equal, can be reordered to reflect the view that some item needs to be a *residual* that balances the balance sheet. This goes somewhat along with the economic method to distinguish between endogenous and exogenous variables. A 'model' described by a single linear equation, such as the balance sheet identity, needs *one* endogenous variable to have exactly one 'equilibrium'. As a first approach, it appears useful to make reserves of banks the residual of the balance sheet (all netting being made on the asset side):

Reserves of banks with the central bank = net open market operations + net use of standing facilities + net autonomous factors.

Table 2.1   *An ideal central bank balance sheet format*

Autonomous factors	
Foreign currency incl. gold	Banknotes in circulation
Investment assets	Government deposits
Other assets	Capital and reserves
	Other liabilities

Monetary policy operations	
OMO I (e.g. reverse operations)	Liquidity-absorbing OMO I (e.g. reverse operations)
OMO II (e.g. outright holdings of securities)	Liquidity-absorbing OMO II (e.g. issuing debt certificates)
Liquidity-injecting standing facility	Liquidity-absorbing standing facility
	Reserves of banks (including those to fulfil required reserves)

Note: OMO: open market operations.

One may interpret this equation as *the supply function of reserves* held by commercial banks with the central bank. To complete a model of the market for banks' reserves with the central bank, the *demand* side has to be added. First, if the central bank imposes reserve requirements, the banks will have a demand for reserves to fulfil these requirements so as to avoid paying a penalty. Second, banks may tend to hold reserves beyond the required level, called here 'excess reserves'. Section 2.4 goes into more detail about the different components of reserves. Once the supply and demand factors for banks' reserves with the central bank have been identified, the basic principle of monetary policy implementation can be stated: *influence through monetary policy instruments the demand and supply of reserves such that their price, namely, the overnight inter-bank interest rate, is close to the target level that has been defined according to the prevailing stance of monetary policy.* This principle will be worked out and illustrated more precisely in Chapter 3.

2.2   SOME CONCEPTS REFERRING TO THE CENTRAL BANK BALANCE SHEET

In the following, a few useful and/or well-known concepts of monetary policy implementation relating to the central bank balance sheet are introduced. (*a*) The *monetary base*, or 'high-powered money', is defined as the sum of banknotes and the current account holdings of banks with the central bank. It has often been considered as a key concept of monetary policy implementation, since it was supposed to be closely linked through the money multiplier to broader monetary aggregates, which themselves were supposed to have a stable relationship with the price level (see Chapters 1 and 8). As illustrated by, for instance, BIS (1980), the 1970s and 1980s were the high tide of the monetary base as an operational target variable (see, for example, Meulendyke 1990, or Pösö and Stracca, 2004). Today, the monetary base is no longer considered to be of particular relevance to monetary policy implementation. Indeed, banknotes, which are an autonomous liquidity factor, are considered to be something fundamentally different from the current account holdings of banks, which are closely linked or equivalent to required reserves, implying that summing up the two items does not create a particularly meaningful quantity. Still, the monetary base, or components of it, may play a useful role as an indicator variable under some circumstances, such as after a financial crisis in a developing country.

(b) The *liquidity position of the banking system vis-à-vis the central bank* is defined as the net sum of monetary policy operations, considered as an asset. The banking system is considered to be in 'liquidity deficit', if this net sum of monetary policy operations is positive. Using the balance sheet identity, it may also be defined as the sum of current accounts and net autonomous factors, the latter considered as a liability item. The sign of the liquidity position is relevant since it has often been argued that monetary policy implementation works better with the banking system in liquidity deficit rather than surplus vis-à-vis the central bank. Second, it has been argued that the deficit should be sufficiently large, such as to ensure that there are no short-term risks of a change of sign of the deficit. Sometimes, central banks take structural monetary policy measures to increase the liquidity deficit. For instance, reserve requirements may be established or increased for this purpose. Alternatively, the central bank may conduct liquidity-absorbing structural monetary policy operations, such as issuing debt certificates. This would not affect the liquidity position as defined above. However, one may define a *short-term* liquidity position, as consisting of the sum of all *short-term* monetary policy operations, that is, excluding long-term or 'structural' operations such as the holdings of outright securities on the asset side and the issuance of debt certificates on the liability side. One may define 'short-term' operations as all operations with a maturity of less than three months, although this is of course arbitrary.

(c) The balance sheet makes it possible to assess how far the central bank concentrates on monetary policy implementation as distinct from auxiliary activities. A perfectly *'lean' central bank balance sheet* may be defined as one in which autonomous factors excluding banknotes are zero, that is, in which the liability side consists only of the monetary base while the asset side displays only monetary policy operations (see also Gros and Schobert 1999). Since all central banks normally display some capital and reserves on their liability side, totally lean central bank balance sheets are rare, if they ever existed at all. It may be useful to define a 'leanness indicator' of central bank balance sheets for cross-central bank comparisons, such as, for instance, the term *1 − (sum of autonomous factor asset items + sum of autonomous factor liability items excluding banknotes)/ twice the length of the balance sheet.* The perfectly lean central bank would accordingly have a leanness of 1, while a very unfocused central bank would have a leanness of close to zero. Unfortunately, it is sometimes not obvious how the balance sheet items should be divided between autonomous factors and monetary policy instruments, especially in the case of outright holdings of domestic and even foreign exchange securities. For domestic outright securities, it may be unclear whether they are to be assigned to *investment* purposes (that is, to autonomous factors) or to *monetary policy.* The relevant question in this context should be what determines the composition and, more importantly, the size of the portfolios. If monetary policy considerations dominate these two dimensions, then the portfolios should be assigned to the monetary policy instruments category. As for foreign exchange reserves, they could be considered as a monetary policy item in the event that the central bank has specified an exchange rate target.

(*d*) This possible ambiguity in the assignment of items to the ideal types elaborated above also relates to the issue of *earmarking* assets against liabilities. An asset item is 'earmarked' to a liability item if a specific link between the two is perceived. For instance, the ECB has on its asset side an investment portfolio which is earmarked to its *capital and reserves* account. More importantly, in the earlier days of central banking, the issuance of banknotes was often linked to the asset side of the balance sheet in so far as banknotes could, under central bank statutes, be issued only if covered by specific counterparts such as gold or trade bills (for an overview of these restrictions, see for instance Keynes 1930: 237–41). Also, today both the Federal Reserve System and the Bank of Japan follow a somewhat related rule, namely, to cover their banknotes by government securities (see, for example, Blenck et al. 2001). Another case is that of a 'currency board', in which banknotes and foreign exchange reserves are linked.

(*e*) Another issue on which the central bank balance sheet should provide at least some information is *the profitability and financial independence* of the central bank. A first interesting item in this respect is the Capital and Reserves account, which is normally an indicator of past profitability and of financial buffers against future losses. The profitability of a central bank in the medium and longer term normally depends mainly on its operating costs and the possible obligation of the central bank, imposed by the government, to engage in loss-making activities such as granting subsidized credit to the government, bailing out banks, and administering prudential supervision activities. The profitability of central banks in the short term can also be heavily affected by changes of exchange rates or of longer-term interest rates if the central bank has considerable exposure in these markets. Last but not least, the profit of central banks depends on the interest rates it charges in its monetary policy operations. For instance, the Bank of Japan in 2003 could hardly make any profit since all its domestic monetary policy assets earned zero or very low returns, while its foreign exchange reserves were subject to revaluation losses.

The central bank balance sheet may reveal useful information on almost all of these profitability factors, since it gives a preliminary overview of central bank activities: does the central bank have substantial claims against the government? Does it have claims against banks or other private economic agents resulting from bail-outs? Are there other balance sheet positions, which hint at costly activities? Does the central bank hold substantial foreign exchange and longer-maturity domestic securities? Of course, the balance sheet can always only be a first indicator on these questions, and the central banks may even aim at a balance sheet format that masks the relevant information. For instance, claims with zero or low returns may be displayed in the balance sheet at nominal, not market, values. Valuation principles of *foreign exchange reserves* are also crucial for extracting from a central bank balance sheet information on its financial buffers: for instance, the Deutsche Bundesbank valued its foreign exchange reserves at their lowest historical exchange rate so as to systematically display a downward bias in the value of the foreign exchange reserves in its balance sheet. To maximize the information content of the balance sheet, it is preferable to revalue from time to time foreign exchange assets and those domestic securities that are unlikely to be held until maturity. Revaluation techniques are relevant also since they impact on the calculation of profits and thus on the disbursement of profit to the central bank's shareholders (normally the government).

In sum, although imperfect, there is no better quick overview of central bank profitability issues than the balance sheet. Lack of profitability of the central bank is important since it is key to the central bank's independence from the government and to the likelihood that the central bank will set monetary policy (that is, short-term interest rates) only according to monetary policy needs. To that extent, the balance sheet also provides information on the credibility of a central bank and the probability of achievement of its ultimate targets, such as price stability (see, for instance, Gros and Schobert 1999; Leone 1993; Vaez-Zadeh 1991; Stella 1997).

2.3   EXAMPLES OF CENTRAL BANK BALANCE SHEETS

Recognizing the relevance of their balance sheets, many central banks early on adopted a policy of publishing them frequently.[2] For instance, the Bank of England started in 1844 with Robert Peel's Act to publish a weekly financial statement (the 'Bank Return') each Wednesday, the format of which has changed only to a limited extent since then. Since its foundation in 1876, the Reichsbank published its balance sheet four times a month on evenly spread specific calendar days (7, 15, 23, and 30/31), and the Bundesbank followed this exact tradition until 1998. It is worth looking at the Reichsbank's balance sheet for 1900 because it provides us indeed with an insight into a key feature of monetary policy implementation by many continental European central banks at the beginning of the twentieth century (Table 2.2).

A number of observations may be made. First, the substantial amounts of metal (mainly gold) on the asset side was a consequence of the gold standard's key feature that banknotes issued were to be redeemed in gold on presentation, such that gold was considered the natural asset of a trustworthy central bank, and central banks were often requested by law to cover a proportion of their banknote issue with gold.

Table 2.2   *Reichsbank financial statement, averages for weekly statements in 1900, in millions of Goldmarks*

Gold and silver	817	Notes in circulation	1,139
Banknotes of other issuing banks	14	Capital, reserves, other	150
Short-term government paper	23		
Discounted trade bills	800		
Lombard lending to banks	80		
Residual	68	Reserves (of banks and others)	513
TOTAL	1,802	TOTAL	1,802

Source: Reichsbank (1925*b*).

---

[2] Two early comparative monographs focusing on central bank balance sheets and their relation to monetary policy implementation are Palgrave (1903) and Käppeli (1930).

Second, besides metal, the asset side of the Reichsbank mainly contains credit granted to banks through borrowing facilities, whereby discounting of bills dominates lombard lending (advances). Outright holdings of securities and open market operations play a negligible role (indeed, there were *no* liquidity-providing Reichsbank open market operations at that time). Monetary policy implementation by the Reichsbank hence consisted mainly setting the discount rate. Since the banks were always structurally short of liquidity, they had massive recourse to the discount facility, and hence the discount rate was guiding quite closely the short-term inter-bank rate.

Third, on the liability side, the reserves are not separated into government deposits and deposits held by banks. However, since no reserve requirements were imposed on banks, the government could be viewed as a player not fundamentally different from the banks, and the need to distinguish them was less pressing. The deposits were non-remunerated for all counterparts, making their high level relative to banknotes astonishing. It gives evidence of the highly developed giro system that the Reichsbank had successfully established since its foundation and that had already become a very popular means of larger value payments before the turn of the century, also thanks to the Reichsbank's benevolent pricing policy (see Reichsbank 1900). One motive for this had been that giro payments were a substitute for banknotes, the issuing rights of which were limited by law.

Fourth, all in all, the Reichsbank balance sheet of 1900 appears to be rather lean as long as we accept that gold has a quasi-monetary policy instrument status in the gold standard. Little involvement of the Reichsbank in government refinancing is revealed on the asset side. Also, the concentration on one genuine monetary policy instrument (discount loans) suggests a well-focused system.

The Reichsbank's case in the early 1920s provides a good example how balance sheets can reveal information not only on monetary policy implementation in the narrow sense but also on prospects for inflation. Indeed, the Reichsbank was used by the German government, as were other central banks by their respective governments, during the First World War to finance budget deficits at interest rates that were too low. While the winners of the war managed afterwards to stabilize their economies and to reduce once again the government debt held by the central bank, the German government increasingly used the Reichsbank as a printing press for money and thus extended its liabilities to it while preventing the Reichsbank from raising interest rates. The Reichsbank balance sheet of 1922 therefore looked rather different from the one of 1900 (Table 2.3).

Table 2.3   *Reichsbank financial statement, end 1922, in millions of Reichsmarks*

Gold and silver	1,005	Banknotes in circulation	1,280,095
Short-term government paper	1,184,464	Capital, reserves, other	180
Discounted trade bills	660,708	Residual	36,150
Lombard lending to banks	774		
		Reserves (of banks and others)	530,526
TOTAL	1,846,951	TOTAL	1,846,951

Source: Deutsche Bundesbank (1976: Table C1–1.01).

Table 2.4   *Reichsbank financial statement, end 1922, percentage changes to end 1921*

Gold and silver	+1	Banknotes in circulation	+1,026
Short-term government paper	+795	Capital, reserves, other	+0
Discounted trade bills	+8,237	Residual	–
Lombard lending to banks	+8,500		
		Reserves (of banks and others)	+1,512

Besides metal, banknotes of other issuing banks, and Capital and Reserves, all positions exploded relative to the year 1900. In particular, short-term government paper has now become the main position on the asset side. Of course, one should admit that this balance sheet in itself would not necessarily reveal the hyperinflationary environment of Germany in 1922. Indeed, today the Bank of Japan and the US Fed follow the policy of covering the issuance of banknotes through government paper. However, in the case of the *Reichsbank*, the big *change* from the financial statement of 1900 should trigger questions, and an examination of the rates of growth relative to end-1921 confirms the hyperinflationary ballooning of the balance sheet (Table 2.4).

The monetary base and the overall size of the balance sheet increased within one year by more than 1,000 per cent, which is an unambiguous indicator of extreme inflationary pressures. The fact that the monetary base growth reveals the inflationary environment suggests that the monetary base may after all be of use as an indicator variable. Under normal conditions, it is less suitable as an indicator variable than broader economic aggregates, since its relationship to inflation is normally less stable. Still, the monetary base has the advantage that it does not rely on balance sheet data to be collected from banks, and it may therefore be in fact a useful indicator under less orderly conditions, in which commercial banks' balance sheets are very unstable or banks are even unable to provide reliable statistics. This does not imply that the monetary base

Table 2.5   *Eurosystem financial statement, 22 December 2000, in billions of euros*

Net foreign assets (incl. gold)	389	Banknotes in circulation	373
Domestic securities and claims towards government	87	Capital, reserves, incl. revaluation accounts	199
Other domestic assets	88	Other autonomous factors	136
OMOs of two weeks maturity	212		
OMOs of 3 months maturity	45		
Borrowing facility	2	Deposit facility	1
		Reserves of credit institutions	114
TOTAL	823	TOTAL	823

Note: OMO: open market operations.

Source: ECB website.

becomes an important magnitude for monetary policy *implementation* in the narrow sense, that is to say, that it becomes an operational target.

The successor of the Reichsbank, after a ten-year interlude of the Bank Deutscher Länder, was the Bundesbank, which is now an integral part of the *Eurosystem*. Relevant to analysing monetary policy operations in the euro area is the balance sheet of the Eurosystem, that is, the consolidated balance sheet of all participating national central banks and the ECB. The Eurosystem financial statement makes it possible to read off the four categories of items outlined above. In total, the published weekly Eurosystem balance sheet contains around fifty items, but in Table 2.5 most have been summarized for the sake of simplicity.

The Eurosystem balance sheet not only makes it possible to distinguish among autonomous factors (with all relevant sub-items), current accounts of credit institutions, and standing facilities, but also shows the different types of open market operations separately. Its reverse open market operations have two weeks and three months maturity, whose operational details are described in, for instance, ECB (2002a). From the balance sheet, we can extract the following key information on the monetary policy implementation of the ECB:

- The ECB does not have a portfolio of securities held outright (that is, acquired permanently, and not only temporarily through, for example, repurchase operations) for implementing monetary policy. Instead, all open market operations are reverse operations, whereby those with two-weeks maturity provide around three-quarters of the total open market operations volume.
- Recourse to standing facilities is only marginal compared with open market operations; that is, it does not serve to cover a relevant part of the liquidity deficit.

- The reserve holdings of commercial banks with the central bank are considerable (they are, on average over the month, to a large extent determined by required reserves).
- With regard to autonomous factors, foreign exchange reserves dominate the asset side, while banknotes are of a similar order of magnitude on the liability side.
- The capital and reserves and revaluation reserves are the third largest autonomous factor item.

The financial statement of the *Bank of England* is even today subdivided into statements from the Note Issuing Department and the Banking Department. Also, assets and liabilities are presented in the opposite manner to the convention of listing assets on the left and liabilities on the right. Table 2.6 displays the Bank of England balance sheet for Wednesday 20 December 2000, though with the conventional presentation and with the Banking and Issue Departments' separate statements consolidated to provide a format as close as possible to the one used above.

The assignment of the Bank of England's securities to monetary policy items is somewhat ambiguous. Also, the balance sheet format does not provide a great deal of detail on the different monetary policy instruments, such as reverse open market operations and the borrowing facility, and it is hence impossible to determine from the balance sheet the relative importance of the different instruments. In any case, outright operations appear to dominate the liquidity supply. The banking system held reserves of £1.5 billion, partly required reserves. Finally, it is noteworthy that there are no foreign exchange reserves in the central bank's balance sheet, since these are held by the Treasury.

The *US Fed* has also had a tradition of publishing a weekly financial statement from its beginnings in 1914 (see, for example, Burgess 1927 and Carr 1959 on detailed descriptions of the Fed's earlier balance sheets). The

Table 2.6   *Bank of England consolidated financial statement, Wednesday 20 December 2000, in billions of pounds sterling*

Premises, equipment, securities	2.3	Notes in circulation	29.4
		Public deposits	0.4
		Reserves and other accounts	11.4
		Capital	0.01
Government securities	18.0		
Other securities	15.9		
Advances and other accounts	6.5		
		Reserves of banks	1.5
TOTAL	42.7	TOTAL	42.7

Source: Bank of England website.

statement is currently published each Wednesday under the title 'Factors Affecting Reserve Balances', which already indicates that the main purpose of the publication is to provide information on the factors affecting the scarcity of reserves, and hence short-term interest rates (Table 2.7).

As in the case of the Eurosystem, the balance sheet is detailed and clearly distinguishes the four categories of positions. Monetary policy operations, and indeed the asset side in general, are dominated by outright holdings of government paper. Repurchase agreements amount only to 5 per cent of the stock of outright portfolios. The borrowing facility (the discount window) is not used in a substantial way. As well, as government paper dominates the monetary policy operations on the asset side, so do banknotes in circulation for autonomous factors on the liability side. Indeed, the balance sheet appears overall to be rather lean. Again, foreign exchange reserves play only a limited role, for two reasons: first, in the US the government and the Fed each hold half of the federal foreign exchange reserves; and second, the US has never targeted foreign exchange rates and therefore traditionally has not needed large foreign exchange reserves.

Finally, consider two more, very different, types of balance sheets. First, Table 2.8 displays that of the *Bank of Latvia*, which presents the

Table 2.7   *US Fed: Factors affecting reserves, Wednesday 20 December 2000, in billions of US dollars*

Gold and other foreign assets	13	Currency in circulation	587
Float	4	Government deposits	5
Other assets	66	Required clearing balances	7
		Capital, other liabilities	18
US government paper bought outright	515		
Repurchase agreement	26		
Discount window	0		
		Reserves of banks	7
TOTAL	624	TOTAL	624

Source: Board of Governors' website.

Table 2.8   *Bank of Latvia financial statement, end December 2001, in millions of Lats*

Net foreign assets	563.0	Notes in circulation	483.6
Other assets	7.3	Government deposits (net)	3.4
		Capital accounts	59.3
Credit to banks	39.4		
		Deposits of banks	63.4
Sum	609.7	Sum	609.7

Source: Quarterly Bulletin of the Bank of Latvia.

case of a small open economy with a currency peg (the currency of Latvia is pegged to the IMF Standard Drawing Right, SDR, basket).

The bank of Latvia conducts some monetary policy operations, and banks hold deposits with it to fulfil reserve requirements, but overall the balance sheet is largely dominated by net foreign assets on the asset side and banknotes in circulation on the liability side. To that extent, the balance sheet reveals a focus on the chosen monetary policy framework of a currency peg.

Last but not least, the balance sheet of the *Bank of Ghana* in Table 2.9 represents the case of a developing country. Claims on the government dominate the asset side of the balance sheet. The net foreign position of the central bank is on the liability side. The balance sheet seems to reveal a dependence of the central bank on the government and a substantial danger of central bank losses, especially if the claims on the government are remunerated at artificially low rates and if the domestic currency is devalued such that the value of net foreign liabilities, measured in domestic currency, increases. Monetary policy operations seem to play a limited role in the operations of the central bank. To judge from the balance sheet, one would not be surprised to observe a high inflation rate in this country. This is further confirmed if one considers the growth rates of balance sheet measures compared with the previous year, as revealed in Table 2.10.

Table 2.9   *Bank of Ghana financial statement, end December 2000, in billions of Cedis*

Claims on government	3,169	Notes in circulation	1,857
Other assets (net)	625	Net foreign liabilities	1,154
		Capital accounts	511
Claims on banks	15		
		Deposits of banks	287
TOTAL	3,809	TOTAL	3,809

Source: Quarterly Bulletin of the Bank of Ghana.

Table 2.10   *Bank of Ghana financial statement, percentage changes between end 1999 and end 2000*

Claims on government	+144	Notes in circulation	+46
Other assets (net)	−8	Net foreign liabilities	−
		Capital accounts	18
Claims on banks	+39		
		Deposits of banks	−7

Note: At end 1999, the Bank of Ghana still had a net foreign assets position of 22 billion Cedis.
Source: Quarterly Bulletin of the Bank of Ghana.

The increase in claims on governments, the switch from a net foreign asset into a net foreign liability position, and the growth of banknotes are not good sign, and indeed year-on year inflation was around 40 per cent in the fourth quarter of 2000 in Ghana. Banknotes have expanded broadly in line with inflation. As in the case of the Reichsbank in 1922, this suggests that monetary items in the central bank balance sheet can, in particular under circumstances of exceptional financial instability, be indicators of inflationary pressures in the economy, and thus be useful for the analysis underlying the setting of the level of the operational target (the short-term interest rate). It should be noted that, contrary to the Reichsbank case of 1922, in which the worst was still to come, inflation in Ghana has fallen since 2000.

It has become clear from the series of examples that structures of balance sheets can differ strongly, depending mainly on three factors:

1. Whether the monetary policy strategy of the central bank focuses (or focused) on foreign exchange rates. In case of a foreign exchange rate target (for example, Bank of Latvia), the optimal size of foreign exchange reserves is normally considerable.
2. Dependence on the government. Central banks that are dependent on governments that pursue unsustainable fiscal policies are likely to end up with huge claims, possibly remunerated at low rates, on the government. Then, their main concern is no longer the appropriate implementation of monetary policy in order to reach some macroeconomic target, but to keep the government solvent or to compensate the losses it accumulates due to the assets imposed on it. Both aims can be achieved by running an inflationary policy, that is, one in which short-term interest rate targets are below the level appropriate for achieving price stability or low inflation.
3. The monetary policy implementation framework, which includes such choices as (*a*) whether to impose reserve requirements and, if so, of which size; (*b*) satisfying structural liquidity needs through open market operations (like most modern central banks) or through a borrowing facility (like, for example, the Reichsbank in 1900); (*c*) the use of outright operations (as in the US and the UK) versus the use of reverse operations for the structural provision of liquidity (euro area).

While the first two issues are beyond the scope of this book, the third is treated in the following chapters. For the time being, it may be concluded that some of the observed differences between central bank balance sheets appear to be well justified on the basis of different environments, while others (for example, the difference between the US Fed's and the Eurosystem's balance sheets) seem to be based more on history and convention.

2.4   AUTONOMOUS LIQUIDITY FACTORS: THE CASE OF THE EUROSYSTEM

It follows from the central bank balance sheet that, if the supply of reserves is supposed to stay constant, and if recourse to the standing facilities is supposed to remain negligible, then the central bank has to precisely *neutralize autonomous factor changes by changes in the volume of outstanding open market operations.* Stabilizing the supply of reserves is, for a given demand for reserves, a necessary condition for stabilizing short-term interest rates. As long as the central bank is unable or unwilling to enter the market continuously through open market operations, this implies for the central bank a need to *forecast* the evolution of autonomous factors. A considerable part of the resources central banks devote to day-to-day monetary policy implementation therefore relates to the forecasting of autonomous liquidity factors. This section thus briefly reviews the time-series properties and the forecasting approach for the most relevant autonomous factors, focusing on the case of the Eurosystem. A relatively detailed description of autonomous factors and their forecasting in the case of the US Fed is provided in Meulendyke (1998). Time-series properties of autonomous factors in EU countries prior to 1999 are described in Escriva and Fagan (1996). Some information on the case of the Bank of England can be found in Butler and Clews (1997). A detailed assessment of the euro area case can be found in Bindseil and Seitz (2001) and ECB (2002*b*).

2.4.1   *Banknotes*

Banknotes are typically one of the largest single items in the central bank balance sheet. The amount of euro banknotes, displayed in Fig. 2.1, exhibits a rather regular weekly, monthly, and seasonal pattern. These patterns reflect social regularities such as the withdrawal of cash before the weekend, the payment of salaries, the summer holiday season, and Christmas shopping. Moreover, this series displays a general upward trend, which temporarily reversed only when the euro banknotes were introduced at the beginning of 2002.

The regularities in the banknote time series suggest an *econometric* forecasting approach. Traditionally, central banks have used both informal methods (charts, looking for similar situations in the past, simple calculus)

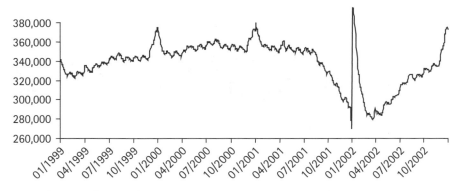

Figure 2.1 *Banknotes of the Eurosystem, 1999–2002, in millions of euros*
Source: European Central Bank.

and econometric forecasts; the latter seem to have been first developed by the Banco d'España (see, for example, Cancelo and Espasa 1987). The model applied by the European Central Bank in its day-to-day forecasting has been presented in Cabrero et al. (2002). Still, it needs to be recognized that 'expert knowledge', that is, elements not easily incorporated in a model, often helps to improve the econometric forecast in particular situations. In any case, forecast errors are significant during special periods such as Christmas. The Eurosystem had particular problems in forecasting banknotes during the cash changeover at the beginning of 2002, and even needed to have recourse to non-regular open market operations to adjust the supply of reserves after realizing the forecasting errors.

2.4.2 *Government deposits*

Already in 1927, Burgess noted that the relationship between the state and the money market is as complicated as the relationship between the state and the church and, indeed, changes in the government's deposits with the central bank have usually represented the most volatile and most unpredictable autonomous liquidity factor. Figure 2.2, covering government deposits with the Eurosystem in the period 1999–2002, reveals that, despite some monthly patterns, many of the changes appear to lack regularity. The volatility of government deposits in the Eurosystem in fact stemmed only from a few national central banks (NCBs), namely, those of Spain, France, Ireland, Italy, and Portugal, although more and more of these NCBs adopted, during the first years of the euro, institutional reforms that led to a reduction of the volatility or at least to increased predictability. It is in principle easy to set up arrangements whereby government flows have no

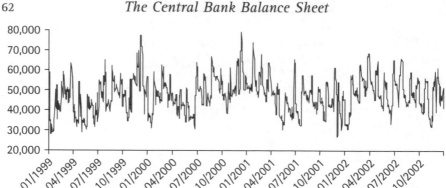

Figure 2.2 *Government deposits in the Eurosystem, 1999–2002, in millions of euros*
Source: European Central Bank.

impact on the supply of reserves. Most euro area governments have adopted the approach of placing all their funds, at least at end of day, with the market, not with the central bank, partially because the return on government deposits with the central bank has been set at zero. Traditionally, however, governments have preferred to avoid the credit risk and operational requirements implied by placing funds in the market, and governments have often even been forbidden by law from placing liquid funds anywhere other than in the central bank. In the traditional setting, which is still relevant in the US and the UK, government deposits are affected by any financial operation conducted by the government, such as debt issuance, redemption and coupon payments, the collection of tax and social security contributions, the acquisition of goods and services, and the payment of wages, pensions, and other social security benefits.

In central banks with volatile government deposits, sizeable resources are devoted to forecast the net liquidity flows resulting from all government transactions with the private sector. This forecasting requires detailed knowledge of institutional factors, and good information flows from the government to the central bank with regard, for instance, to debt issuance activities. Econometric techniques are of little help since they do not easily capture complex institutional factors. Despite all efforts invested in forecasting government deposits, they remain for many central banks the most important source of unintended changes in money market conditions, and this is indeed also the case for the Eurosystem.

2.4.3   Net foreign assets

The level and time-series properties of net foreign assets of central banks typically depend on the size of their currency area and on the foreign exchange rate regime. *Small currency areas'* central banks tend to have relatively large net foreign assets, in order to be able to stabilize their exchange rate through foreign exchange interventions. Then, the changes of net foreign assets depend on international economic conditions and the dedication of the central bank to achieving a certain exchange rate target. In the case of *large currency areas*, such as the US or the Eurozone, the volatility of the level of foreign exchange reserves is likely to be lower because exchange rate interventions are rare. Apart from changes induced by foreign exchange interventions, changes of net foreign assets also occur when the central bank acts as foreign exchange counterpart of the government. Indeed, the government normally makes use of the central bank's foreign exchange reserves when paying bills or issuing and redeeming debt in foreign exchange. The central bank then readjusts its foreign exchange reserves to their previous level depending on, for example, market conditions. Moreover, the level of foreign exchange reserves may of course change when a central bank reassesses its need for foreign exchange reserves and therefore deliberately reduces or increases their level. Finally, changes of net foreign assets *without* effects on domestic money market conditions are those related to the earning of interest (in foreign exchange) and to revaluation (for example, if the exchange rate between the US dollar and euro changes, then the value, expressed in the balance sheet in euro, of a given amount of US dollars also changes). In the case of the Eurosystem, all of the factors mentioned above sometimes had an effect on net foreign assets whereby the quarterly revaluations dominate, as suggested by Fig. 2.3. These revaluations are, as mentioned, balanced by an opposite change in some revaluation account, such as to leave all other balance sheet items unchanged.

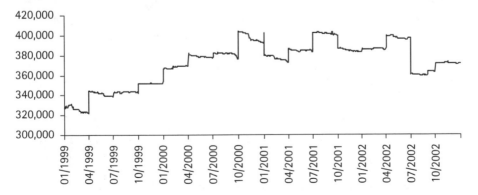

Figure 2.3 *Net foreign assets of the Eurosystem, 1999–2002, in millions of euros*
Source: European Central Bank.

2.4.4   Domestic financial assets not related to monetary policy

Outright holdings of securities purchased in the secondary market may be more attractive than reverse monetary policy operations for income generation, since they allow diversification into longer maturity. As already mentioned, it may not always be obvious how to distinguish between domestic financial assets that are *monetary policy* assets and those that are mainly *investment* assets. In the case of the Eurosystem, a clear separation between monetary policy assets and other securities is necessary since the nature of the assets determines who controls them. While the ECB controls monetary policy operations, the NCBs are in principle entitled, according to Article 14.4 of the ECB/ESCB (European System of Central Banks) Statute, to perform functions other than those related to monetary policy, and those functions may imply the holding of securities portfolios. Indeed, all NCBs and the ECB have some 'own funds' or other investment portfolios they manage under risk/return considerations. In the case of other central banks, there is no comparable need for a clear distinction between the two types of assets. As Fig. 2.4 reveals, the Eurosystem's financial assets that are not related to monetary policy are relatively stable. Furthermore, the forecasting of this item is normally considered easy since its changes are under the full control of the central bank.

2.4.5   Items in course of settlement ('float' of the payment system)

Payment system float is created whenever the crediting and the debiting of the accounts of banks with the central bank related to inter-bank

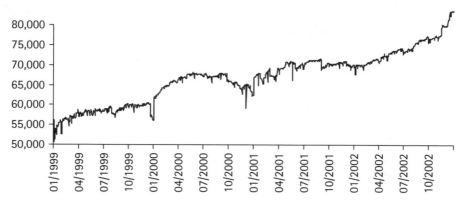

Figure 2.4   *Net financial assets of the Eurosystem, 1999–2002, in millions of euros*
Source: European Central Bank.

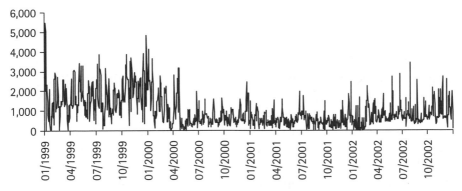

Figure 2.5 *Items in course of settlement in the Eurosystem, 1999–2002, in millions of euros*

Source: European Central Bank.

payments do not occur simultaneously. It can be both liquidity-providing (appearing on the asset side of the central bank balance sheet) or liquidity-withdrawing (appearing on the liability side of the balance sheet). For instance, cheques which are credited before being debited inject liquidity (create an asset-side float). In contrast, *transfers* have, if any, the opposite effect. The relevance of float thus depends on the specification of the payment system. In the euro area, a majority of national central banks do not exhibit any float, and the overall volatility created by the float is limited (see Fig. 2.5). In the US, the float is still a considerably more important source of shocks to the supply of reserves, due to the persisting popularity of payment by cheques (Blenck et al. 2001: 44; see also Carr 1959).

2.4.6 *Quality of forecasts of autonomous factors at different horizons*

The *time horizon over which*, in day-to-day monetary policy implementation, *autonomous factors need to be forecast* depends much on the operational framework of a central bank. In the case of the Bank of England, with its reserve maintenance period of one day and daily open market operations, by far the most relevant forecasting horizon is the end of the same day and, therefore, most forecast resources are invested in its case into this short-term perspective. In the case of the US Fed, with its two-weeks reserve maintenance period, relatively low reserve requirements, and open market operations on most business days, the relevance of forecasts of autonomous liquidity factors over several days and even up to the end of the reserve maintenance period is somewhat greater, although the same-day horizon is still most important. Finally, in the case of the Eurosystem with its weekly open market operations and a reserve maintenance period of one month, accurate forecasts over a one-week horizon are most crucial.

Internally, the Eurosystem produces separate forecasts for all the main autonomous factors. The national central banks transmit forecasts of their respective national autonomous factors on a daily basis to the ECB, which then integrates them into an aggregate euro area autonomous factor forecast. Table 2.11 provides, for the second semester of 2002, the volatility of the main autonomous factors as well as the forecasting errors, both over three different time horizons, namely for $T + 1$, $T + 5$ and $T + 10$.

It appears that the effectiveness of forecasting, if measured by the ratio of forecast errors over volatility, is greatest for the two items which are most volatile, namely, banknotes and government deposits. This mainly reflects the larger amount of resources devoted to the forecasting of these two key time series. For the US, a similar table for $T + 1$, found in Federal Reserve Bank of New York (2002: 9), shows similar orders of magnitude. In its spring 2003 quarterly bulletin (p. 19), the Bank of England also provides standard deviations of $T + 1$ errors, but distinguishes between forecasts made at 9.45 a.m., at 14:30 p.m., and at 16:20 p.m. The standard deviation of forecast errors of the sum of autonomous factors amounted in February 2003 to £81 million, £61 million, and £37 million at these three points in time during the day, respectively.

Finally, it may be remarked that, among the three central banks considered here, two—the European Central Bank and the Bank of England—*publish* their forecasts of autonomous liquidity factors. The ECB, when announcing its weekly open market operation, provides the average net sum of autonomous factors until the day before the settlement of

Table 2.11 *Autonomous liquidity factors in the euro area, second half of 2002,*
standard deviations of changes and of forecast errors at three different
forecasting horizons, in billions of euros

	T + 1	T + 5	T + 10
Banknotes	1.1 / 0.2	4.1 / 1.4	7.8/2.8
Government deposits	4.5 / 0.4	10.0 / 2.0	12.0 / 3.4
Net foreign assets	0.4 / 0.1	0.8 / 0.4	11.4 / 0.9
Domestic financial assets	0.4 / 0.2	0.8 / 0.6	1.3 / 1.0
Float	0.7 / 0.1	0.8 / 0.3	0.8 / 0.8

Source: European Central Bank.

the subsequent open market operation. The Bank of England publishes twice a day a forecast for the same day. The role of the publication of liquidity forecasts in steering short-term interest rates will be taken up in Chapter 3.

2.5 A CLOSER LOOK AT THE RESERVE HOLDINGS OF BANKS

The reserve holdings of banks with the central bank were presented above as a residual of the central bank balance sheet. The balance sheet could accordingly be considered as the list of all *supply* factors of reserves. Required reserves and excess reserves, in contrast, would be the main *demand* factors. This section looks closer at excess reserves and some other sub-categories of reserves which have played or play an import role in monetary policy operating procedures.

Excess reserves are defined as those reserves that do not contribute to the fulfilment of reserve requirement. Excess reserves actually play an important role in the practice of forecasting liquidity needs for the calibration of open market operations, as the following demonstrates. Reserve holdings in a system *without* required reserves are always excess reserves. In a system *with* reserve requirements that need to be fulfilled on average over a reserve maintenance period (for example, one month), the evolution of excess reserves in the course of the reserve maintenance period normally cannot be extracted from the aggregate central bank balance sheet figures, since excess reserves are a phenomenon *at the level of individual banks*. While on a certain day of a reserve maintenance period one bank may still not have fulfilled its required reserves, such that all its daily reserves are contributing to fulfilment of its required reserves, others may already be holding excess reserves since they fulfilled their entire accumulated requirement earlier in the reserve maintenance period. This is an important issue for the implementation of monetary policy, since it determines how many additional reserves will be needed before the end of the reserve maintenance period in order to allow fulfilment of aggregate reserve requirements without tension.

Consider the example, given in Table 2.12, of a reserve maintenance period of five days in a monetary area with three banks subject to reserve requirements, each having a reserve requirement of $10 million, and the simple balance sheet identity being $R = M-A$, that is, reserves of banks equal open market operations minus autonomous factors (from here onwards, open market operations M will be considered to be netted on

Table 2.12   *An example of excess reserves accumulation within the reserve maintenance period, in millions of dollars*

	Day 1	Day 2	Day 3	Day 4	Day 5	Average
M (outstanding open market operations)	50	50	40	40	40	44.0
A (autonomous factors)	22	7	5	9	16	11.8
R (reserves = $M - A$)	28	43	35	31	24	32.2
Reserves of bank 1 (R1)	8	25	15	4	0	10.4
Reserves of bank 2 (R2)	20	18	15	2	1	11.2
Reserves of bank 3 (R3)	0	0	5	25	23	10.6
XSR of bank 1	0	0	0	2	0	0.4
XSR of bank 2	0	0	3	2	1	1.2
XSR of bank 3	0	0	0	0	3	0.6
XSR − total	0	0	3	4	4	2.2
Remaining reserve fulfilment needs at day's end	122	79	47	21	0	–

the asset side of the balance sheet and autonomous factors A on the liability side, such as it is indeed the case for the three central banks in our sample). The table assumes a certain path of M, A, and R, and individual reserve holding paths of the three banks, also implying a certain individual and aggregate excess reserves path. The last row of the table indicates the remaining needs of banks to fulfil reserve requirements. At the beginning of the maintenance period, these needs amount to $150 million; at end of day 1, they have declined by the sum of current accounts on day 1. The same logic applies to the other days, whereby excess reserves of course do not contribute to reducing the remaining need to fulfil reserve requirements. Once a bank has fulfilled its accumulated reserve requirements over a reserve maintenance period (such as bank 2 on day 3), then all reserves it holds on subsequent days are excess reserves.

As mentioned, it is obviously not possible to measure the intra-maintenance period path of excess reserves on the basis of the aggregate reserve figures. However, this path is relevant to the central bank calibrating its open market operations at the end of the reserve maintenance period. Suppose, everything else unchanged, that bank 2 would have held on its account on day 3 not $15 million but $30 million, and bank 1 would have held not $15 million but zero, such that the aggregate amount of reserves would have been unchanged (for instance, an end-of-day payment of $15 million from bank 2 to bank 1 could have failed, and bank 2 may have been unable to access a deposit facility). Then, total excess reserves on day 3 would have been higher by $15 million, and in the morning of the last day of the maintenance period banks would have had a residual need to fulfil reserve requirement not of $21 million but of $36 million. Since the total amount of reserves available on that day, as determined by the central bank balance sheet, was, however, only $24 million, the banking system would have been short by $12 million of reserves, and inter-bank overnight rates would have soared. If the central bank had been aware of the large accumulation of excess reserves on day 3, it could of course have increased its open market operations volume correspondingly on days 4 and 5.

In the case of the Eurosystem (the US case being described by, for instance, Beek 1981; Dow 2001), Fig. 2.6 reveals the average amounts of excess reserves per reserve maintenance period during the first three and a half years of the euro.

Excess reserves' averages per maintenance period had an expected value of €707 million and a standard deviation of €34 million. The minimum value within the period considered was €437 million (in the maintenance period ending on 23 September 1999), while the maximum was €1,668 million (in the maintenance period ending on 23 January 2002, that is, covering the euro cash changeover). Another pattern that emerges is that maintenance periods ending on weekends also exhibit above-average levels of excess reserves. Indeed, from the start of monetary union until May 2002, the average amount of daily excess reserves in reserve maintenance periods ending on Sundays was €877 million, against €674 million in all other reserve maintenance periods (excluding

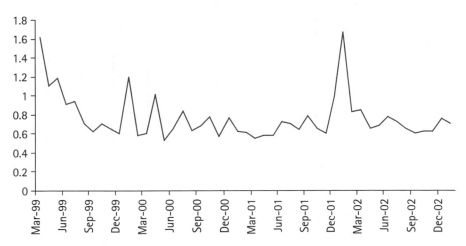

Figure 2.6   *Average excess reserves per maintenance period, 1999–2002, in billions of euros*

Source: European Central Bank.

the first three in 1999). As Fig. 2.7 reveals, the intra-reserve maintenance
period evolution of daily excess reserves exhibits a similar pattern in
every maintenance period, with a low level at the start of the period and
then a rapid build-up during the last few days. The time series is, however, not really monotonously increasing within the reserve maintenance
period. For instance, there is sometimes a local peak at the end of the
calendar month. Figure 2.7 also reveals that the reserve maintenance
period covering the introduction of euro banknotes and the withdrawal
of the old national banknotes (ending on 23 January 2002) saw the
accumulation of exceptionally high excess reserves early in the reserve
maintenance period.

The increasing trend of daily excess reserves within each maintenance
period obviously stems from the fact that the number of banks which
have already fulfilled their required reserves and which may hence
generate excess reserves if they are exposed to a positive liquidity shock
at the end of the day (and do not have recourse to the deposit facility)
increases monotonously. Bindseil et al. (2004) show that there are no
indications from euro area data that excess reserves would depend
on liquidity conditions or on short-term interest rates. Therefore, in the
weekly calibration of open market operations, they can effectively be
treated as an *exogenous demand factor*, which needs to be forecast

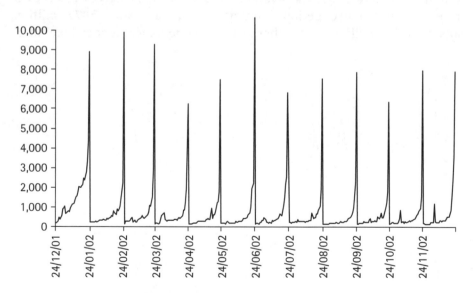

Figure 2.7   *Excess reserves in the euro area, 24 December 2001 to 23 December*
2002, in millions of euros

Source: European Central Bank.

similarly to autonomous factors. The fact that excess reserves are not interest-rate elastic implies that *no* factor on the market for reserves is interest-rate elastic, apart from the recourse to standing facilities (the supply of liquidity through open market operations may, of course, also be interest-rate elastic if the central bank handles it in this way). This will be key to the simple model of liquidity management presented in Chapter 3.

Some banks tend to under-fulfil their reserve requirements and hence to produce *reserve deficiencies*. This is, however, rare since it is associated with a penalty. For instance, in the case of the Eurosystem, penalties correspond to the rate of the borrowing facility plus 2.5 per cent, such that any bank aware of a deficiency should prefer at the end of the reserve maintenance period to have recourse to the borrowing facility. In the euro area, the sum of the deficiencies per monthly reserve maintenance period is normally below €10 million. The following relationship between required reserves (RR), actual reserves (R), excess reserves (XSR), and reserve deficiencies (RDs) holds under the definitions adopted *on average over the reserve maintenance period*, the upper bars indicating that such averages are meant:

$$\overline{RR} = \overline{R} - \overline{XSR} + \overline{RD} \tag{2.1}$$

This identity normally does not hold for single days of the reserve maintenance period (if the reserve maintenance period has more than one day), since required reserves only need to be held on average over the reserve maintenance period.

One may now consider some definitions of sub-categories of reserve holdings that have played an important role in the US Fed's implementation of monetary policy (see, for example, Meulendyke 1998: 36) and that have been discussed in the reserve position doctrine literature over decades. Nearly from the start of the Federal Reserve System in 1914, the Fed distinguished between *non-borrowed reserves* (NBR) and *borrowed reserves*, whereby borrowed reserves are simply defined as the reserves obtained from recourse to the discount window, the US Fed's borrowing facility (B, for recourse to the borrowing facility):

$$R = NBR + B \tag{2.2}$$

From the Fed's balance sheet identity, $R = M + B - A$ (M being open market operations and A being autonomous factors), it follows that $NBR = M - A$. Actually, from 6 October 1979, for three years the Fed claimed to follow a *non-borrowed reserves targeting* procedure, and afterwards for a few years a *borrowed reserves targeting* procedure. In the

1950s and 1960s the Fed focused in its operating procedures on *free reserves* (FR) as one money market indicator (see, for example, Meigs 1962; Dewald 1963). Free reserves were simply defined as the difference between excess reserves and borrowed reserves (again being properly defined only as average over the reserve maintenance period):

$$\overline{FR} = \overline{XSR} - \overline{B} \tag{2.3}$$

The interpretation of monetary policy implementation procedures focusing on these magnitudes is taken up in Chapters 7 and 8.

2.6   A CLOSER LOOK AT THE RECOURSE TO STANDING FACILITIES

In monetary policy implementation, it is necessary to distinguish clearly between two different kinds of recourse to standing facilities; and the failure to do so may actually have been one of the most important sources of confusion in the twentieth century's debates on monetary policy implementation. The two are driven by different motivations from the side of credit institutions. Consider them in turn. Under the assumption of *perfect inter-bank markets and large reserve requirements*, recourse to standing facilities should take place in principle only at the end of the reserve maintenance period and should basically reflect the *aggregate* lack or surplus of accumulated reserves relative to the given demand for reserves.

This type of use of the standing facilities will be called in the following the *aggregate recourse*. During the reserve maintenance period, the buffers provided by the reserve requirement system should be sufficient to allow the aggregate banking sector to average out transitory reserve deficits or surpluses. Also, this type of recourse to standing facilities should by definition always be one-sided, that is, a simultaneous aggregate recourse of the banking system to both a liquidity-providing and to a liquidity-absorbing standing facilities can never occur. Aggregate recourse to standing facilities is a priori symmetric for the two facilities: an aggregate surplus of reserves at the end of the reserve maintenance period implies recourse to the deposit facility (if any such is offered), an aggregate deficit of the same magnitude implies a corresponding recourse to the borrowing facility. It is hence possible to talk only of the 'net recourse to standing facilities', defining a net recourse to marginal lending (depositing) as a positive (negative) net recourse to standing facilities. This type of recourse should be considered *as a residual of the central bank balance sheet over the reserve maintenance period*, since it follows logically from the other average magnitudes of the central bank balance sheet.

If the *assumption of perfect inter-bank markets is abandoned*, then further recourse to standing facilities may occur at a non-aggregate level at any point in time of the maintenance period. Such recourse has little to do with the aggregate liquidity situation, but mainly reflects transaction costs or failures in the payment systems and non-anticipated end-of-day payment flows which occur too late to allow a correction via the inter-bank market and which cannot be averaged out through reserve requirements (Holland 1970 and Hester 1970, for example, focus on this type of recourse). This type of recourse may be called *individual recourse*. Reflecting the very different nature of the two types of recourse to standing facilities, their analysis needs to be separated correspondingly.

In a framework like that of the Eurosystem, individual recourse *is fully exogenous* to the aggregate availability of reserves. It becomes relevant for reserves because it is normally not symmetric, that is, the recourse to either of the two standing facilities due to market imperfections does not necessarily neutralize the other in its effect on the supply of reserves. From the point of view of monetary policy implementation, this type of recourse can be considered as *exogenous and its nature is to be considered similar to that of an autonomous liquidity factor.*

Consider the following three examples of individual recourse to standing facilities that occurred in the euro area.

1. On Friday 29 January 1999, a national technical component of the euro area payment system TARGET failed, and numerous inter-bank payments could not be processed. The result was a recourse to the borrowing facility of €8.7 billion and a recourse to the deposit facility of €0.7 billion, implying over the weekend a total accumulated net reserve injection of €24 billion.
2. On Friday 20 December 2002, in an environment of tight conditions in the market for reserves, one bank deposited more than €1 billion in the deposit facility for unknown (probably technical) reasons, and thereby further withdrew more than €3 billion of accumulated reserves from the market.
3. On 30 December 1999, the last business day before 2000, despite ample availability of reserves, banks took €11.4 billion recourse to the borrowing facility for safety and window-dressing purposes.

In ECB (2002*b*), an attempt is presented to separate aggregate and individual recourse to standing facilities. According to the chosen method, aggregate recourse and individual recourse each account, on average, for around half of the overall recourse to the standing facilities in the euro area. The average daily recourse to each of the standing facilities amounts to around €300 million.

2.7 HOW TO ORDER THE CENTRAL BANK BALANCE SHEET?

Defining, from the perspective of monetary policy implementation, the residual of the balance sheet—that is, the item that is considered to balance the balance sheet—means determining which balance sheet variables are to be considered exogenous and which endogenous in the one-equation 'model' which is a balance sheet. It thus means making out of the balance sheet, which is an *identity*, a basic *modelling tool* for monetary policy implementation. In the short term, which is relevant for monetary policy implementation, autonomous factors (A) and required reserves (RR) are in any case exogenous (the latter at least under lagged reserve accounting, which is today standard). In Section 2.1, actual reserves (R) were presented as the residual of the balance sheet on a daily basis, hence $R = M + B - D - A$. This ordering of items around the balance sheet identity, however, does not make sense for maintenance period averages. On average over the maintenance period, other items should be considered as endogenous. If one sets in equation (2.1) reserve deficiencies at zero for the sake of simplicity $(RD = 0)$, then one obtains on average over the maintenance period $R = \overline{RR} - \overline{XSR}$. This will be used in the following.

One may distinguish now the case in which open market operations are given (for instance, because they are conducted only from time to time and the last operation of the reserve maintenance period has already taken place), and the one in which they are not.

If open market operations are given: With regard to excess reserves (XSR) and the recourse to standing facilities, we need to distinguish the cases in which a deposit facility exists from those where it does not. Call *Di, Bi* the *individual* recourse to the deposit and borrowing facility, respectively, and *Da, Ba* the corresponding *aggregate* recourse, such as defined in Section 2.6.

Now, consider first *the case of existence of a deposit facility* (for example, the Eurosystem and Bank of England). Then, the residual of the balance sheet over the reserve maintenance period is the variable $\overline{Ba} - \overline{Da}$, that is, the net aggregate recourse to standing facilities, and the appropriate conceptual ordering of the balance sheet identity is thus:

$$\overline{Ba} - \overline{Da} = \overline{RR} + \overline{XSR} - \overline{M} - \overline{Bi} + \overline{Di} + \overline{A} \qquad (2.4)$$

Either $\overline{Ba}$ or $\overline{Da}$ is zero, the other being positive, depending on the sign of the expression on the right. Note that generally $\overline{Ba},\overline{Da},\overline{Bi},\overline{Di},\overline{RR},\overline{XSR}$ cannot take negative values, while $\overline{M},\overline{A}$ can.

In the *absence of a deposit facility* (such as in the US), one needs in addition to distinguish between two types of excess reserves, namely, those that are due to banks' individual liquidity management and those that occur due to an aggregate excess of reserves: $XSRi$ and $XSRa$. In fact, $XSRa$ precisely takes over the role of the aggregate recourse to the deposit facility, while $XSRi$ will now cover both the excess reserves and the individual recourse to the deposit facility which arose in the case of existence of a deposit facility. (In case of a deposit facility, $XSRa = 0$ and $XSR = XSRi$.) Therefore:

$$\overline{Ba} - \overline{XSRa} = \overline{RR} + \overline{XSRi} - \overline{M} - \overline{Bi} + \overline{A}, \tag{2.5}$$

whereby either $\overline{Ba}$ or $\overline{XSRa}$ is zero, the other being positive, depending on the sign of the expression on the right.

If open market operations are still to be determined by the central bank: The use of open market operations to achieve the aims of monetary policy implementation is discussed in more detail in Chapters 3 and 5. Here, assuming the availability of both a borrowing facility and a lending facility, one may simply assume that open market operations are used by the central bank so as *to avoid aggregate recourse to standing facilities*, since the latter is normally related to market rates moving towards the respective standing facility rate. Setting Ba and Da to zero, we obtain open market operations as being determined by the rest of the balance sheet. Taking the perspective of the central bank at the moment of the allotment decision in its open market operation, and assuming that the open market operation covers exactly one reserve maintenance period, one may write:

$$\overline{M} = \overline{RR} + E[\overline{XSR} + \overline{A} + \overline{Di} - \overline{Bi} \,|\, I_t] \tag{2.6}$$

whereby $E[. \,|\, I_t]$ is again an operator indicating expectations by the central bank based on available information at time t of the allotment decision. If one makes open market operations endogenous in the sense of equation (2.6), but considers the entire reserve maintenance period from the *ex post* perspective, the aggregate recourse to standing facilities becomes again the endogenous variable according to the following equation:

$$\overline{Ba} - \overline{Da} = \overline{XSR} + \overline{A} + \overline{Di} - \overline{Bi} - E[\overline{XSR} + \overline{A} + \overline{Di} - \overline{Bi} \,|\, I_t] \tag{2.7}$$

In words: from an *ex post* perspective, the balance sheet residual is the net aggregate recourse to standing facilities; it is determined by the difference between the actual exogenous liquidity factors and the central bank's forecast of these factors at the moment of the (last) open market operation of the reserve maintenance period.

3

The Control of Short-Term Interest Rates

In Chapter 2 it was explained why central bank open market operations need first of all to react to changes in autonomous liquidity factors so as to ensure that the supply and hence the scarcity of reserves is not affected by those factors. In this chapter, short-term interest rates are introduced as an operational target of the central bank, and open market operations will be modelled as an instrument to achieve this operational target, in conjunction with standing facilities and reserve requirements. This corresponds to current central bank practice and will be discussed further in Chapters 7 and 8. The modelling will remain simple, to allow a focus on the main issues and the mechanics of interest-rate control. There is no doubt that modelling real-world monetary policy implementation involves additional challenges due to the institutional complexities of markets that create various idiosyncratic effects. Most of the literature in this field has put the emphasis on capturing the empirical properties of overnight interest rates, and then possibly providing a model to capture those specific effects.[1]

3.1 WHY FOCUS ON THE SHORTEST POSSIBLE MATURITY, THE OVERNIGHT RATE?

Before proceeding, it should briefly be explained why central banks tend to focus on the *overnight* interest rate in monetary policy implementation,

---

[1] It would be beyond the scope of the book to review this rich and heterogeneous literature, of which at least the following should be mentioned (all of the literature focuses on the US or euro area cases, nothing comparable apparently having been written on the UK): Ho and Saunders (1985), Campbell (1987), Spindt and Hoffmeister (1988), Kopecky and Tucker (1993), Angeloni and Prati (1996), Hamilton (1996, 1997, 1998), Clouse and Elmendorf (1997), Nautz (1998), Clouse and Dow (1999), Furfine (2000), Angelini (2002), Bartolini, Bertola, and Prati (2001a, b, 2002), Hartmann, Manna, and Manzanares (2001), Hayashi (2001), Perez-Quiros and Rodriguez-Mendizábal (2001), Bindseil and Seitz (2001), Ejerskov, Moss, and Stracca (2003), Cassola and Morana (2003), Gaspar, Perez-Quiros, and Rodriguez-Mendizábal (2004), Whitesell (2004), and Würtz (2003).

that is, why they normally set an implicit or explicit target for that short-est of all rates and not for a somewhat longer-term rate, like the one-, three-, or twelve-months rate. It could be argued that the latter rates are more relevant to monetary policy transmission, so why not target them directly? According to Borio (1997: 296), there were in his sample of fourteen central banks of industrialized countries eleven with an overnight, one with a 30-days, and two with 30–90 days interest-rate targets. In the meantime, the three latter ones (of Belgium, Netherlands, UK) all have also embraced the overnight maturity. The main problem with targeting rates of maturities longer than overnight are the anom-alies this implies for time-series properties of shorter-term rates and thus for the yield curve. In contrast, targeting short-term interest rates does not imply any anomaly for the yield curve or for the time-series proper-ties of longer-term rates. Consider as an example the case of a central bank that would target the 90-day rate (that is, approximately the three-months rate). Assume also that the central bank is predictable in its changes of interest rate targets, and that it achieves market rates at its target level with a high degree of precision (both of which are clearly desirable). Concretely, assume that on day τ it is expected to reduce its 90-day target rate from 5 per cent to 4 per cent. What does that imply, at least in theory, for the overnight rate around day τ if the expectations hypothesis of the term structure of interest rate holds? The 90-day hori-zon on $\tau - 1$ and on τ obviously overlaps by 89 days. The expectations hypothesis, in its simplified linear form (see equation 1.13 for the exact form), tells us that ($i_{90,t}, i_{1,t}$ are the 90-day and overnight interest rates on day t, respectively): $i_{90,t} = \sum_{i=0}^{89} i_{1,t+i}/90$. Therefore the difference in the 90-day rate between $\tau - 1$ and τ has to be translated in terms of overnight rates exclusively into the overnight rates on day $\tau - 1$ and $\tau + 89$, such that $(i_{1,\tau - 1} - i_{1,\tau + 89}) = 90(i_{90,\tau - 1} - i_{90,\tau})$. Assuming that $i_{1,\tau + 89} = 4\%$, this implies $i_{1,\tau - 1} = 94\%$, which would clearly represent an anomaly. It appears particularly disturbing since it consists of a strong temporary *increase* of the overnight rate, although the overall level of rates is lowered. It should also not be forgotten that the overnight market is a very important and liquid segment of the inter-bank market since it is at this maturity that all the unexpected short-term liquidity fluctuations are adjusted. For instance, the average daily volume of inter-bank overnight lending of fifty-two banks in the euro area reporting this data has been around €40 billion in recent years.

In contrast, if a predictable central bank targets an overnight rate of 5% until $\tau - 1$, and then moves its target on τ to 4%, the 90-day rate will simply have moved on $\tau - 89$ from 5% to approximately 4.99%, and on each of the following days lower by approximately 1 basis point. Therefore, the adaptation of longer-term rates takes place in the smoothest possible way if the overnight rate is changed in a predictable way. If the central bank would like to see an earlier decline in 90-day rates, it simply needs to cut its overnight rate earlier (which, under the assumption of predictability, triggers a correspondingly earlier start of the decline of the 90-day rate).

3.2 TWO STYLIZED MODELS OF THE MARKET FOR RESERVES AND INTEREST RATES

The demand for reserves by banks normally stems either from reserve requirements or from a 'demand' for excess reserves (or 'working balances'), or from both.[2] *Reserve requirements* are determined by the central bank according to some formula referring to the liability side of the credit institutions' balance sheets. At least under the presently applied *lagged* reserve accounting systems (see Chapter 6), reserve requirements are fixed from the first day of the reserve maintenance period. *A demand for excess reserves*, in contrast, requires that banks face some payment uncertainties, as suggested first by Orr and Mellon (1961).

The modelling in the present chapter and in much of the remainder of this book is based on Poole (1968). Poole pointed out that two different approaches need to be distinguished in the practice of central bank liquidity management, depending on which of the two factors dominates the demand for reserves. Both are briefly presented below, after which it is argued that the first of the two is, at least today, much more relevant.

3.2.1 *The aggregate liquidity management model*

The relevance of this approach is most obvious in the case of efficient markets, large reserve requirements and averaging, as represented by the

---

[2] As was argued in Chapter 2, excess reserves in the case of high reserve requirements and existence of a deposit facility do not reflect a demand for working balances but rather some kind of transactions cost, and can be treated like an exogenous factor.

euro area, for instance. In the euro area, banks have to fulfil reserve requirements of around €130 billion on average over a reserve mainte- nance period of one month. Short-term fluctuations of actual reserves of the banking system rarely push the daily reserves below €100 billion, and the absolute minimum of actual reserves in the first five years of the euro has been €63 billion. In such a setting, one may reasonably assume that the demand for working balances does not matter, and this is indeed postulated by the aggregate liquidity model. This does not imply that there are no excess reserves, but only that excess reserves can be treated as a fixed exogenous mark-up to required reserves.

Like any financial market, the market for reserves in the aggregate liq- uidity model is interesting owing to its *uncertainty*. Assume for a moment that there is no uncertainty regarding autonomous factors or regarding the liquidity supply through open market operations in the remainder of the reserve maintenance period, and thus that no news would emerge during that period on any of the factors relevant for the overnight inter- est rate. Then, equation (2.4), $\overline{Ba} - \overline{Da} = \overline{RR} + \overline{XSR} - \overline{M} - \overline{Bi} + \overline{Di} + \overline{A}$, suggested that there will normally be an aggregate recourse to either one or the other of the two standing facilities.

A deterministic aggregate recourse to one standing facility at the end of the reserve maintenance period, however, implies that the competitive price in the market should correspond to the respective standing facility rate, since this rate represents the marginal value of reserves at the end of the maintenance period. This is in line with Bagehot's (1873: 58) early insight regarding the inherent instability of money markets to the effect that only the central bank could limit the implied volatility of rates, for instance by offering standing facilities (see Chapter 1).

In the following, for the sake of simplicity it will be assumed that $Bi = 0$, $Di = 0$ (and hence $B = Ba$, $D = Da$), $XSR = 0$, $RR = 0$. The last assumption may warrant an explanation: the key feature of reserve requirements in the present context—namely, to allow for averaging within a reserve maintenance period—is preserved by allowing over- draft of the reserve accounts of commercial banks at end-of-day. In other words, banks are allowed to 'average around zero' without limits within the reserve maintenance period. The property that market rates will cor- respond in the entire reserve maintenance period to one or the other standing facility rate may then be expressed as follows, where $i_1 \ldots i_T$, i_D, i_B are the overnight market interest rates on the T days of the reserve maintenance period, and the rates of the deposit and borrowing facilities at the end of the maintenance period, respectively. After the mentioned simplifications, (2.4) reduces to $\overline{B} - \overline{D} = \overline{M} - \overline{A}$ and thus:

$$\overline{M} > \overline{A} \Rightarrow (\overline{B} = 0; \overline{D} = \overline{M} - \overline{A}; i_1 = i_2 = \ldots i_T = i_D)$$
$$\overline{M} < \overline{A} \Rightarrow (\overline{B} = \overline{A} - \overline{M}; \overline{D} = 0; i_1 = i_2 = \ldots i_T = i_B)$$

(3.1)

The result that overnight interest rates are constant within the reserve maintenance period, which is a particular case of the celebrated martingale property (see, for example, Hamilton 1996), also follows from the fact that holding reserves on any day of the maintenance period contributes equally to fulfilling reserve requirements. A time series x follows a martingale if and only if $E(x_{t+1} | I_t) = x_t$. Therefore, in the hypothetical case of anticipated differences between overnight rates within the reserve maintenance period, an arbitrage opportunity would emerge, which is not compatible with a competitive equilibrium in the money market.

Now, one may consider the more interesting and relevant case in which the liquidity supply and the rates of the standing facilities are subject to *uncertainty*. It was the Radcliffe Report (Radcliffe et al. 1959: 121), which, around ten years before Poole (1968), was the first to explicitly mention a lucid *probabilistic* concept of the reserve balance as determining the short-term level of interest rates:

The level of rates of interest in the money market therefore depends on the current level of the rate being charged by the Bank for loans from the Discount Office, and on the market's expectations as to the trend of the (discount) rate and as to the extent to which they are likely to be obliged to borrow from the Bank at this rate.

It is assumed that the money market participants have a homogeneous information set I_t at the time of each market session $t = 1 \ldots T$. The basic relationship between quantities and prices (overnight rates) under the assumptions made above (especially the one of perfect inter-bank markets and averaging) is then described by the following equation, in which $f_{(\overline{M} - \overline{A}|It)}$ is the probability density function money market participants assign during the trading session to the random variable $\overline{M} - \overline{A}$:

$$\forall t = 1 \ldots T: i_t = E[i_B | I_t] P(\text{"short"}) + E[i_D | I_t] P(\text{"long"})$$

(3.2)

$$= E[i_B | I_t] \int_{-\infty}^{0} f_{(\overline{M} - \overline{A}|It)}(x) dx + E[i_D | I_t] \left(1 - \int_{-\infty}^{0} f_{(\overline{M} - \overline{A}|It)}(x) dx \right)$$

This is a rather obvious extension of what the paragraph quoted above from the Radcliffe Report had described: the overnight rate on any day will correspond to the weighted expected rate of the two standing facilities, the weights being the respective probabilities that the market will be 'short' or 'long' of reserves at the end of the maintenance period before having recourse to standing facilities. Equation (3.2) may be considered as *the fundamental equation* of monetary policy implementation.

It should be noted that, also in the case of uncertainty, the banks' possibility of averaging reserve fulfilment implies the *martingale property* of the overnight interest rate, that is, that the overnight rate on any day corresponds to the expected overnight rates on the following days of the same reserve maintenance period. However, in the case of uncertainty, news will constantly emerge in the course of the maintenance period with regard to the factors determining the overnight rate, and thus the overnight rate will normally *not* be constant from an *ex post* perspective. It should also be highlighted that the martingale property holds only under the assumptions of the model outlined above. In practice, some deviations from the martingale property are common.[3]

Apart from expectations of standing facility rates, the perceived density function $f_{(\overline{M} - \overline{A}|It)}$ will obviously be crucial. Since the central bank controls open market operations, it should also be able to exert influence on $f_{(\overline{M} - \overline{A}|It)}$. As will be explained further below, this requires mainly (*a*) forecasting of autonomous factors, (*b*) understanding the expectations formation of the market, and (*c*) building up an appropriate reputation.

3.2.2   *The individual shock model of liquidity management*

For instance, banks in the UK are not able to average the fulfilment of their reserve requirements, and reserve requirements are very low. In this case, the banks' demand for working balances, such as modelled by Orr and Mellon (1961), is also likely to be relevant to determine the money market equilibrium (see also, for instance, Freixas and Rochet 1997: 228–9). The demand for working balances depends on the efficiency of the payment system and of the commercial banks' liquidity management, as well as, more generally, on the uncertainties relating to payment flows. The latter factor in particular varies considerably from one business day to the next. Also, the (changing) degree of market concentration and competition is likely to play a relevant role. Therefore, when steering short-term interest

---

[3] For a discussion of the martingale property of overnight rates, an empirical analysis for the US, and a tentative model to explain the observed deviations from it, see Hamilton (1996). For the euro area, see also Perez-Quiros and Rodriguez-Mendizábal (2001), Bindseil, Weller, and Würtz (2003), and Würtz (2003).

rates, the central bank needs to assess constantly the demand for working balances based on all these market imperfections, in order to provide the appropriate amount of reserves through open market operations.

To obtain a basic idea of central bank liquidity management under such circumstances, one may capture the payment system uncertainties by assuming that, *after the inter-bank market has closed*, individual liquidity shocks occur that may leave the bank either short of, or with excess, reserves. From this one may derive a demand for positive reserves independently of reserve requirements. Assume that there is no deposit facility. Assume further a large number N of identical banks, and that the available total amount of liquidity, $M - A$, is equally spread before the payment system shock. Denote thus by $q = (M - A)/N$ the reserve holdings of each bank before the liquidity shock. Assume that normally distributed white noise (that is, independently and identically distributed and zero expected value) shocks s_j, $j = 1 \ldots N$ with variance σ_s^2 and such that $\sum_{j=1}^{N} s_j = 0$ take place after the inter-bank market has settled and affect reserve holdings of individual banks. If a bank ends the day in overdraft, it has to make use of the borrowing facility, even though the aggregate banking sector is not in a deficit position. It is assumed that there is no deposit facility. Therefore, the expected costs of going overdraft when holding an amount of reserves q, $C(q)$, will be for a typical bank ($\phi(x)$ is the density of the standard normal distribution):

$$C(q) = i_B \int_{-\infty}^{-q} (q + x)\phi(x/\sigma_s)dx \qquad (3.3)$$

The marginal cost of holding reserves has to be traded off against the expected marginal costs of going overdraft. For a given amount of available reserves in the system, the equilibrium market interest rate, which is the opportunity cost of holding reserves, will have to ensure that banks are indifferent between holding one more unit of reserves and not doing so. Hence, the market equilibrium is defined by the following equation:

$$-\frac{\partial(C(q))}{\partial q} = i \qquad (3.4)$$

Since the total volume of open market operations, M, is in a simple linear relationship with q for given A, it is easy to show that for any level of uncertainty $\sigma_s^2 \in \Re_+$, the central bank can control i within $]0, i_B]$ by choosing an appropriate $M \in \Re_+$. The central bank, of course, needs to know the level of $\sigma_s^2 \in \Re_+$ perceived by the market, which is only a model proxy for several factors that are much more complicated in practice.

3.2.3 *Intermediate cases*

Actually, both the Federal Reserve System and the Bank of England may be considered to be cases in between the aggregate and the individual shock models of the reserve market. In the US, reserve requirements, which have to be fulfilled on average over a two-week reserve maintenance period, are at a relevant although relatively low level. Hence, the Fed will, in its steering of the Fed funds rate, not be able to avoid totally looking at the demand for working balances, especially on days with outstanding payment system activity. Clouse and Elmendorf (1997) attempt to model such a complex intermediate case. Also, Woodford (2001*b*: 36–8) models a kind of intermediate case, in which aggregate liquidity conditions are built into the individual banks' demand for reserves function. This model is simple and elegant, but is not designed for a reserve maintenance period with several days. Gaspar, Peres-Quiros, and Rodrigues-Mendizábal (2004) extend the model of Woodford (2001*b*) to a reserve maintenance period with several days, which leads to a series of technical challenges.

Also, the Bank of England is ultimately an intermediate case, since the effective overnight rate, being the average of the overnight rates agreed in transactions over the trading day, also reflects views of the banking system on end-of-day *aggregate* conditions. Indeed, during the day banks can overdraw their account with the central bank. To that extent, at, for example, 11.00 a.m., individual payment system shocks are not yet as relevant as at the end of the day for banks. In fact, the day can be viewed as a maintenance period with a series of trading sessions, whereby fulfilment of (zero) reserve requirements is only measured at the very end once. The pure working balances model as expounded above would apply only if the overnight rate is determined in *one* market session limited to *one* moment in time, which is followed by payment system shocks, before assessment of fulfilment of (zero) reserve requirements. In fact, therefore, the aggregate liquidity model is somehow relevant to every central bank in the world, while the individual shocks model is not necessarily so. This motivates why the following focuses on the *aggregate* model, although it is kept in mind that some central banks also have to take into account elements of the individual shocks model.

3.3 STEERING SHORT-TERM INTEREST RATES

Two tools are available according to equation 3.2 to the central bank to steer the short-term market interest rate: the rates of the standing facilities, and the reserve supply through open market operations. Therefore, central banks have in principle *one degree of freedom for achieving their operational target rate*. The question of how to make the best use of this degree of freedom is probably the oldest of all questions in central-bank monetary policy implementation. Two extreme approaches can be distinguished: the open market operations approach, and the standing facility rates approach.

Under the *open market operations approach*, the rate of the borrowing facility is set at a rather high level, such that it is unlikely that the stance of monetary policy will ever require a higher target rate. Then, through open market operations policy—that is, through the control of the probabilities of the market being long or short at the end of the reserve maintenance period—the market rate is steered in the wide corridor between zero and the high borrowing facility rate, depending on the prevailing stance. Therefore, the standing facility rate never needs to be adjusted. Apparently, no central banks have so far adopted this approach *in its pure form*, but elements of the approach have often been present. Riefler (1930: 28) claims that elements of this approach prevailed during the 1920s in the US: 'Induced through open market operations, changes in the volume of member bank indebtedness have been used since 1922 both to tighten and to ease the money markets, independently of changes in discount rates.' It was also applied to some extent by the Fed during the 1970s, when changes in the federal funds target were much more frequent than changes of the discount rate. This is illustrated by Fig. 3.1 for the years 1974 and 1975.

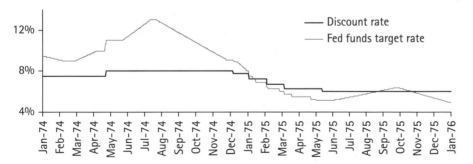

Figure 3.1 *Open market operations approach (partial): discount facility rate and federal funds target rate in the US during 1974–1975*

Source: Federal Reserve Board website.

Note that some of the changes of the spread between the discount rate and the federal funds target rate may also have been implemented through variations in the intensity of suasion towards banks not to use the discount window, that is, variations of the non-interest-rate costs of using the window.

Under the *standing facility rates approach*, the scarcity of reserves, in the sense of the probabilities of recourse to each of the standing facilities, is always kept constant, but standing facility rates are varied with the monetary policy stance. A first variant of this approach is to always maintain liquidity conditions such that banks have quasi-deterministically to have recourse to *one* standing facility, and market rates are pegged to this standing facility rate. This approach was followed by many central banks at the beginning of the twentieth century, when frequent open market operations were not yet common, as illustrated by the Deutsche Reichsbank's balance sheet presented in Chapter 2. A second variant of this approach is the one applied by, for instance, the Bank of England, the ECB, and the central banks of Australia, Canada, and New Zealand. Accordingly, 'neutral' reserve market conditions are kept within a corridor set by two standing facilities, 'neutrality' being defined ideally as an equal likelihood of an aggregate end of reserve maintenance period recourse to each of the two standing facilities. Then, according to the aggregate model provided above, the money market rate should be in the middle of the corridor set by the facilities. Under both the Reichsbank and the ECB approaches, the central bank therefore keeps liquidity conditions constant when changing the monetary policy stance, and merely moves the rates of its standing facilities. The approach is illustrated by Fig. 3.2 of ECB rates for the period 2000–2 in the euro area (the minimum bid rate in the main refinancing operations is the rate the ECB normally aims at in the short-term money market, as suggested by ECB 2002*b*).

In the event that the central bank offers only a borrowing facility and no deposit facility, and sets its target overnight rate below the rate of the borrowing facility, the standing facilities rates approach is no longer possible in its pure form. Indeed, when the target rate and the borrowing facility rate move up or down in parallel, the distance between the target rate and the lower zero bound to the interest rate changes, and hence the probability of being long or short needs, *ceteris paribus*, to be adjusted accordingly through open market operations. A *symmetric* corridor around the target rate set by borrowing and deposit facilities makes it possible to avoid the need to adjust liquidity conditions in that case. It also makes it possible to ignore the probability distribution of autonomous factor shocks, as long as this distribution is symmetric (this point is developed below). One may

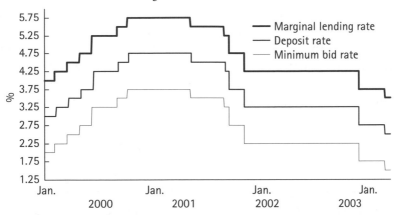

Figure 3.2 *Standing facilities rate approach: standing facility rates and,
as proxy of target rate, minimum bid rate set by ECB in its
weekly open market operations, 2000–2002*

Source: European Central Bank, *Monthly Bulletin.*

therefore say that the standing facility rate approach in its purest form
is achieved only with a symmetric corridor (as with the ECB's approach), or
with the identity of the target rate and a single standing facility rate (as with
the Reichsbank's approach).

Generally, it seems that the open market operations approach is much
more challenging for the central bank and less transparent, especially if
the central bank's target rate is not published. It may be facilitated if the
central bank sets a target rate such as the US Fed funds target, and if the
open market operations of the central bank are high-frequency *reverse*
operations of short maturity, such that they have elements of standing
facilities themselves (that is, banks can be confident that they will
receive, if they wish, liquidity at a certain price through them). Indeed,
Cook and Hahn's quotations from the *Wall Street Journal* suggest that
this is how the Fed operated during the 1970s. For instance, for 1974,
Cook and Hahn (1989: 348) quote the *Wall Street Journal* as follows
(other quotations are very similar):

The Federal Reserve System has apparently eased its credit stance another
notch . . . As recently as a week ago, . . . the central bank absorbed funds when the
following day's rate dipped to 10% and injected . . . funds at the $10^{1}/_{2}$% level.
The Fed's open market movements will be closely watched this week to determine
the new intervention points, which many specialists believe will be $9^{1}/_{2}$% to absorb
reserves and 10% to inject them.

Chapter 7 reviews in more detail the liquidity management practice of
the three selected central banks during the twentieth century and their

choices between the two approaches. A formal representation of the approaches other than the symmetric corridor approach (which is presented in Section 3.4 in more detail) is also provided there. It will be shown that most central banks have moved in recent years to a standing facilities rate-based approach, and this is considered to be part of the new view of monetary policy implementation outlined in Chapter 8.

3.4   THE SYMMETRIC CORRIDOR APPROACH

To illustrate the basic working of the control of the overnight interest rate, this section provides simple examples of the symmetric corridor approach. The alternative approaches (the Reichsbank approach in 1900, the open market operations approach, and so on) are analysed again in Chapter 7, where these approaches are reviewed in their historical context.

3.4.1   *A one-day maintenance period*

Consider now a very simple reserve maintenance period of one day with the following sequence of events. First, the central bank conducts an open market operation with published allotment amount M (which also corresponds to the outstanding open market operations volume). Second, the inter-bank market session takes place and the overnight rate is determined that clears the market. Third, the realization of autonomous factors takes place and is published. Finally, banks have recourse to standing facilities and the day and reserve maintenance period ends. It is assumed that the central bank and the market have the same information set. Figure 3.3 summarizes the sequence of events.

Under the symmetric corridor approach, the central bank always has to keep reserve market conditions neutral, which means in equation (3.2) that P('short') = P('long') = ½. Then, equation (3.2) becomes very simple:

$$i = \frac{i_B + i_D}{2} \tag{3.5}$$

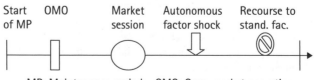

MP: Maintenance period;   OMO: Open market operation

Figure 3.3   *Sequence of events in stylized reserve maintenance period*

Achieving any target rate i^* then implies simply setting the standing facilities correspondingly around the target rate, whereby the width of the corridor can be set according to technical considerations. For symmetric distributions of the density function of A, P('short') = P('long') = $\frac{1}{2}$ requires only $M = E(A)$. Example: If A is $N(10,1)$, and $i^* = 5\%$, then one may achieve $i = i^*$ by setting $i_B = 6\%$; $i_D = 4\%$; $M = E(A) = 10$. Consider now how the central bank needs to react to two specific exogenous changes.

First, *if the target rate i^* changes*, the corridor of standing facilities needs to be shifted in parallel. The central bank, in contrast, *does not need to change its open market operations* since the relationship $M = E(A) \Rightarrow (i_B = i_D)/2$ is independent of the level of the target rate. *Thus, the volume of outstanding open market operations is not affected by a change in the stance of monetary policy*, which is of course rather the opposite of what proponents of reserve position doctrine (see Chapter 1) had in mind. It should also be noted that the fact that under the symmetric corridor approach open market operations are not relevant to implementing a change of market rates has nothing to do with the idea of 'open mouth operations' made popular by Guthrie and Wright (2000). To change market rates, it is indeed not enough for a central banker to open his or her mouth, but the central bank needs to effectively adjust rates of standing facilities in the relevant reserve maintenance period.

Second, *when the density function of A changes*: first, the *mean* of autonomous factors changes constantly, reflecting moves in its main elements such as banknotes, government deposits, and foreign exchange assets. Second, higher-order moments of autonomous factors, such as their variance, also change in permanence. On some days there may be little uncertainty with regard to the autonomous factors, while on others, as for instance tax payment days (affecting government deposits), important shopping days (affecting banknotes), or periods with foreign exchange turbulence (affecting foreign exchange assets in the event of intervention), the uncertainty will be considerable. As long as the density function remains symmetric, the volume of outstanding open market operations needs only to be adapted such that $M = E(A)$ is maintained, that is, M needs to be shifted simply in parallel to $E(A)$. This property greatly facilitates the calibration of open market operations in day-to-day practice. As is shown in Chapter 7, this property, in contrast, does not hold for interest rate targets within an asymmetric corridor. In sum, the central bank can steer interest rates perfectly in such a simple model setting, and this does not even appear to be very challenging.

3.4.2   *A one-day reserve maintenance period with three inter-bank sessions and new information on autonomous factors emerging in between these sessions*

The Bank of England operates in a system without averaging, thus with a one-day reserve maintenance period. Nevertheless, it does not achieve a perfect stability of overnight interest rates (see, for instance, Table 3.1), in contrast to what the previous paragraph seems to suggest. Why? The intra-day sequence of events is in fact somewhat more complex than the one set out in the previous example. In particular, market trading is spread over the entire day, and during the day news on autonomous factors emerges and changes the probabilities that the market assigns to being long or short at the end of the day. To capture this, one may subdivide the shock affecting autonomous factors into a series of accumulating white noise terms which are revealed step by step during the day. For instance, let $A = \eta_1 + \eta_2 + \eta_3$, the three noise terms being uncorrelated and each being distributed normally with expected value zero, that is $\eta_j \approx N(0, \sigma_\eta^2), j = 1, 2, 3$, such that $A \approx N(0, 3\sigma_\eta^2)$. Let there also be three market sessions, one immediately after the open market operation, one after η_1 is revealed, and one after η_2 is revealed. This sequence of events is summarized in Fig. 3.4.

The central bank may now still control the interest rate in the first market session, but not the one in the two subsequent ones, since these will normally be affected by the previously revealed autonomous factor shocks (which are supposed to become public immediately after they happen). Thus, an effective overnight interest rate, which would be a weighted average of the rates in the different market sessions—for example, $i = (i_1 + i_2 + i_3)/3$—would regularly tend to deviate from the target rate. Assume now for the sake of simplicity of notation that $i_B = 1$, $i_D = 0$. Then the interest rate in market session 1 will simply be, for

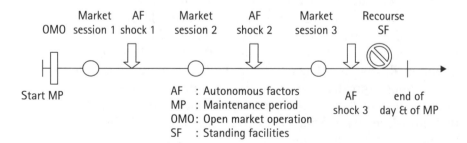

Figure 3.4   *A one-day maintenance period with three inter-bank sessions*

$M = E(A) = 0$ ($\Phi(\ )$ is the cumulative standard normal probability distribution):

$$i_1 = P(-A < 0|I_1) = P(-(\eta_1 + \eta_2 + \eta_3) < 0)$$

$$= \Phi\left(0/\sqrt{3\sigma_\eta^2}\right) = 1/2 \tag{3.6}$$

For a given first autonomous factor shock $\tilde{\eta}_1$, the interest in the market session 2 will be :

$$i_2 = P(-A < 0|I_2) = P(-(\tilde{\eta}_1 + \eta_2 + \eta_3) < 0) = \Phi\left(\tilde{\eta}/\sqrt{2\sigma_\eta^2}\right) \tag{3.7}$$

For given first and second autonomous factor shocks $\tilde{\eta}_1, \tilde{\eta}_2$, the interest in the market session 3 will be:

$$i_3 = P(-A < 0|I_3) = P(-(\tilde{\eta}_1 + \tilde{\eta}_2 + \eta_3) < 0)$$

$$= \Phi\left(\left(-\tilde{\eta}_1 - \tilde{\eta}_2\right)/\sqrt{\sigma_\eta^2}\right) \tag{3.8}$$

The variances of i_2, i_3 and $i = (i_1 + i_2 + i_3)/3$ can be calculated accordingly, whereby $Var(i_3) > Var(i_2) > Var(i_1) = 0$. Of course, the Bank of England could reduce again the volatility of rates by conducting a second and a third open market operation during the day. That is actually what it tends to do (see Chapter 5). Still, as in reality both the market and the diffusion of autonomous factor shocks are continuous over time, even this is not enough for complete control of short-term interest rates.

3.4.3 A three-day reserve maintenance period

Consider now the case of a three-day reserve maintenance period with an open market operation (with three days maturity) only on its first day, as shown in Fig. 3.5.

The figure is similar to the previous one, with the exception of the two additional end of days. Actually, under the assumptions made here, namely, unlimited averaging of reserve fulfilment, the two cases are very similar, since the end of days do not represent any particular constraint on their own. Distinguish now between autonomous factors on each of the three days, A_1, A_2, A_3, and set $A_1 = \eta_1$, $A_2 = \eta_2$, $A_3 = \eta_3$ with the shocks having the same properties as above. One now obtains the interest rate equation for day 1, again for M = 0:

$$i_1 = P(-(A_1 + A_2 + A_3)/3 < 0|I_1) = P(-(\eta_1 + \eta_2 + \eta_3))/3 < 0)$$

$$= \Phi\left(0/\sqrt{\sigma_\eta^2/3}\right) = 1/2 \tag{3.9}$$

It is left to the reader to write out the second- and third-day interest rate equation.

Consider now the case in which the central bank conducts one operation with one-day maturity on each day of the maintenance period, before the respective market session. Assume the allotment policy $M_1 = 0$; $M_2 = \tilde{\eta}_1$, $M_3 = \tilde{\eta}_2$, that is, the central bank always neutralizes as soon as possible autonomous factor shocks. It is easy to verify that this allotment strategy allows again a perfect stabilization of interest rates within the reserve maintenance period, since in each market session expectations with regard to the liquidity conditions prevailing at the end of the reserve maintenance period tend to be balanced. Note that the same result is actually achieved for the allotment strategy $M_1 = 0$; $M_2 = 0$, $M_3 = \tilde{\eta}_1 + \tilde{\eta}_2$, as long as the market is indeed aware of this allotment strategy of the central bank. If it is aware, it will be confident that the central bank will only delay the correction, through an open market operation, of the first day's autonomous factor shock. If not, it will have biased expectations after observing this shock, and the market session on day 2 will thus result in an interest rate different from 0.5. This example suggests two findings which are key in the day-to-day practice of liquidity management. First, there may be open market strategies that are distinct in terms of the distribution of liquidity supply across the reserve maintenance period, but that are actually equivalent in terms of the implied interest rate path if they lead to the same accumulated liquidity supply. Second—and this is normally a precondition for this equivalence to hold—it is important that the market has a clear picture of the central bank's strategy of liquidity supply across different open market operations within the reserve maintenance period.

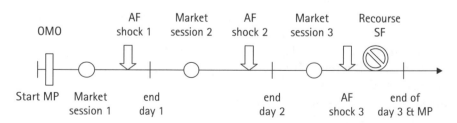

Figure 3.5   *A three-day maintenance period with one open market operation*

3.4.4 A two-day reserve maintenance period with uncertainty about the level of the standing facility rates at the end of the maintenance period

Now, the focus turns to expectations of changes of policy rates, that is, standing facility rates. Assume that the monetary policy decision-making body (the Federal Open Market Committee, FOMC, in the case of the US, the Monetary Policy Committee, MPC, in the case of the Bank of England, and the Governing Council in the case of the ECB), meets just after the first market session has taken place. For the sake of simplicity of notation, also assume that there is only one autonomous factor shock η at the very end of the maintenance period, such that $A \approx N(0, \sigma_\eta^2)$. Thus, the sequence of events shown in Fig. 3.6 is obtained.

Assume the case of expectations of rate changes *upwardly* biased and, concretely, that the market assumes that there is a 50 per cent likelihood that interest rates will be raised by 50 basis points, such that, starting from $i_{B, t-1} = 1; i_{D, t-1} = 0$ one obtains $E(i_{B, t}|I_t) = 1.25; E(i_{D, t}|I_t) = 0.25$. Under the assumption that $M_t = 0$ (and two days maturity of the operation), one would thus obtain according to equation (3.2), $i_t = 0.75$, that is, the expectations directly affect overnight rates. On day $t + 1$, depending on the decision taken, one obtains either $i_{t+1} = 0.5$ (if rates were not hiked) or $i_{t+1} = 1$ (if rates were hiked).

An interesting question in this context is this: can the central bank prevent market rates from anticipating the standing facilities rates change through a specific allotment policy? The market interest rate on day 1 is:

$$i_t = P(2M_t - \eta < 0|I_t) + 0.25 = \Phi\left(2M_t/\sqrt{\sigma_\eta^2}\right) + 0.25 \qquad (3.10)$$

Since $\Phi(\ )$ is a monotonous continuous function, it is invertible, and therefore, if the desired i_1 is 0.5, then the central bank simply needs to allot $M_t = \sqrt{\sigma_\eta^2}\Phi^{-1}(0.25)/2$. However, unavoidably, news of the interest rate decision will move rates away and, due to the continued unbalanced

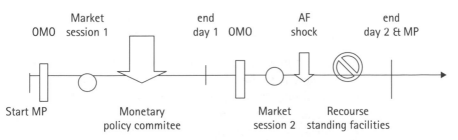

Figure 3.6 *A two-day maintenance period with a potential interest rate decision*

liquidity conditions, interest rates on day 2 will obviously be in the middle of neither the old nor the new corridor.

What more can the central bank achieve by adding an open market operation on the second day, that is, after the interest rate decision has been taken? First, it should be noted that the central bank *can in the event of biased rate change expectations never achieve an interest rate path within the maintenance period according to the actual mid-point of the corridor.* This would violate the martingale property, since it would imply (in the case considered here) $i_t < E(i_{t+1} | I_t)$. What the central bank can achieve, however, is stability of rates over the maintenance period at the level it desires, for example, at the old or possible new mid-point of the corridor. For this, it needs only to set $M_t = 0$ and M_{t+1} *contingent* on the rate change decision. Assume the interest rate level the central bank wants to achieve over the entire reserve maintenance period is 0.5 (the old mid-point of the corridor). Then, the central bank simply needs to ensure that, in the event that the rate hike takes place, it counteracts its effect through a more ample allotment decision on day 2, such that also in the event that the rate hike materializes, market rates stay at 0.5. Thus, the allotment rule of the central bank needs to be:

If the corridor remains unchanged: $M_{t+1} = 0$.

If the corridor is shifted upwards by 0.5%: $M_{t+1} = \lim_{x \to 0} \sigma_\eta \Phi^{-1}(x) = \infty$.

If a 100 basis points corridor is shifted upwards by 50 basis points, then the former mid-point becomes the floor of the corridor, and hence one needs to make the likelihood of recourse to the deposit facility equal to one to keep rates at the old mid-point. In practice, supplying excess liquidity of, for example, $3\sigma_\eta$ would be enough to bring the market rate as close as 1 basis point to the new floor of the corridor.

To derive these results, it was assumed that the central bank can indeed always allot in its open market operations whatever amounts it wishes, which requires that counterparts always submit sufficient bids. This is actually not guaranteed, as Chapter 5 demonstrates in the case of fixed rate tenders.

3.5   A SIGNAL EXTRACTION PROBLEM

In the previous section, it was implicitly assumed that there are no information asymmetries between the central bank and the money market participants. Now, the model will be enriched by assuming that the central bank knows more about future autonomous factors than the market. It will be shown that such asymmetries, and whether the central bank decides to reduce them, are of key importance for the way the overnight market rate is determined. The specific model presented below will be one illustration of how to model more complex settings of monetary policy implementation on the basis of the general framework presented above. The reader who is less keen on calculus may move directly to Section 3.6, and will still be able to follow the rest of this book.

In June 2000, the ECB took the decision to start publishing, together with the announcements of its weekly main refinancing operations, part of its internal forecasts of autonomous liquidity factors (see ECB 2000), joining the Bank of England and the Bank of Japan, for instance, which have adopted a similar policy. The Fed, in contrast, never publishes autonomous factor forecasts. In any case, even with the publication of autonomous factor forecasts, it seems that signalling issues are almost omnipresent in day-to-day liquidity management, and it is hence worth looking at a basic model to understand the underlying issues.

Again, the same one-day reserve maintenance period as described by Fig. 3.1 is assumed. Consider the following additional specifications regarding information asymmetries between the central bank and the market. The allotment amount M is immediately published at the moment of allotment. If applicable, the central bank publishes its forecast of autonomous liquidity factors at the same time. Autonomous liquidity factors are now assumed to be composed of two white noise elements, with $A = \varepsilon + \eta$, ε, η being identically and independently normal distributed random variables with an expected value of zero and variances $\sigma_\varepsilon^2 \in [0,1]$, $\sigma_\eta^2 = 1 - \sigma_\varepsilon^2$. The total variance of autonomous factors per day is hence standardized to 1. The central bank is assumed to have perfect forecasts of ε but it has no prior information on η. The higher σ_ε^2, the better is the quality of liquidity forecasts of the central bank for the autonomous factors on day 1. The money market participants are assumed to have no prior information on either of the two variables. This assumption seems to contradict the Hayekian idea of information being dispersed among many individual actors within the economy. However, it appears in practice that the central bank always has more prior knowledge than market players regarding autonomous liquidity factor flows, and that it never obtains information that is valuable in terms of autonomous factor forecasting out of the bids submitted by banks in open market operations.[4] As explained in Chapter 2, central banks indeed

---

[4] The opposite conjecture—that central banks do extract valuable information held by market participants from the bids submitted by banks in open market operations—has been put forward by, for instance, Nautz (1997).

invest considerable amounts of resources into the forecasting of autonomous factors, using also various sources of information the market cannot access (for instance, on Treasury flows and on its foreign exchange operations). It is assumed furthermore that information asymmetries between market participants are not relevant and that inter-bank interest rates fully reflect the publicly available information.

Here, a purely 'quantitative' approach is adopted by assuming that the central bank does not have an interest rate target but only a *net borrowing facility target*, which is denoted in the following by γ.[5] The target γ may change from one maintenance period to the other. Even under an interest rate targeting approach, the central bank may sometimes set a quantitative target reflecting some pedagogical aim (for example, to provide more or fewer incentives for the market to participate in open market operations) or to give a signal about, for instance, possible future changes of standing facility rates. Assume that, from the point of view of the market, γ follows a white noise process, that is, that it has an expected value of zero and a variance of $\sigma_\gamma^2 \in \Re_+$. Formally, the open market operation volume is assumed to be chosen by the central bank as $M = \arg\min\{E(\gamma - (M - A))^2 \mid \varepsilon = \varepsilon_0\}$, that is, M is chosen by the central bank, which knows ε, such that the expected squared difference between the end of period liquidity situation and the liquidity target is minimized. It is straightforward to show that this implies $M = \varepsilon + \gamma$. The cases of published and non-published autonomous factor forecasts are considered in turn.

If the central bank does *not* publish its autonomous factor forecasts, the overnight inter-bank interest rate is determined in this case by the following equation:

$$i = P(M - A < 0 \mid M = M_0) \tag{3.11}$$

In words: the interest rate equals the probability that there is an end of reserve maintenance period shortage of liquidity, knowing that $M = M_0$. Counterparts observe the allotment amount M_0 and know the linear structure $M_0 = \varepsilon + \gamma$. Applying the standard signal extraction formula, one obtains the following estimators for the unobserved variables, after observing $M = M_0$:

$$E(\gamma \mid M = M_0) = \frac{\sigma_\gamma^2}{\sigma_\gamma^2 + \sigma_\varepsilon^2} M_0, \quad E(\varepsilon \mid M = M_0) = \frac{\sigma_\varepsilon^2}{\sigma_\gamma^2 + \sigma_\varepsilon^2} M_0 \tag{3.12}$$

[5] In Bindseil (2001, 2002), it is also assumed that the central bank has a stochastic interest rate target. This case is somewhat more complicated.

The variances of the errors of the estimates will be:

$$E(\gamma - E(\gamma|M = M_0))^2 = \sigma_\gamma^2 - \frac{\sigma_\gamma^4}{\sigma_\gamma^2 + \sigma_\varepsilon^2},$$

$$E(\varepsilon - E(\varepsilon|M = M_0))^2 = \sigma_\varepsilon^2 - \frac{\sigma_\varepsilon^4}{\sigma_\gamma^2 + \sigma_\varepsilon^2}$$

(3.13)

The overnight rate in the inter-bank market will amount to:

$$i = P(M - A < 0|M = M_0)$$

$$= \int_{-\infty}^{0} f_{(M-A|M=M_0)}(x)dx = F_{(M-A|M=M_0)}(0)$$

(3.14)

To specify $f_{(M-A|M=M_0)}$, note that the expected value of the underlying random variable is: $E(M - A \mid M = M_0) = E(\varepsilon + \gamma - \varepsilon - \eta \mid M = M_0) = E(\gamma \mid M = M_0)$. Its variance is $Var(M - A \mid M = M_0) = Var(\gamma - \eta \mid M = M_0) = Var(\gamma \mid M = M_0) + Var(\eta \mid M = M_0)$. Hence, $(M - A \mid M = M_0)$ is normally distributed with an expected value of $\sigma_\gamma^2/(\sigma_\gamma^2 + \sigma_\varepsilon^2)M_0$ and a variance of $\sigma_\gamma^2 - \frac{\sigma_\gamma^4}{\sigma_\gamma^2 + \sigma_\varepsilon^2} + 1 - \sigma_\varepsilon^2 = \frac{\sigma_\varepsilon^2\sigma_\gamma^2}{\sigma_\gamma^2 + \sigma_\varepsilon^2} + 1 - \sigma_\varepsilon^2 = 1 - \frac{\sigma_\varepsilon^4}{\sigma_\gamma^2 + \sigma_\varepsilon^2}.$

Therefore, using the Gaussian (standard normal) cumulative density function, one can write:

$$i = \Phi\left(\frac{-E(M - A|M = M_0)}{\sqrt{Var(M - A|M = M_0)}}\right) = 1 - \Phi\left(\frac{\sigma_\gamma^2/(\sigma_\gamma^2 + \sigma_\varepsilon^2)M_0}{\sqrt{1 - \sigma_\varepsilon^4/(\sigma_\gamma^2 + \sigma_\varepsilon^2)}}\right)$$

$$= 1 - \Phi(Z)$$

(3.15)

The random variable Z has an expected value of zero and a variance of $Var(Z) = \sigma_\gamma^4/(\sigma_\gamma^2 + \sigma_\varepsilon^2 - \sigma_\varepsilon^4)$.

As indicated by the mean squared errors of the estimated values of the liquidity target and the autonomous factor forecast, the signal extraction will not be perfect and the relationship between the liquidity target and the resulting interest rate will hence be noisy.

If the central bank *does* publish its autonomous factor forecasts, publishing forecasts of autonomous factors is equivalent to reducing the uncertainty with regard to γ to zero and the residual uncertainty with regard to the end of maintenance period liquidity position to $\sigma_\eta^2 = 1 - \sigma_\varepsilon^2$. The expected end of maintenance period liquidity position is γ, which can be extracted perfectly. Hence, interest rates will be determined by the following relationship:

$$i = P(M - A < 0 | M = M_0, \varepsilon = \varepsilon_0)$$

$$= \int_{-\infty}^{0} f_{(M-A|M=M_0, \ \varepsilon=\varepsilon_0)}(x)dx = F_{(M-A|M=M_0, \ \varepsilon=\varepsilon_0)}(0) \tag{3.16}$$

where $f_{(M - A \ | M = M_0, \ \varepsilon \ = \ \varepsilon_0)}$ is the density function of a normally distributed random variable with expected value γ and variance $1 - \sigma_\varepsilon^2$. Hence:

$$i = \Phi\left(-\gamma/\sqrt{1 - \sigma_\varepsilon^2}\right) = 1 - \Phi\left(\gamma/\sqrt{1 - \sigma_\varepsilon^2}\right) = 1 - \Phi(Z) \tag{3.17}$$

with $Var(Z) = \sigma_\gamma^2/(1 - \sigma_\varepsilon^2)$.

Without going to the details, the following conclusive observations, which can easily be verified by calculus, can be made:

- As already noted, under public autonomous factor forecasts, the market can perfectly extract both the autonomous factor forecast and the reserves target of the central bank, while under private forecasts signal extraction remains noisy.
- Related to that, under public forecasts, any reserve target can be mapped precisely into an interest rate target, which is achieved without noise. Under private forecasts, the relationship between the reserve target and the interest rate will always remain noisy.
- A given liquidity target leads on average, under published autonomous factor forecasts, to a stronger reaction of interest rates than under private autonomous factors, since in the latter case the market will tend to assign a part of the deviation of the allotment volume from the normal level to the non-observed autonomous factor forecasts.
- Under published autonomous factor forecasts, the better the quality of autonomous factor forecasts, the stronger will be the reaction of interest rates to a given deviation of the allotment from neutral. The opposite holds under private autonomous factors.

3.6   ACTUAL PRECISION OF CONTROL OF THE OVERNIGHT INTEREST RATE

Before we examine in more detail in the following chapters how the three selected central banks have effectively employed the instruments of monetary policy to steer short-term interest rates, it would be useful to look briefly at how precise each of them currently is in this job. Figure 3.7 shows for 2002 for the Bank of England, the Fed, and the ECB the short-term interest rate target and the effective overnight rate. The target is, in the case of the Fed, obviously the Fed funds target rate. In the case of the ECB, it is assumed to be the minimum bid rate in its main refinancing operations, and, in the case of the Bank of England, the repo rate (note that the latter two rates are in the middle of the standing facilities corridors). The effective overnight rate is measured as 'sterling overnight index average' (SONIA) for the UK, 'euro overnight index average' (EONIA) for the euro area, and the effective federal funds rate for the US. Table 3.1 summarizes this by providing key statistics, namely, the average spread between the target rate and the effective rate (to check for a bias), the standard deviation of this spread, and the standard deviation of day-to-day changes of this spread (to measure volatility). It appears that the degree of control of short-term interest rates around the target rate is rather heterogeneous. The Fed outperforms the other two central banks, which makes sense since it alone commits explicitly to an overnight interest rate target. In terms of average spread, the Fed is very close to zero with −1 basis point, while the ECB and the Bank of England are at +/−8 basis points, respectively. The average spreads are in any case smaller than the smallest change of official interest rates by any of the three central banks in the last decade, which has been by 25 basis points. One may therefore say that the average spread is within the perceived margin of error in the definition of the monetary policy stance, and thus sufficiently small. The standard deviation of the UK spread is outstanding among the three central banks at 55 basis points, and is mainly explained by the absence of a reserve requirement system. It needs, however, to be noted that SONIA always remained in the +/−100 basis point range defined by the two standing facilities the Bank of England offered, illustrating the effectiveness of the facilities and suggesting how important standing facilities are indeed for limiting moves of overnight rates. Also, the low serial correlation of the spread appears to be consistent with the absence of averaging, which implies that each day is distinct from the others in terms of factors determining the overnight rate. In the case of the ECB, two features stand out. First, there is clearly more serial correlation in the spread than for both other central banks, which reflects the one month reserve maintenance period. Second, especially in the first half of the year, one observes a monthly upward or downward spike of the spread, which reflects end of reserve maintenance periods. In the case of the Fed, there seems to be far less serial correlation of the spread, but nevertheless one

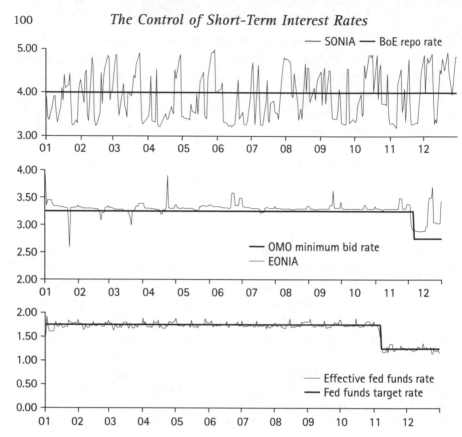

Figure 3.7   *Implicit or explicit short-term interest rate target and effective overnight interest rate of Bank of England, ECB, and Fed, January–December 2002*

Source: Respective central banks.

Table 3.1   *Deviation of overnight interest rate from target and volatility, 2002, in basis points*

	B of England	Fed	ECB
Average value of spread	−8	−1	8
Standard deviation of spread	55	5	13
Standard deviation of day-to-day changes	52	6	10

Source: Respective central banks.

gains an impression of a pattern reflecting the 14 days reserve maintenance period. Indeed, such a pattern is confirmed by the literature (see, for instance, Hamilton 1996).

   Whether volatility of overnight rates is problematic from a monetary policy point of view depends on whether it is transmitted to maturities which are deemed directly relevant for decisions of economic agents, such as perhaps the three-, six-, and twelve-month rates and above (see, for example, Ayuso, Haldane, and Restoy 1997).

3.7 CONCLUSIONS

The impact of monetary policy operations (open market operations and standing facility rates) on short-term money market interest rates in principle reflects a simple probabilistic relationship proposed first by Poole (1968). With *two* instruments and *one* target rate, central banks have, however, one degree of freedom in their approach, and the way they make use of this degree of freedom is crucial for the simplicity and transparency of monetary policy implementation. Indeed, the calibration of open market operations becomes rather complex especially if information asymmetries between the market and the central bank are considered. It appears that the symmetric corridor approach, chosen *inter alia* by the Bank of England and the ECB, is rather convenient (which becomes even clearer when compared with the alternative approaches presented in Chapter 7). Under this approach, changes in the monetary policy stance—that is, changes of the targeted market overnight rate—do not imply a change in the outstanding volume of open market operations. It is argued that this has little to do with the concept of 'open mouth operations' advanced by Guthrie and Wright (2000), since the market rate change is driven by a concrete action, namely, the change in standing facility rates (or expectations thereof).

The simple examples given of interest rate control revealed that the timing of open market operations within the reserve maintenance period, relative to inter-bank market sessions and diffusion of news on autonomous factors, was crucial to the degree of control over the overnight interest rate. It appeared that, generally, the control was greater the closer the conduct of the last open market operation was to the end of the reserve maintenance period. It was also shown that, in the case of several open market operations within the reserve maintenance period, further degrees of freedom emerge in terms of the assignment of the overall allotment volume to the different operations. It was agued that, in such cases, the reputation of the central bank in terms of its liquidity management strategy was crucial. Finally, it was shown that, in the event of a possible change in standing facility interest rates within the reserve maintenance period, the central bank can, through a contingent allotment policy, engineer constant market rates, but it cannot steer market rates to be constantly at the mid-point of the standing facilities corridor.

In Section 3.5, it was argued that signal extraction problems tend to be key to many issues of day-to-day liquidity management. The following more general conclusions may be drawn from the signal extraction model. First, the details of the time structure and information asymmetries are crucial in modelling richer settings of the steering of overnight rates by a central bank. Second, modelling the control of the overnight rate through open market operations rapidly becomes complex in the case of information asymmetries (even in a one-day reserve maintenance period under strongly simplifying assumptions). Third, this potential complexity suggests that the central bank should keep its approach to monetary policy implementation simple and transparent and thereby avoid the equilibrium determining the overnight rate being so complex as to be fully understood neither by the money market participants nor by the central bank itself.

4

Standing Facilities

In each of this and the following two chapters, one of the three main monetary policy instruments is reviewed, namely, standing facilities (this chapter), open market operations (Chapter 5), and reserve requirements (Chapter 6). The focus is on comparing the use of the instruments through time and across the three selected central banks. Standing facilities are the oldest of the three monetary policy instruments. Standing facilities are defined as monetary policy operations which eligible counterparts of the central bank can use *at their discretion at any moment* during business hours and in particular at the end of the day. The central bank fixes the exact conditions of access, such as, first of all, the interest rate, but also the paper eligible for rediscounting, repurchasing, or pledging, and possibly other operational rules.

Every central bank before 1914 quoted at almost any time at least one official discount rate at which it was prepared to discount eligible paper. Standing facilities basically remained the dominant monetary policy tool until the 1920s, when they started to be more and more replaced, at least for structural liquidity provision, by open market operations (see, for example, Bloomfield 1959).

While it is in the very nature of standing facilities that access to them is, under the conditions set, at the discretion of counterparts, central banks have often deviated from this purist approach and have imposed (*a*) quantitative restrictions per counterpart; (*b*) restrictions obtained through a sufficiently narrow definition of the set of eligible paper; (*c*) 'moral' restrictions in the sense that counterparts were advised that, as far as possible, recourse to standing facilities should be avoided and that excessive recourse may have negative consequences; and (*d*) disincentives obtained by associating the use of standing facilities with an *ex post* administrative procedure. Furthermore, in fact, most central banks made clear that they could in principle always refuse to discount without giving reasons.

4.1   WHY STANDING FACILITIES?

In the previous two chapters, a simple model of monetary policy implementation was expounded in which standing facilities played a key role
in allowing a simple and effective steering of short-term interest rates.
However, such a positive assessment was not standard in the twentieth
century. An example of a recent totally different perception can be found
in the textbook classic by Mishkin (2004: 403), who explains that 'the use
of discount policy to conduct monetary policy has little to recommend'.
In contrast to Mishkin, Chapter 3 concluded that a standing facility
rate-based approach would be simpler than one based mainly on open
market operations to achieve whatever intermediate or final target. The
negative view on standing facilities in the US in fact goes back to the
1920s, and was reinforced by monetarists like, for example, Friedman
(1960), who strongly criticized at least the specification of standing facilities prevailing in the US. This chapter, as well as Chapters 7 and 8, sheds
some light on this astonishing divergence of views and in particular on
where the negative assessment comes from. Only a closer look at the
earlier history of US monetary policy implementation in the twentieth
century will eventually make it possible to understand these older US
views and explain why the Fed took so long to return to a less negative
attitude towards standing facilities.

Before proceeding, we need briefly to explain why, contrary to
Friedman (1960: 35–45) and Mishkin (2004), abolishing standing facilities per se is difficult.[1] Consider what would happen in the event of
the absence of a borrowing facility. Recall first from Chapter 1 the
insight of Bagehot (1873) that the money market tends to be in short-
term disequilibrium and, if the central bank were absent, interest rates
would either sky-rocket or fall to zero most of the time. Thus, standing
facilities (or, equivalently, standing facility-like open market operations)
are a necessary condition for avoiding extreme short-term interest rate
volatility (and a corresponding increase of volatility of longer-term
interest rates). To turn to today's practicalities, note that modern payment
systems allow for intra-day overdrawing of the accounts of banks with
the central bank, in the UK and in the euro area against collateral, in the
US without the need for collateral. If a bank ended the day in overdraft
in the absence of a borrowing facility, an overnight overdraft would
become fact and the central bank could only impose a penalty on the

---

[1] According to Borio (1997: 303, 310) the Netherlands and Spain did not have a borrowing facility
at that time. However, they had a penalty system for end of day overdrafts, which did not impose
prohibitive costs either.

bank. Since the surcharge associated with the borrowing facility can in principle always be equivalent to the level of a penalty, no fundamental difference between the two arises from that side. Still, there are two respects in which the two differ. First, with a borrowing facility, collateral needs to be provided and the central bank is hence insured against credit risk. Second, the borrowing facility is much more efficient and streamlined, and does not require the procedural burden normally associated with a penalty. Therefore, it seems always preferable for the central bank to grant a borrowing facility, and possibly impose a rather high rate on it to give banks an incentive not to end the day in overdraft.

The consequence of a very high penalty rate for non-fulfilment of reserve requirements or a very high borrowing facility rate (for example, 1,000 per cent) would be a higher demand for excess reserves, which would indeed make end of day overdrafts or borrowing extremely rare. The demand for excess reserves would, of course, fluctuate depending on the current payment uncertainties, and so therefore would the overnight interest rate, as long as the central bank did not continuously fine-tune its liquidity supply through open market operations. In particular, such a system would imply a considerable end of maintenance period volatility, since the effective corridor of standing facilities would be so huge (for example, 0–1,000 per cent). To hold the interest rate at, say, 5 per cent in such a corridor after the last open market operation of the reserve maintenance period requires the probability of the market being short (if no individual payment shocks are expected) to be 0.005 per cent. If autonomous factors then change surprisingly, huge changes of overnight rates follow. Of course, the central bank can minimize such volatility by holding the last open market operation of the reserve maintenance period very late in the day. But, of course, in so doing the central bank basically would restore a kind of standing facility, contradicting the assumption that the central bank dislikes this instrument.

That the absence of standing facilities can lead to extreme interest rate volatility is illustrated by the experience of the US before 1914. Burgess (1927: 278–9) quotes a report by the Senate Banking and Currency Committee of November 1913 which gave evidence of the incredible volatility of interest rates before the setting up of the Fed: '... during the year 1907 the range of interest for money was from 2 to 45% in January, from 3 to 25% in March, from 5 to 125% in October, from 3 to 75% in November, and from 2 to 25% in December.' As Friedman (1960: 35) himself summarized, the Federal Reserve system was created by men whose views on the goals of central banking were shaped by the money panics during the national banking era. The solution to the problem of panics reflected in the Federal Reserve Act was the discount window, whose purpose was 'to provide an elastic currency'. Of course, a modern central bank—and this was Friedman's counter-argumentation (1960)—may also attenuate extreme fluctuations through very regular open market operations.[2] However, as mentioned, such open market operations would in effect not be so different from standing facilities.

The rest of this chapter proceeds as follows. Section 4.2 overviews the key issues in defining a system of standing facilities. Sections 4.3, 4.4, and 4.5 review in turn the cases of the three selected central banks. Section 4.6 is dedicated to an important misunderstanding, regarding recourse to standing facilities, which has appeared in the debates over two centuries: the 'reversed causation fallacy'. Section 4.7 concludes.

4.2   TYPES OF STANDING FACILITIES AND KEY ISSUE

Borrowing facilities have two aims. First, they serve as a monetary policy instrument and thereby contribute to steering short-term interest rates. Second, they contribute to the stability of payment flows and to financial stability in so far as they ensure that banks can always overcome temporary liquidity problems as long as they have eligible paper for recourse to the borrowing facility. Historically, recourse to a liquidity-providing standing facility was therefore sometimes not very clearly distinguished from emergency liquidity assistance. Indeed, the US discount window had a reputation for revealing structural liquidity problems, and the Fed for a long time did not really try to overcome this problem through reforms.[3]

Today, there is consensus among central bankers that the two should be fully separated, to make sure that the one is as far as possible at the discretion of commercial banks while the other is as far as possible at the discretion of the central bank. Consider now the different types of borrowing facilities in turn.

Discount facility in the original sense. In a classical rediscounting operation, the holder of an eligible bill (for example, a commercial bill with residual maturity of less than three months) sells the bill to the central bank outright (that is, for good), whereby the price charged in the transaction is determined by 'discounting' the nominal value of the bill

---

[2] M. Friedman (1982) was even more radical in this respect by arguing that the central bank should not even conduct any 'defensive' open market operations.

[3] A famous example was the one of Continental Illinois in May 1984: having serious liquidity problems, the bank took US$3.6 billion recourse to the discount window on 11 May, which became public *inter alia* through the Fed's balance sheet. This created the persistent perception of a link between recourse to the discount window and financial problems. See also Clouse (1994).

through the 'discount' rate. In the first two decades of the twentieth century, monetary policy was still more or less equivalent to 'discount policy', that is, to defining the discount rate and the eligibility criteria for bills, since both lombard lending (see below) and open market operations were of limited relevance. Today, no major central bank offers any longer a discount facility in the original sense, although the US still uses this term for its lombard facility. Classical discounting is still used in the twenty-first century by some developing countries' central banks, for instance by the Central Bank of Egypt. Until the first decades of the twentieth century, classical rediscounting was preferred by central banks to lombard loans due to some kind of *real bills doctrine*, which in its original sense states that banknotes which are lent in exchange for 'real bills', that is, titles to real value or value in process of creation, cannot be issued in excess (see, for example, Reichsbank 1900; Green 1987; McCallum 1986; Meltzer 2003). The origin of the real bills doctrine lies in eighteenth-century England and possibly relates to the fact that usury laws prevented the Bank of England's discount rate from being set above 5 per cent. Therefore, when the appropriate Bank rate would have been higher, the Bank of England tried to limit the gold drain by restricting the set of eligible paper, for example to 'real bills', claiming that this type of paper had specific properties since it represented real commerce. H. Thornton (1802: 252–3) had already convincingly refuted the real bills doctrine:

If it should be said that the bank [Bank of England] loans ought to be afforded only to traders, and on the security of real bills, that is to say, of bills drawn on the occasion of an actual sale of goods, let it be remembered that real bills ... may be multiplied to an extremely great extent; and moreover, that it is only necessary sufficiently to extend the customary length of credit, in order to effect the greatest imaginable multiplication of them.

One may add that real bills also can be multiplied by multiplying the number of layers in trade. Despite Thornton's arguments, the real bills doctrine turned out to be astonishingly persistent and seems to have played an important role in the first decade of the Fed (see Meltzer 2003). Echoes of the real bills doctrine even seem to have survived until the 1990s. For instance Deutsche Bundesbank (1995: 100) explains that 'the trade bills purchased by the Bundesbank are those drawn between enterprises and/or the self-employed *on the basis of deliveries of goods and services*' (emphasis added).

Lombard facility (or 'advance' facility). Recourse to a lombard facility means obtaining a credit from the central bank with given maturity as specified by the central bank, and pledging (or repoing) some eligible paper for the duration of the credit. This has two particular advantages over discounting, namely, standardization of the maturity of operations, and allowing for a wider set of eligible paper in terms of maturity and risk characteristics. It was mainly in the 1950s that more and more central banks developed a preference for advances over discounting (Tamagna 1963: 79–80), which was also due to a large extent to the growth of long-term government debt during the Second World War, which could easily be pledged.

Deposit facility. Central banks have only recently discovered the advantages of liquidity-absorbing facilities for monetary policy implementation. Indeed, a deposit facility is somewhat less important since it is not needed to support financial stability. Still, it was shown in Chapter 3 that a symmetric corridor system makes the steering of short-term interest rates a rather simple matter when the target rate is not identical to a standing facility rate. But this was not recognized by central banks for a long time, possibly also due to the general passion for open market operations and monetary quantities.

In the following review of the histories of the specification and use of standing facilities by the three selected central banks, a series of issues will emerge again and again, namely: (*a*) What determines recourse to the borrowing facility? (*b*) Should there be non-price controls of recourse to standing facilities of any kind? (*c*) Should the banking system be structurally dependent on the discount window? (*d*) Should the discount rate always be close, or in a well-defined relationship, to the market rate? Related to that: how often should it be adjusted? It is worth spending some more time on the Bank of England's experience in the eighteenth and nineteenth centuries, when all of these questions arose for the first time.

4.3   THE BANK OF ENGLAND

4.3.1   *Before the twentieth century*

The Bank of England had already acquired rich experience of this instrument in the nineteenth century and, indeed, many of the issues relating to its appropriate use arose during this period.[4]

---

[4] Detailed treatments of the nineteenth-century London discount market and of the operations of the Bank of England in this market have been provided by King (1936) and Wood (1939). This section draws primarily on the former book. A more general history of the pre-1914 Bank of England also containing evidence on operations is Clapham (1944). Meltzer (2003: 19–64) surveys nineteenth-century Bank of England policy. Sayers (1976) is rich on policy operations for the period 1891–1944.

Instruments similar to bills of exchange were already in use in England in the twelfth century. However, the instrument was long discouraged by law since fungible claims were considered evil (at least in England; for the role of the bill of exchange in early European trade in general, see, for example, de Roover 1963). Legal reform after the end of the Middle Ages removed barriers to the use of bills. In England, central bank laws played an important indirect role in promoting the bills market in the early eighteenth century. In Acts of Parliament from 1708 and 1742, the Bank of England's monopoly over banknote issuance was protected by the prohibition on other banks having more than six partners. Therefore, the country banks remained small and local, implying that they could not bridge areas with surplus and deficit funds, and the bill broker became indispensable as a connecting link. In the middle of the eighteenth century, bills of exchange must have become a key instrument, and Adam Smith could praise this fact in 1776 in his *Wealth of Nations* as substantial financial progress. He also mentioned the three months maturity of bills, which would be kept as a standard in central bank operations until the twenty-first century. For instance, the discount facility offered by the Bundesbank until 1998 set the maximum time to maturity of bills at three months, and the Eurosystem introduced in 1999 a so-called longer-term refinancing operation with three months maturity, still maintained today.

Already before the nineteenth century, the market most of the time had systematic recourse to rediscounting bills with the Bank of England (King 1936: 71), and indeed, the market was rather dependent on the Bank and not always happy with its sometimes restrictive policy. Applying a policy of quantitative restriction was probably unavoidable at least sometimes until 1833 because the usury law set a 5 per cent ceiling on interest rates. The following declaration of a committee of protesters of 1797 suggests that such restrictions were indeed relevant (quoted by King 1936: 72):

That the Committee . . . are of opinion that it is important to the Mercantile Interest of the Country . . . that the practice of Discounts should be extended to and continued upon the Scale stated . . . and that therefore, if the Bank of England is incompetent to afford this necessary and reasonable Aid, it will be requisite that some other Public Establishment should be created . . .

It was to remain a topic for central banks until the end of the twentieth century whether access to its borrowing facility should be regulated purely through the price mechanism (the borrowing facility rate) or, in addition, through deliberately narrowing eligibility criteria, quantitative limits, administrative restrictions, or moral suasion.

4.3.2   A first episode of over-loose Bank rate policy and its aftermath (1822–1825)

The first example of expansionist monetary policy by the Bank of England through over-loose Bank rate policy was the episode of 1822–5. Liberal changes in the law regulating the issue of banknotes were combined with a cut in the Bank rate to 4 per cent and a softening of eligibility criteria for bills in so far as maximum maturity was extended from 65 to 95 days. Abundant credit was thus made available to finance many unsound speculative projects. In 1825, the Bank of England became aware of the serious problems and suddenly reversed its policy by refusing to discount. The result was financial panic and the famous first massive emergency liquidity assistance by the Bank of England, which has since been recognized to be a major responsibility of any central bank (see Section 1.2.5).

The years preceding the crisis of 1825 may be regarded as *the first case of expansionist monetary policy through standing facility rates policy.* The sudden refusal to rediscount was a reversal of this policy with at the same time a switch to a policy of *quantitative* restriction. The question of applying interest rate policy or quantitative restrictions also remained a key issue of monetary policy implementation in the twentieth century, and even the 1979–82 US experiment may in principle be subsumed under this debate (see especially Chapters 7 and 8). The normal sequence of events was, first, an expansionist interest rate policy; second, a need for restrictive policy; third, restrictive measures encompassing *quantitative* restrictions; finally, abandonment of this approach because of its disturbing side-effects.

4.3.3   A period of distrust against discounting (1825–1844)

As a consequence of the crisis, the Bank of England adopted a new doctrine according to which it aimed to back one-third of its liabilities in gold and the rest in securities, and whereby the note issue should fluctuate only when the public was paying in or withdrawing gold. The rule implied that the Bank of England would no longer be discounting bills. In practice, the rule was applied less stringently, in such a way that, at least in theory, there should no longer be regular and structural discounting, which is not too far from today's central bank practice. Following King (1936: 78), the Bank exactly reversed its previous approach under which discount operations had to be a central part of its credit control. This approach prevailed between 1825 and 1844. It is worth quoting Horsley

Palmer (Governor from 1830 to 1833) from Committee minutes of 1832 on the approach during that episode (King 1936: 79):

Horsley Palmer declared that so long as the Bank was well supplied with other readily marketable securities, private discounts were one of the 'worst means' of regulating issues, for they interfered with the action of the London private banks . . . The Board therefore preferred that its rate should be generally above the market rate, 'thereby not to interfere with the employment of money actually in existence' and argued that the Bank should be a 'bank of discounts' only in times of emergency . . .

The issue addressed here—whether or not the market should be structurally dependent on standing facilities—is another classic question of monetary policy implementation, in which Horsley Palmer's view that the central bank should *not* interfere with the money market by offering a standing facility on which banks are structurally dependent seems to have eventually prevailed (although today's motivation would be somewhat different).

The Bank rate was still kept rather stable in the period 1824–44 (yearly averages between 4.00 per cent and 5.10 per cent, whereby the rate remained unchanged at 4.00 per cent in eleven of the twenty-one years; King 1936: 80). The Bank simply stopped discounting in case of excess liquidity, and inter-bank rates then dropped below the Bank rate. When liquidity became again scarce, market rates climbed towards the Bank rate and discounting automatically resumed. A consequence of the rigidity of the Bank rate even after the usury law had been repealed was that, in time of financial expansion and high demand for discounts, the Bank again relied on *quantitative* restrictions when it wished to limit the expansion. The public outcry against such measures was, however, apparently always very strong, and an observer judged in 1844 that 'a rate of discount by the Bank of 8 per cent or 10 per cent would have been considered preferable to some of the limitations which prevailed' (King 1936: 82). Consistent with the supposedly diminished role of the discount facility, the period 1824–44 also witnessed the first open market operations, which are reviewed in more detail in Chapter 5.

4.3.4 *A second episode of over-loose Bank rate policy (1844–1847), and a second crisis*

Economic fluctuations during the last years of the 1830s again directed the attention of the Bank and the public to the importance of controlling money and credit, which resulted in the well-known 'Currency School' vs

'Banking School' controversy. The Currency School, which promoted the idea that the note issue needs to be controlled so as to ensure that their volume fluctuates automatically with bullion holdings, eventually prevailed over the Banking School. Corresponding principles were embodied in the Bank Charter Act of 1844, the so-called Peel's Act. All Bank of England notes above a fiduciary value of £14 million were to be backed by their equivalent in bullion, existing private issues were to be limited, and new ones prohibited. The Bank was separated into a Note Issue Department and a Banking Department, still evident today in its weekly return (see Chapter 2). The Act also seemed to be, to put it in modern terms, a triumph of rules over discretion, since the power to manipulate the issue of banknotes was in theory taken away from the Bank. The Banking Department made the best of it and concentrated on competitive operations, including again discounting under its so-called *new discounting policy*. Of course, the freedom to set the discount rate was now limited by the restriction on banknote issuance, that is, by the required central bank reserves of bullion relative to the issued banknotes. The new discounting policy consisted of keeping the discount rate close to market rates, which is consistent with relevant discounting taking place continuously. Also, the discount rate started to be handled in a much more flexible way. Market rates and discount rates moved closely together, and *the perceived causality was that the Bank was following the market*. The publicly stated view of the Bank of England that it was *following* the market rather than *controlling* market rates, is a further key issue of monetary policy implementation that will appear again and again up to the present. King (1936: 109) quotes Commons committee minutes of that time saying 'there is no reason why the Bank should not vary the rate of interest in the same way as any discount broker, or any other parties discounting would do'. It was contended that the public attached too much importance to variations in Bank rate and, with the object of correcting this 'misapprehension', towards the end of 1844 the Bank even temporarily suspended the regular issue of Bank rate notices.

Of course, according to the aggregate liquidity model presented in Chapter 3, the central bank cannot really 'follow the market' directly through discount rate changes since the spread between the discount rate and the market rate is supposed to depend mainly on the needs of the banks to have recourse to the discount facility to cover their liquidity needs (see also Section 4.6). To this extent, lowering the discount rate leads, *ceteris paribus*, to a further fall of the market rate, although at least the absolute difference between the two will decline. Also, indirect effects may imply a closing of the spread: when the economy acquires momentum due to an over-loose interest rate policy of the central bank, the demand for banknotes may expand and gold may be withdrawn. Both imply an increase in refinancing needs of the market towards the central bank, and thus eventually higher discounting and a fall in the spread between market and Bank rate. Through this channel, 'following the market' may thus indeed eventually be successful, although the price is obviously the triggering of an unsustainable economic boom (see also Section 4.6).

The new discounting policy indeed led to Bank rates lower than ever before (2.5 per cent in 1844/5) and higher income from discounts than in any year since 1825 (Clapham 1944: ii. 433). The combination of this loose policy and a railway-related stock market boom resulted after a lag in a dramatic fall of the Bank of England's metal reserves. The Bank reacted in 1847 once again by increasing rates and by restricting access to the discount facility through a narrowing of the set of eligible bills. A stock exchange panic developed, combined with an incipient bank run. Uncertainty about banking failures made inter-bank interest rates soar to previously unknown levels, and it was suddenly clear that it was up to the Bank of England to save the financial system by lending again without quantitative limits. It did so, and the prohibition laid down only three years earlier in the bank act regarding note issuance was temporarily suspended.

4.3.5 *From 1847 to 1914*

After the crisis of 1847, the Bank adopted a more careful strategy towards safeguarding the stability of the currency, and according to King (1936: 166), the post-1847 behaviour of the Bank was not too different from its practice in the first decades of the twentieth century. Before 1844, it had normally kept the Bank rate above market rates. Between 1844 and 1847, it had aggressively 'followed the market'. Finally, after the crisis of 1847, it adopted an intermediate course, keeping the rate close to but normally somewhat above the market rate, with only a seasonal heavy recourse by banks. Meltzer (2003: 51) comes to the conclusion that from around 1844 the Bank of England 'gradually accepted money market rates as the principal indicator of current monetary policy'. While this approach was not always followed in the twentieth century, and is criticized by, for example, Meltzer (2003: 51), it is today again regarded as standard by central banks. In Chapter 8 it will be presented as one of the key elements of the 'new view' on monetary policy implementation.

The Bank adopted a wiser policy in the subsequent crises of 1857 and 1866, namely, not to restrict quantities but to always lend, if necessary at high rates (Meltzer 2003: 48). Still, the Bank made other mistakes. In 1858, it restricted access to the Bank of England's discount facility *of discount brokers*, which were the most active money market players at that time. According to King (1936: 200), Sheffield Neave, Governor of the Bank in 1857–9, was 'obsessed by the problem of the bill market's reliance upon the bank'. Instead of viewing this as the consequence of the market's liquidity deficit vis-à-vis the central bank, the Bank decided to narrow the set of its eligible counterparts, which from today's perspective does not appear to be a helpful measure to reduce the liquidity deficit. On 16 March 1858, Neave explained the new rule (according to the Lords' Committee minutes reported by King 1936: 201) as eventually aiming at quantitative restrictions:

Hitherto the discount brokers have had access to the Bank at all times for discounts; the change made now is to decline giving them discounts any longer. . . . The object is to keep the resources of the Bank more within her own compass, and not to give the opportunity to the discount brokers, who accumulate such very large sums in their hands, to rely entirely and totally for cashing their bills upon the Bank of England.

Unsurprisingly, 'the announcement was received with open hostility in the bill market' (King 1936: 201). Also, the Lords' Committee concluded during an interrogation of Neave that the new approach was inconsistent: it was supposed to protect the Bank in the case of a crisis, but in the event of a crisis it was very difficult to enforce it. Indeed, the first real test of the new regulation came with a stock market crash in Easter 1859. The unwillingness of the Bank to discount in a flexible way to bill brokers seriously aggravated the repercussions of the crisis. A similar crisis emerged in 1860 for the same reasons. In succeeding years the topic continued to be discussed in an emotional way between the market and the Bank, but without the Bank giving in. The continued application of the rule 'resulted in constant derangement of the credit position, and extreme instability of rates' (King 1936: 216).

During the 1880s and the 1890s, the big topic for the Bank of England was to 'make Bank rate effective': due to excess liquidity, market rates often tended to lie again clearly below the discount rate. The Bank no longer made the mistake of responding to this by lowering the Bank rate. But it was concerned when a clear increase in interest rates required by the macroeconomic environment (mainly international flows of gold) could not be easily engineered due to a very weak demand for rediscounting. In such cases, the Bank sometimes borrowed directly in the market or sold

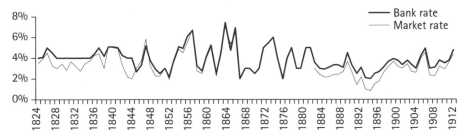

Figure 4.1 *Bank rate and market rate in the UK: Yearly averages, 1824–1914*
Sources: King (1936); Clapham (1944).

consols (perpetual fixed-income securities): that is, it *absorbed liquidity through open market operations to bring market rates close to the Bank rate*. According to King (1936: 311–12), the Bank acquired definitive control from 1898 onwards. Normally, the market was structurally short of liquidity, such that some borrowing always occurred. 'There was no longer any doubt that the Bank *could* control the market; and the average differentials [between the Bank rate and the market rate] revealed that, despite occasional spasms of unusually fierce competition or of pronounced monetary ease, the Bank in general *did* control it.' King (1936: 315) continues: 'From about 1900 onwards, the main concern of the Bank seems to have been not how to impose its own rate on the market, but how to avoid imposing upon the trade of the country a rate often dictated solely by external influences.' In other words, monetary policy *implementation* was eventually mastered, with the fundamental issue of the correct macroeconomic strategy and stance of course left to the central bank.[5]

Figure 4.1 shows Bank rate and, for a sub-sample, also discount *market* rates, for the period 1824 to 1914. Market rates were usually at or around one percentage point below Bank rate, but short-run fluctuations were of course much more intense and could drive market rates to zero or, when eligible paper was scarce, even above Bank rate. To reveal how volatile Bank rate in fact was, Fig. 4.2 shows Bank rate for one selected year, 1873. In this year Bank rate was changed 24 times, varying between 9 per cent and 3 per cent. Although volatility in this year was clearly above average, from five to ten changes of Bank rate a year were quite normal in the second half of the nineteenth century.[6]

---

[5] For the period from 1890 to the 1930s, Sayers (1976) provides a detailed overview of 'how to make Bank rate effective' through liquidity-absorbing open market operations and how the discount window was operated. On open market operations to make Bank rate effective, see Sayers (1976: 38, 297–313); on eligibility for discounts and advances, see Sayers (1976: 33–4, 272–83).

[6] On Bank rate policy in the second half of the nineteenth century and the first decades of the twentieth century, see also, for instance, Hawtrey (1938) and Sayers (1981).

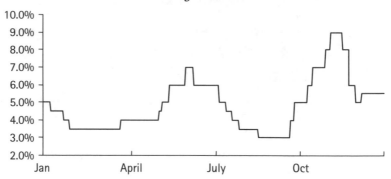

Figure 4.2　*Bank of England Bank rate in 1873*
Source: Clapham (1944).

The volatility of Bank rate and the serial correlation of its changes revealed in Fig. 4.2 also well explain why the Bank preferred to maintain a positive spread of around one percentage point between the market rate and Bank rate. For instance, Bank of England Deputy Governor Harvey reported in the Macmillan Committee's hearings in 1929 both the problem and one element of the solution adopted by the Bank (Sayers 1976: iii. 149):

Of course, it may mean that at certain periods, if the market have [*sic*] apprehensions that the Bank rate is going to rise, if they see ahead a possibly lengthy period of high rates, they may say to themselves: 'well, we had better clear out some of our bills before the rates go up; we will take them to the Bank at once and discount them; it is better to go there and get rid of them, release our funds and be able, when the rates has gone up, to replenish our portfolio at a higher rate.' There the Bank has to protect itself by limiting the currency of the bills, which it will take. It may say: 'Yes. Whilst we will give the discount market the accommodation it requires, we will only advance to it ordinarily for a minimum period of a week, or we will discount bills, it may be, having two or three weeks to run.'

The problem with a speculative use of the discount facility in the event of expectations of a rate hike indeed becomes obvious in view of Fig. 4.2 and the fact that eligible bills normally had a maturity of up to three months. In principle, the combination of frequent and correlated (thus predictable) changes would have allowed banks to circumvent rate hikes by the central bank, at least for three months, by covering all refinancing needs for this period through massive three-months bill discounting whenever rate hike expectations emerged. The technique described above by Deputy Governor Harvey is *one* way to limit the phenomenon. The classic technique of the Bank of England of maintaining a spread of around one percentage point between Bank rate and market rate is another one. This spread ensures that speculative borrowing emerges only when rate hike expectations over the period of eligibility of bills exceed this spread.

4.3.6 *From 1914 to today*

According to Haase (1962), discounting remained the most important monetary policy instrument only until 1914. Thereafter, outright holdings of securities dominated, and recourse to the borrowing facility was always more limited, such as to keep market rates clearly below the Bank rate. Indeed, data provided by Haase (1962: 102) suggests that discount and lombard lending between 1932 and 1959 usually amounted to less than 5 per cent of the total domestic assets of the Bank of England. The lombard rate was normally 50 basis points above the discount rate, but in later years the two rates tended to be equal. According to Haase (1962: 106), the Bank of England was in the 1920s the first central bank to use systematically the interplay between open market operations and standing facility rates to steer market rates at a certain level relative to the Bank rate, as in the model presented in Chapter 3. According to the Deputy Governor of the Bank of England in the hearings of the Macmillan Committee in 1929, the spread between market rates and the discount rate was at a 'minimum of about 1 per cent', which also suggests that there was no large structural recourse to the discount facility (Sayers 1976: iii. 150). Tamagna (1963: 69–74) highlights the Bank of England as the best example of a central bank that had only one borrowing rate, while many others had multiple penalty rates increasing with the level of the recourse (for example, the Banque de France had three rates, plus a rate for advances). Between 1932 and 1951, the discount rate remained at 2 per cent (apart from three months in 1939). Interestingly, however, it lost its relevance especially during the war years, when the Bank of England effectively adopted an additional standing facility at 1 per cent with a zero per cent spread towards market rates. As Sayers (1953: 394) explains:

Intervention in the bill market . . . not merely remained continuous but became automatic, as the Bank dropped all pretence of holding the initiative. The Bank's primary contribution to the policy of the 'three per cent war' was in fact to hold the Treasury Bill rate at 1 per cent, by standing ready at all times to operate either way in the market at that price.

Such a policy was continued until 1951. The fact that these were officially open market operations on the part of the Bank of England, although they were in the nature of a standing facility, illustrates the potential ambiguity in distinguishing between the two. The Bank rate played the role of the main official rate until 1972, when it was substituted by the 'minimum lending rate', that is, a rate of open market operations, and hence an implicit target rate (see also Cramp 1987). In 1981, the 'Minimum Band 1' dealing rate was instead introduced.[7] Bank of England (1988: 17) describes the borrowing facilities provided in the 1980s to counterparties. Accordingly, these

provide discount houses with a supplementary means of balancing their positions after the Bank's main operations in eligible bills have been concluded. . . . Each discount house's facility is in two tranches, each for an amount equal to the capital base of the discount house. Facilities are adjusted quarterly in line with changes in the capital base of each discount house . . . Drawings on the second tranche will normally bear a higher rate of interest than those on the first tranche. The rates on which these facilities are available on a particular day are at the discretion of the Bank. The facility may be activated by personal application to the Head of the Money Market Operations Division at the Bank. Prospective borrowers are invited to state the amount they wish to borrow before being told the terms on which the funds will be made available.

It appears that the borrowing facilities were quantitatively restricted and that their price was even unknown at the moment a commitment was made with regard to the amount borrowed. Also, the two tranches and the personal application appear complicated. This seems to reflect the recurring view (also prevalent in the US during most of the twentieth century) that non-price disincentives are needed against using the facility, and that their true full price should be preferably non-transparent. In 1997, new procedures were adopted for daily open market operations, and the occasion was also used to make standing facilities once again more transparent and less administrative (Bank of England 1997):[8]

The Bank will therefore be prepared to make available, to the settlement banks only, between 3.50 pm and 3.55 pm a late repo facility at a rate $1/4$% above the repo rate applied in the Bank's open market operations. The Bank will be prepared to provide liquidity, normally up to the amount of any late swing it identifies in the system's need for liquidity, to any settlement bank, whether or not it is one of the Bank's counterparties in the open market operations. An individual settlement bank will not

[7] A move from open market operations (being close to standing facilities) to more genuine open market operations with variable rate tenders was considered in 1982. Bank of England (1982: 89) explains: 'Behind these proposals lay the desire to introduce a system which, while preserving the Bank's ability to influence short-term rates, would generally permit market forces a greater role in determining their structure. To allow such play for market forces, the system of pre-determined dealing rates had to be abandoned.' Still, in practice, fixed-rate tender open market operations have continued to prevail in the UK to the present day.

[8] In 1997, the 'repo rate' was introduced to replace the Minimum Band 1 rate as the main policy rate.

be permitted to apply for more than the total of the forecast shortage remaining at that stage, but the Bank will not otherwise place any predetermined limits on individual banks' access to this facility.... The operation will be conducted in the form of repo, and normally with an overnight maturity as at present, unless the Bank specifies otherwise. Paper eligible for use in this facility will be the same as for the Bank's open market operations.

Although quantitative restrictions remain, they do not appear to be binding on normal occasions. Four years later, the system was again adjusted, and a plus or minus 100 basis points *corridor system* was introduced: that is, a *deposit* facility was offered for the first time (Allen 2002; Bank of England 2002*a*). Furthermore, for settlement banks only (these are a small number of banks with a special relationship with the Bank of England since they provide settlement services to other banks), a further round of recourse to an overnight repo facility is foreseen after the round of first recourses, whereby, interestingly, the price to be paid by settlement banks in that late repo depends on the reason for the recourse (Bank of England 2002*a*: 12):

On days when the residual forecast shortage reflects only a late revision to the day's forecast shortage by the Bank of England . . . funds are normally provided to the settlement banks at the official repo rate . . . However, on days when there is a remaining shortage but there has been no late change to the forecast (and, therefore, the settlement banks should reasonably have been able to take the necessary funds from the Bank of England earlier in the day) funds are provided at a higher rate, normally 150 basis points above the official repo rate.

The contingent specification of the rate charged at the last round of access seems to reflect fairness considerations, that is, banks should not pay for the central bank's forecasting errors. The drawback is, of course, a higher degree of complexity. Nevertheless, the specification reflects a modern view on the appropriate specification of standing facility which is that it should (*a*) be quantitatively quasi-unlimited but effectively only for 'marginal' needs; (*b*) leave little discretion on the part of the central bank regarding pricing and general conditions; and (*c*) be conducted as an overnight operation.

4.4 THE FEDERAL RESERVE SYSTEM

The history of the US Fed's discount window in the twentieth century appears from today's perspective rather mysterious. Instead of restricting access via the price mechanism, it was defined in a rather opaque way, with administrative procedures and moral suasion key to limiting its use.

In contrast to similar episodes at the Bank of England in the nineteenth century, the Fed maintained such an approach throughout the century; and it was only in 2002 that the Fed eventually took a decisive step towards modernizing its borrowing facility.

For the entire twentieth century, a US bank taking recourse to the discount window had in fact technically two options: to take an advance or an actual discount. The rates applied to both variants were *equal*: that is, the Fed never charged, as the Reichsbank did, 100 basis points more for an advance. While in the early days of the Fed discounts were the more important means of access to Federal Reserve credit, at least from the 1960s virtually all funds obtained through the discount window took the form of advances (Board of Governors 1974: 70). Still, the name of the borrowing facility was not changed accordingly.

The Fed in fact always distinguished several types of recourses to the discount window, of which the 'adjustment credit loan' was the most relevant. The other types were 'seasonal credit', given to a limited number of banks in vacation and agricultural areas, and 'extended credit', provided to banks that had more serious liquidity problems. Sometimes this latter category, which is close to emergency liquidity assistance, was also called 'emergency credit' (see Holland 1970: 145; Clouse 1994). Quantitative restrictions and administrative procedures differed among the three sub-categories.[9] For instance, in 1970 access to the adjustment credit was split into two tranches (see Holland 1970: 145). The first, called 'basic borrowing privilege', triggered no administrative procedure other 'than general discouragement of net selling of Federal funds by borrowing banks', and the only further restriction was that the borrowing bank 'must not have been found to be in unsatisfactory condition'. The quantity limit for the basic borrowing privilege was calculated according to the capital stock, whereby a sub-proportional increase was apparently meant to support small banks: it corresponded to 40 per cent of the first $1 million of capital, plus 20 per cent of the next $9 million, plus 10 per cent of the rest. Furthermore, frequency was limited to six out of thirteen (or thirteen out of twenty-six) consecutive reserve maintenance periods. If banks borrowed beyond their basic borrowing privilege, no further limits were defined, but an appraisal and, where necessary, supervisory action was triggered.

---

[9] The rates of these three sub-categories were normally the same. For adjustment credit loans, the Fed in the early 1920s introduced temporarily 'progressive rates', that is, incremental rates increasing with the volume of the recourse. The adoption of progressive rates in 1920 was for the purpose of distributing Federal Reserve Bank credit more evenly among the member banks. However, as 'they created hardship to some individual member banks', they were soon abolished again (Goldenweiser 1925: 42).

4.4.1 *Shaping of the discount window, 1914–1924*

During most of that period the financial system was structurally dependent upon borrowing. Scarcity of eligible paper was never an issue (Riefler 1930: 20). A detailed description of the early years of the Fed and the role of the discount window may be found in Meltzer (2003) and also in Sprague (1921) and Harris (1933). Meltzer describes the Fed at that time as too decentralized a system, with too many commercial bankers at the top and too much Treasury power in decision making. The result was that it could not conduct an appropriate discount rate policy before 1920. Tension between the Federal Reserve Board and the Reserve Banks had already emerged before business started in 1914. One of the earliest acts of the Board was to rule that the Reserve Banks could not announce or change discount rates until they had been approved by the Board. In contrast, in early 1915 the conference of Governors of Federal Reserve Banks approved a resolution giving the Reserve Banks full power to initiate discount rate changes without pressure from the Federal Reserve Board (Meltzer 2003: 77–8). The structure of discount rates was remarkably complicated and, for instance, in 1917 Federal Reserve banks quoted heterogeneously up to more than seven different discount rates depending on the maturity and type of paper (Meltzer 2003: 84).

While discount rates were in 1914 considered to be *penalty rates*—that is, above market rates—following the example of the Bank of England, as early as 1917 this idea was given up and market rates stood above discount rates, reflecting some non-price restrictions. Discount rate policy from 1917 to 1919 was dominated by the Treasury insisting that short-term rates should remain low in order to limit the costs of the war department. Furthermore, preferential discount rates were stipulated for Treasury paper, such that most discounted paper was soon of that type and no longer of a commercial bill nature. The preferential rate thus soon became the key rate. Although some Federal Reserve banks repeatedly proposed to increase rates, all such requests were rejected by the board under the influence of the Treasury. *The solution that was attempted was to keep rates low, but to intensify efforts to persuade the banks to borrow moderately, which of course implied that market rates increased to levels above the discount rate.* Only in November 1919 did the Federal Reserve System eventually begin to raise discount rates, whereas the moral suasion approach was retained as a complementary tool, in theory substituting for a part of the needed rate increase.[10]

---

[10] For instance, Goldenweiser (1925: 48) confirms that moral suasion was a key element of the disincentives against the use of the discount window already in the early 1920s: '... the Federal

In April 1920, Congress passed the Phelan Act, which allowed *progressive* discount rates. The idea was to penalize *heavy* use of the facility. The choice of the exact formula was left to the Federal Reserve banks. The selective application of progressive rates by the different Federal Reserve banks implied shifts of borrowing from the more restrictive to the less restrictive Reserve districts. In March 1923 Congress repealed the provision, and since then progressive rates have never again been applied in the US (see Wallace 1956 for a more detailed account of this episode).

The result of the failure to raise discount rates (and market rates) during the First World War was an extraordinary increase in inflation from 2 per cent in 1915 to 11.0, 17.0, 18.6, and 13.8 per cent respectively in the succeeding years (Meltzer 2003: 91). When the Federal Reserve System started in 1919 to reverse this inflation so as to restore the gold standard at the old parity, the costs of deflation were high. The unemployment rate rose from 4 per cent on average in 1920 to 12 per cent on average in 1921. Furthermore, in the context of monetary policy *implementation*, the Fed did not manage until 2002 to restore a 'rational' borrowing facility with unlimited access at a penalty rate, such as to set a ceiling to the market rate.

Statements and reports from that time suggest that it was not clear to the Fed that a precondition for restoring a penalty rate system (with market rates below the discount rate) would have been an injection of reserves through open market operations to reduce the dependence of the banks on the discount window. Consider the following episode from 1921 reported by Meltzer (2003: 125). In 1921, the Board asked the Governors how the discount rate should be set. Replies reflected a rather peculiar understanding of monetary policy implementation. Most Governors took the view that discount rates should be set slightly above market rates. For instance Governor McDougal of Chicago, expressing the majority view, argued that 'If the reserves of the Federal Reserve System were to be safeguarded against misuse and to be held available for legitimate seasonal requirements . . . the discount rate policy should be one which should hold those rates as high or slightly higher than the prevailing rates in the commercial centers.'[11] This position reveals confusion about causalities and ignores the insight that the spread between the discount rate and the

---

reserve banks disapprove the practice of borrowing reserve bank funds, which are a joint reserve of credit belonging to all the members, for the purpose of increasing the earnings of an individual bank. When a reserve bank finds that a member bank is borrowing for such a purpose it uses its influence against the continuance of such borrowing.'

[11] Apparently, only Governor Strong from New York took a dissenting view and, anticipating reserve position doctrine, felt that the volume of borrowing through the discount facility was 'absolutely the fundamental and controlling factor'.

market rate depends on the need to have recourse and the non-price disincentives against using the facility. The same confusion over causalities will be observed in US academic and (to a lesser extent) central banking literature throughout the century. Since the reversed causality fallacy is likely to have been key to the delay in the reform of the discount window, it is discussed in more detail in Section 4.6.

Even after 'discovering' open market operations in the early 1920s, the Fed failed to see, or at least to make use of, this tool to restore a penalty discount rate. In the meantime, mysterious concepts like 'the tradition against borrowing' had gained currency. From the end of the 1920s, thinking started to turn more and more to reserve position doctrine (see Section 1.3.2), and borrowing through the discount window was more and more regarded as a nuisance that did not deserve reform since open market operations were anyway considered the only desirable tool.

Meulendyke explains the US discount window puzzle mainly by the Fed's over-decentralization during its first decade.[12] The Federal Reserve System came into being at a time of strong discomfort with concentration of power in Washington. Two previous central banks had been dissolved in the nineteenth century, in part because of regional distrust of concentrated power. The Federal Reserve was created as a decentralized system to deal with seasonal agricultural needs and to ease or prevent financial panics. It was not seen as an organization to make monetary policy. Discount policy fell to the semi-independent regional banks, with varying degrees of oversight from the board in Washington. The US economy was much more decentralized then, and one region could be in a recession while another was prospering. It was assumed that different parts of the country could have different levels of credit stringency at the same time, although improved communication and transportation and the Federal Reserve's funds transfer services were soon uniting the country financially. Still, the regional banks never wanted to give up their power over the discount facility. Consequently, discount policy was always poorly linked with open market policy. Eventually, the system of subsidized credits with administrative constraints took on a life of its own and was used to restrain credit growth.

4.4.2 *Some further* ex post *interpretations of the early Fed experience*

In the 1920s, Fed officials like Goldenweiser still looked for excuses as to why the Fed had not copied the Bank of England penalty rate system. He

---

[12] The author gratefully acknowledges Meulendyke's detailed suggestions on this issue.

cited certain not very specific financial and institutional differences (see also Burgess 1927: ch. 11):

Bank rate in England has traditionally been above the open market rate, and this relationship has been considered as an essential part of credit administration by a central institution. . . . there are sufficient differences in the nature of the money market and in the character of services rendered by the Bank of England and the Federal reserve banks, to make it impossible to follow British precedents in American banking practice. (Goldenweiser 1925: 46)

Keynes (1930: 213), as a proponent of reserve position doctrine, also judged excessive the recourse to the discount window in the first years of the system, instead of noting that the Fed simply failed, under Treasury pressure, to sufficiently raise the discount rate in time. He continued:

The history of the Federal Reserve System since the war has been, first of all, a great abuse of the latitude thus accorded to the member banks to increase the 'advances' of the Reserve Banks, and subsequently a series of efforts by the reserve authorities to invent gadgets and conventions which shall give them a power, more nearly similar to that which the Bank of England has, without any alteration of the law. The first phase, before the flaw in the system had been discovered, was clearly seen in the great inflation of 1920. For in 1920 those responsible for the management in the Federal Reserve System had not yet realised the enormous latent possibilities of inflation resulting from its failure to imitate the Bank of England system . . . Since that time, the Federal Reserve Board has been working out, largely empirically, methods of control of its own not borrowed from London. In the first place, pressure is put on the member banks to restrain their use of rediscounting facilities with the Federal Reserve Banks by criticising them, asking inconvenient questions, and creating a public opinion to the effect that it is not quite respectable for a member bank, or good for its credit, to be using the resources of the Reserve Bank more than its neighbours.

While Keynes's description is likely to reflect more or less the US Fed's interpretation of events at that time, two aspects in particular of his reasoning are not easy to understand from today's perspective. First, from a financial market arbitrage point of view, the strong differentiation between open market operations and recourse to the borrowing facility is difficult to justify; second, from the perspective of Chapter 2, one misses in Keynes's reasoning a reference to the central bank balance sheet, which provides for the relationship between open market operations and borrowing at the discount window. Indeed, if one feels that recourse to the discount window is too great, one should simply inject funds through open market operations. If instead the feeling is that the economy and money and credit are on too expansionary a path, one should raise the targeted short-term inter-bank rate (for example, by raising the discount rate: see Chapter 3). Keynes (and US Fed central bankers of that time, like the Bank of England on occasion in the nineteenth century) did not appear to distinguish between the two issues. Keynes felt that high levels of borrowing at the discount window were per se inflationary: liquidity injection through open market operations to reduce borrowing would on this interpretation mean pouring petrol on fire.

Forty years after Keynes, Holland (1970: 140) described the pre-1920 Fed episode mainly as a consequence of the fallacious real bills doctrine:

In the early years of the system, both the quantity and quality of discounting were supposed to be controlled by the requirement that only short-term self-liquidating paper (so called 'eligible paper') could be accepted as collateral for borrowing from the Reserve Banks. Resting as it did both on fallacious doctrine (that of 'real bills') and an assumed old world institutional structure that American business and finance did not replicate, this control device soon was found wanting. To achieve more effective control of discounting, both in total and at the individual bank level, supplementary reliance was placed on variations of the discount rate charged and on administrative counselling by System officials.

It is difficult to believe that the Fed really had such a strong version of the real bills doctrine in mind and that it had not noticed from studying the experience of old-world central banks that it would need to adjust discount rates to stabilize prices and the economy. As well, the reliance on Treasury bills in discounting from 1917 to 1921 raises doubts about the role of the real bills doctrine. And it remains unclear what Holland means by 'old world institutional structures' which could be responsible for fundamentally different requirements for monetary policy implementation, an argument already used by Goldenweiser.

4.4.3 *From 1925 to 2002*

In any case, the 'tradition against borrowing'—that is, non-price disincentives—was substantial only a few years after the launch of the Federal Reserve System. The aversion of banks against borrowing increased further in the early 1930s, when bank failures became more frequent and a greater recourse to the discount window was considered to be a signal for a possible weakness of a bank. Such reluctance was less relevant between 1934 and 1950, since during this period market rates were very low and banks generally held large excess reserves, such that there was practically no use of the discount window. When excess reserves had again disappeared in the 1950s, Fed policy continued to be stringent against discounting and a Fed 'Report on the Discount Mechanism' in 1954 concluded that 'routine reserve provision be accomplished almost entirely through open market operations' (Meulendyke 1992: 37; see also Tamagna 1963: 74). Regulations that were adopted after 1954 again guided discount officers to distinguish between 'appropriate' and 'inappropriate' borrowing. In particular, the relevant committee disallowed borrowing to profit from interest rate differentials.[13]

The surprising perception of the relationships among open market operations, the discount rate, and market rates, and the counter intuitive conclusions that were drawn, are further illustrated by the following interpretation of discount rate policy during the 1930s by Friedman and Schwartz (1963: 514–15):

> With respect to discount policy, the Federal Reserve was misled by the tendency, present recurrently throughout its history before and since, to put major emphasis on the absolute level of the discount rate rather than on the relation to market rates. The rate in the thirties was low in comparison with rates in earlier periods but, as we have seen, it was much higher compared with market rates than it had ever been. By relevant standards, the discount policy was abnormally tight, not easy . . . With discount rates so high relative to market rates, discounting was an expensive way to meet even temporary needs for liquidity. Banks, therefore, had an incentive to rely on other sources of liquidity, including the accumulation of larger than usual reserves.

Discount rates were 1.5 per cent and 1 per cent after 1934 and short-term market rates were most of the time clearly below 0.5 per cent, reflecting mainly credit risk (not scarcity). But since the discount window was in any case not used (it was not at all 'effective', to use the nineteenth-century UK term), it is not easy to understand where effects of a further lowering of the discount rate could have come from. The last sentence by Friedman and Schwartz quoted above suggests that it is *up to the banks* to decide on the aggregate amount of excess reserves they wish to hold, which is not true in the event of absence of a deposit facility (according to equation 2.5 in Chapter 2, aggregate excess reserves in the US 1930s case should have been $\overline{XSR} = \overline{M} + \overline{Bi} - \overline{RR} - \overline{A}$).

After reviewing in detail all the defects he sees in the US discount window as specified during the 1950s, M. Friedman (1960: 35–45), does not propose to reform the discount window, but to simply abolish it. Brunner

---

[13] One of the rare critical articles of that time on the policy of administrative restriction is Smith (1958). See Anderson (1965) for an official mid-1960s assessment of the functioning of the discount window.

(1970: 135) finds that 'one could easily argue that the discount mechanism is a quaintly antique institution of minor relevance', while Hester (1970: 151) formulates that 'among the service facilities provided by a Federal Reserve Bank, none seems more antiquated than the discount window' (for a US commercial bank's view of that time, see Atkinson 1970). Although the discount window was eventually kept, for the obvious practical reasons set out in Section 4.1, it seems plausible that mistakes about the causation between borrowing, market rates, and the discount rate, and more generally the lack of an appropriate model of the use of the borrowing facility contributed to delays in the implementation of reforms. This is all the more astonishing as clearer ideas about the relevant relationships had been well-known in the UK since the nineteenth century and were also repeated by contemporaneous studies such as Radcliffe et al. (1959).

A series of banking crisis in the 1980s again prompted the perception that discount window borrowing could be a sign of financial weakness. According to Meulendyke (1992: 41), as more banking crises developed and were then resolved, the reluctance to borrow became alternately more and less severe, but never returned to its pre-1984—that is, pre-Continental Illinois—crisis levels. The changing reluctance made the relationship between borrowing and the market-discount rate spread so unstable that the Fed eventually gave up its borrowed reserves target to return to federal funds rate targeting in the last years of the 1980s.[14] Figure 4.3, which

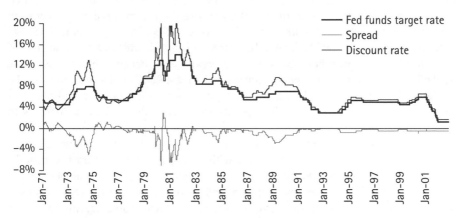

Figure 4.3   *Federal funds target rate, discount rate, and spread, 1971–2002*
Source: Board of Governors' website.

---

[14] A model of the instability of discount window borrowing is also provided by Hanes (1999), who focuses on the role of administrative criteria regulating the recourse to the window.

covers the period from 1971 to 2002 and shows the federal funds target rate and the discount rate as well as the spread between the two, reveals that for this period the discount rate was indeed almost always below market rate, which confirms that up to the end of the twentieth century access to the discount facility was limited through non-price means.

4.4.4　*The 2002 reform*

While academic economists had repeatedly called for the amendment or abolition of the discount window, Hakkio and Sellon (2000) were perhaps the first Fed economists to discuss openly fundamental reforms of the discount window towards the end of the twentieth century. They suggest that a lombard-type facility with a rate above market rates would probably be preferable, but mention a series of technical issues which would need to be addressed. It was only in May 2002 that eventually the Fed embarked on fundamental reform of its discount window, labelling the new borrowing facility 'primary credit'. It now mentioned all the arguments in favour of reform that had probably been applicable to the US since the 1920s (Board of Governors 2002*a*: 3; see also Madigan and Nelson 2002):

A below-market discount rate creates incentives for institutions to obtain adjustment credit to exploit the spread between the discount rate and the market rates for short term loans . . . Because of the restrictions necessitated by a below-market discount rate, a substantial degree of Reserve Bank administration is associated with adjustment credit. In particular, the Reserve Bank may need to review each prospective borrower's funding situation to establish that the borrower has exhausted other reasonably available sources of funds and that the reasons for borrowing are appropriate. Because that evaluation necessarily is subjective, achieving a reasonable degree of consistency in credit administration across the System is difficult. The administration of and restriction on discount window credit create a burden on depository institutions that reduces their willingness to seek credit at the discount window.

In light of the drawbacks associated with the current below-market discount window programs, the Board believes that the interests of depository institutions, the Federal Reserve System, and the economy more generally would be served more effectively by an above-market rate lending program. . . . Primary credit usually would be extended at an above-market rate, which should essentially eliminate the incentive for institutions to seek discount window credit simply to exploit the usual spread between the discount rate and short-term market rates. Eliminating this incentive would reduce sharply the need for administration regarding the extension and use of Federal Reserve credit . . . As a result, the discount window should become a more effective policy instrument.

After consulting the market, in November 2002 the Fed eventually announced the implementation of the changes. It retained some quantitative and qualitative restrictions on the use of the primary credit facility, but its difference from the modern specifications of other central banks was largely reduced. Furfine (2003), who makes a first preliminary analysis of the working of the new discount window, suggests that a certain 'irrational' reluctance on the part of banks to borrow from the window seems to remain.

4.5 THE REICHSBANK, DEUTSCHE BUNDESBANK AND EUROPEAN CENTRAL BANK

Germany's central banks relied for a longer period of time than those of the US and the UK on heavy use of a borrowing facility in monetary policy implementation.

4.5.1 *The Reichsbank*

The Reichsbank, like many other continental central banks at that time, from its foundation in 1876 until 1914 followed a policy of strictly relying on the discount facility. Indeed, Section 17 of the Reichsbank Act prescribed that the Reichsbank *must* hold ready, for all its notes not covered by gold, discounted bills maturing at the latest in three months, for which, as a rule, at least two solvent parties were liable (for detailed reviews of the German discount market before 1914, see Prion 1907 and Plenge 1913). Compared with Prussia's Bank's Law of 1846, which served as a model for the Reichsbank Law of 1876, this represented a further triumph of a kind of real bills doctrine to the extent that under the Prussian Bank Law a sixth of the banknotes not covered by metal could be covered by advances. Bills submitted always needed the acceptance of the drawee. Furthermore, again in line with the real bills doctrine, the business origin of the bills was considered relevant, whereby the main reason advanced was, however, that *credit risk* was deemed to be lower for bills with relevant business background (Reichsbank 1900: 130):

The knowledge of the economic purpose of the bill, also of the circumstances to which it owes existence, is of great importance in judging with certainty of its redemption on the day of maturity. In general, the requirements of the Bank are met only by a bill which, in the moment of the formation, starts from a completed transfer of property between the parties liable on it and is destined on maturity to balance this transfer. This is especially true of so-called merchandise bills

(Warenwechsel). Such bills, which originate in the purchase or sale of merchandise, are an investment specially suitable for the Reichsbank, since the goods which are delivered into the hands of the debtor as equivalent for the bill are by nature suitable for quick turnover. The resale of them gives the debtor funds for the redemption of the bill on maturity.

Under Article 15 of the Reichsbank Act, the Reichsbank needed always to publish its current rate of discount. It is worth reviewing briefly some facts on bills collected by the Reichsbank. According to Reichsbank (1925a: 63), the share of discounts in the total domestic financial assets of the Reichsbank between 1876 and 1913 was never below 80 per cent, except in one year where it was 72 per cent, confirming that the balance sheet of the Reichsbank of 1900, shown in Table 2.2, was typical.[15] In 1900, 55.5 per cent of bills were for amounts of 500 marks or less, and only 11.2 per cent were for more than 3,000 marks (one mark had a purchasing power of between five and ten US dollars or euros today). The yearly average size of bills never exceeded 1,727 marks before 1900. In the same year, the average remaining maturity at time of transmission was 35 days. The number of firms or persons directly or indirectly admitted to the discount business of the Reichsbank was 63,000 in 1900. Each of these had a specific total credit line, whereby the sum of credit lines exceeded the sum of total credit needs so greatly that it did not amount to a restriction on overall credit through rediscounting. Any of these parties could hence in principle become the direct counterpart of the Reichsbank for a discount credit, in contrast to today's policies whereby central banks do operations only with banks or even only with a small set of primary dealers. Around 43 per cent of credit takers were among the mercantile class, including only 3.8 per cent of bankers. Industry contributed 30 per cent of borrowers and agriculture 14 per cent. Losses relating to non-performing bills were insignificant. Around 0.01 per cent of the value of bills was not paid immediately at maturity by any of the liable parties, and 0.003 per cent was actually never paid. However, with respect to the latter figure, 'the Reichsbank in its (first) 25 years of its existence has been free from great political and serious economic crises' (Reichsbank 1900: 152–64), an important point that seems to anticipate the somewhat sad last 30 years of its existence.

---

[15] It is thus interesting that at the same time Deutsche Bundesbank (1976: 278) reveals that the spread between the Reichsbank's discount rate and the market rate (Privatdiskontsatz) was always positive and normally of the order of 100 basis points. This finding, which would appear to contradict any arbitrage logic, may be due to, for example, a different type of paper underlying the two types of operations.

Section 13, paragraph 3, of the Bank Act permits *advances* (lombard loans) on gold, silver, securities, bills, and merchandise stored in Germany. The securities permitted are interest-bearing bonds of the Empire, payable to the bearer, and those of German and foreign states, German communal corporations, other domestic bonds guaranteed by the state, certificates of agricultural, communal, and other land banks under state supervision, and of German joint-stock mortgage banks. The Reichsbank (1900: 173) explained its relative aversion against lombard loans as follows:

Lombard loans–that is, advances on deposited securities–are for modern banks of issue of far less importance than bill purchases, not because they are of smaller economic value, but because lombard advances cannot be used as cover for notes. So far as rapid and certain realization is concerned, loans on collateral can not be compared with bills carefully chosen in accordance with banking principles. Characteristics from which the kind of credit claimed in the lombard loan can be inferred are, as a rule, wanting ... These deficiencies in individual lombard loans and therefore in all lombard investments, cannot be obviated through the safety of the pledge, even by observing the most careful limits in making advances. This safety and the realization of outstanding claims really depend on whether the market is in a position to take securities in case of a compulsory sale. Experience has shown that this cannot be reckoned upon with certainty.

The scepticism, once again, seems to reflect primarily not some kind of real bills doctrine but rather credit-risk control considerations. The Reichsbank hence tended to charge 1 per cent more on lombard than on discount loans, for 'keeping lombard claims within the bounds dictated by prudence'. Furthermore, Section 13, paragraph 3, of the Reichsbank Act specified considerable haircuts as risk control measures, whereby advances were limited to three-quarters of the market value of German securities and half of the market value of foreign securities. The *maturity* of the lombard loans was in practice overnight, since both the Reichsbank and the borrower could discontinue the loan on any day. However, the Reichsbank also sometimes imposed longer minimum maturities in order to provide disincentives against what it perceived to be an abuse of the facility it offered. Indeed, after a few years a trend emerged of heavy recourse to the lombard facility at end of months and especially end of quarters, apparently for settlement purposes, and a high demand for banknotes as a means of payment on these dates. In the 1880s, therefore, the Reichsbank started to increase the minimum maturity of lombard loans over the month-end to make this recourse more expensive. Since 1887, the minimum maturity of lombard loans covering the end of the quarter was set at a full fourteen days 'to prevent any

abuse on the part of the Bourse' (Reichsbank 1900: 191). The natural
consequence of this policy was to create even stronger market rate peaks
on the relevant dates. Today, this obsession of the Reichsbank to avoid
seasonal recourse to the lombard facility appears misplaced, since one
would argue that the higher liquidity needs on settlement dates are a
transitory phenomenon that should be accommodated in order to avoid
transitory fluctuations of short-term interest rates. The lombard facility
would today be considered the most appropriate way to provide this liquidity at a limited mark-up, and lengthening the minimum maturity of
the facility achieves exactly the opposite. Indeed, already in the first half
of the nineteenth century the Bank of England created special advances
to smooth the end of quarters and to avoid 'great fluctuation to market
rates . . . so harmful to trade' (King 1936: 84).

Bopp (1954: 55–6) analysed the specific question whether, in the case of
the Reichsbank before 1914, further restrictive measures were taken with
respect to actual access to the discount facility beyond those generally
specified. He concluded that they were not: apparently, the Reichsbank
could be fully relied on to accept paper on the known conditions, such that
the Reichsbank discount window qualified as a genuine standing facility.
Also, Keynes (1930: 58) explained the low reserve holdings of German
banks with the Reichsbank by reference to the almost universal readiness
of the Reichsbank to accept eligible paper for discounting, and interprets
this as a weakness in the monetary control exercised by the Reichsbank.

In any case, the Reichsbank had no problems with safeguarding its
currency by maintaining gold convertibility consistently from 1876 to
1914 by means of discount rate policy. In this period, it varied discount
rates between 3 per cent and 7.5 per cent, rates above 6 per cent being
experienced only during three months at the end of 1907 (Reichsbank
1925a: A95; for a detailed description of the discount rate policy of the
Reichsbank until 1900, see Reichsbank 1900: 216–87). A question that
indeed seems to remain is how the Reichsbank avoided speculative use
of its discount facility in circumstances of rate hike expectations. It was
shown above that the Bank of England had addressed this issue with
qualitative restrictions of eligible collateral (mainly a reduction of the
maximum maturity of eligible paper) and the policy of keeping market
rates around one percentage point below Bank rate through an adequate
open market operations policy. Probably, the Reichsbank too restricted
eligibility criteria under such circumstances or applied moral suasion,
although it is not easy to find evidence for this conjecture.

The Reichsbank stuck to its focus on the discount facility as a monetary
policy instrument during the First World War and the inter-war period,

although claims against the government soon became the largest item on the asset side of the balance sheet. An interesting episode is that of a temporary discontinuation of the discount facility in 1924 when, after the stabilization of the mark had in principle succeeded, speculative pressure on the currency was re-emerging. The measure was announced on Saturday, 5 April 1924, to take effect from the following Monday. Hjalmar Schacht (1955), President of the Reichsbank from 1923 to 1929 and from 1933 to 1939, describes the episode as follows in his autobiography:

The step we had taken was in direct contradiction to all the traditional rules concerning central banks. It was also probably the first time in economic history that a central bank deliberately refused to grant credit. According to traditional principles the idea was that a central bank should discount at any time, and counteract an excessive influx of bills simply by increasing the discount rate. But . . . no discount policy would avail to win a race against devaluation of currency. The Reichsbank's action aroused absolute panic in the business world . . . I had to give the foreign exchange hoarders a shock and leave them no time to extricate themselves from the dilemma . . . People must understand once and for all that the Reichsbank would make use of any means to ensure the stability of the Mark. Meanwhile, 'destroyer of German industry' was the least opprobrious epithet coined for my benefit. The only reproach that I did take seriously was that of injustice towards decent business folk. For the rest, reproaches left me cold. By means of most careful treatment of our customers we began to counteract injustices during the days and weeks that followed. We did not decrease our portfolio but maintained it at the same level. Any bank, which came back to the Reichsbank from matured bills was used to grant credit to those businesses in special need for it. Since the Reichsbank controlled nearly four hundred undertakings and subsidiaries throughout the country, this policy soon proved its worth. The hoarders, on the other hand, did not get their expired credits, nor were they granted fresh credits. So they were obliged to resort to the same action which I had forced them to adopt at the end of November 1923, namely to hand over their hoarded foreign bills to the Reichsbank in return for Reichsmark. The results of this action were surprisingly swift and surprisingly effective. Between the 7th April and the 3rd June 1924, that is to say within fifty-seven days, no less a sum than eight hundred million marks in foreign exchange bills returned to the German Reichsbank. . . . On 3rd July the Reichsbank was able for the first time (since the war) to meet all demands for foreign bills in full; and it continued to be in a position to do so until the financial crash of 1931 once again put a stop to it.

The episode is also described in Reichsbank (1925a: 153). In fact, it seems that the Reichsbank squeezed the market through its restrictive refinancing policy and obliged especially the 'hoarders' of foreign exchange to bring this foreign exchange to the Reichsbank to obtain domestic liquidity, which they could no longer obtain in the market (or apparently only at prohibitive prices). The administrative elements of the procedure (distinguishing between good and bad counterparts submitting bills) of course appear rather discretionary and inefficient, especially given that a well-developed inter-bank market existed at the time. Indeed, as a consequence of Schacht's measures, according to Pentzlin (1980: 69) overnight and one-month market rates stood in April 1924 at around 45 per cent, and stock market prices declined between April and June by 50 per cent. In the following seven years, the threat of such a squeeze (together with improved economic conditions) was apparently sufficient to prevent further speculative attacks on the Reichsmark and thus to ensure full convertibility. Although Schacht is wrong to claim that this was the first time 'in economic history' that a central bank was refusing to discount (the previous section describes two cases in which the Bank of England did so in the first half of the nineteenth century), it may well be the case that the German episode of 1924 is the only one for which it can be claimed—also *ex post*—that it was appropriate and successful. Also, Vocke (1973: 94), Governor of the Bank Deutscher Länder in 1949–59, takes the view that the restrictive credit policy of 1924 was 'one of the most brilliant achievements of Schacht'.

A detailed description of the Reichsbank's policy in the fatal years between 1930 and 1933 may be found in Luther (1964), who was its Governor during this period. He hints at the traditionalist thinking in the bank's board, although US reserve position doctrine also had already been noticed: 'despite this constraining legacy, the board of course did not stick to outdated principles. The powerful "open market policy" originating in the US had been remarked by all members. The "minimum reserves policy", in contrast, of which the great importance is now recognised, had not yet left the American territory' (1964: 82–3). In the crisis year 1931, Luther had noted in his diary, again concerning his supposedly dogmatic colleagues in the Reichsbank Board: 'Until [19]23 they had not understood the quantity theory, and now they exaggerate it in a ridiculous way' (1964: 251). Luther also reports the softening of eligibility criteria for bills accepted for rediscounting in the course of 1931, arguing that at least this proves that the Reichsbank was doing something to react to the financial crisis (1964: 253).

After 1933, the real bills doctrine served to justify the Nazi government's and the Reichsbank's argument that their system of 'Mefo-Wechsel' was not inflationary. Mefo-Wechsel were trade bills issued by a company (Metall-Forschungsgesellschaft) founded especially for that purpose and for which the Reichsbank guaranteed eligibility for discounting. Effectively, they were a kind of short-term government paper with the option of being discounted at any moment with the central bank. According to Schacht (1955: 314–18), the Mefo-Wechsel represented a full success in so far as they became much-used short-term paper in inter-bank transactions (that is, they were not systematically discounted with the Reichsbank as soon as they were issued) and as they were not inflationary due to their real bills character. This view is convincingly challenged by Vocke (1973: 102), who argues that the Mefo-Wechsel were simply a quasi-unlimited guarantee by the Reichsbank to finance the government, 'a deadly sin for a central bank'. Only when the use of Mefo-Wechsel became too excessive even in the eyes of Schacht was the total amount to be discounted by the Reichsbank limited to 12 billion Reichsmark. Attempts of the Nazi government to refinance through other means led in January 1939 to the famous memorandum from the Board of the Reichsbank to Hitler, which led Hitler to replace Schacht, Vocke, and certain other members of the board with more submissive individuals.

4.5.2 *The Bundesbank*

Following Tamagna (1963: 72), discount borrowing has been used in Germany extensively since the Bank Deutscher Länder was established in 1948 and, indeed, discount lending continued playing a key structural role until the 1980s. However, already in the early 1950s discount *quotas* were defined for the banks in the form of limits on the total recourse to the discount window calculated according to liability-side balance sheet items of the banks and the type of bank, that is, in a rather administrative and discretionary way. During most of the 1950s and 1960s, quotas were not used since the strong growth of foreign exchange reserves of the Bundesbank limited the need of the banks to obtain further Deutschmark reserves with the Bundesbank through monetary policy operations. Thus, the discount rate represented most of the time an effective ceiling for market rates. It was only from 1978 onwards that quotas were systematically used, such that the discount rate became more of a floor than a ceiling for market rates, since banks would reduce discounting to zero before market rates could fall below the discount rate. The role of a real borrowing facility was taken over by the lombard facility, of which the rate was still set at 100 basis points above the discount window. The two rates thus formed a kind of corridor for the short-term interest rate.[16] Hence, the Bundesbank was, at least among our three

---

[16] Of course, the floor for market rates was effective only if the *maturing* of discount credits on a given day was sufficient, such that not renewing them absorbed sufficient reserves. The Lombard

selected central banks, the first to implement the idea of a full corridor for short-term interest rates through standing facilities.

In addition, the Bundesbank created in the 1950s a technique of open market operations which was actually, according to the definition of the two types of instruments adopted here, close to another liquidity-absorbing standing facility. There was a phase in 1957 in which liquidity was over-abundant due to an increase in the Bundesbank's foreign exchange reserves. In its annual report for 1957, the Bundesbank explained its technique as follows (see also Tamagna 1963: 62):

The Bundesbank has adhered to the principle of selling money market paper according to the market's needs, and taking it back again on the terms in . . . force. . . . The Bank leaves the initiative in open market operations largely to the market. However, it indirectly exerts influence on the volume of such transactions through the level of the . . . rates . . . Open market policy ensures that, apart from relatively short-term fluctuations, money market rates cannot drop below the level of the selling rate.

The substitution of structural recourse to standing facilities by genuine liquidity-providing open market operations started in the case of the Bundesbank only in the early 1970s, the first repo operation being conducted by the Bundesbank in April 1973 (Deutsche Bundesbank 1983: 23). According to Deutsche Bundesbank (1994), it was only in 1985 that the volume of open market operations surpassed the volume of discount lending.

Finally, it is noteworthy that changes of the lombard and discount rates normally had until 1998 an important signalling effect, since they were less frequent than changes of the open market operations rates. For the Deutsche Bundesbank (1994b), 'setting the discount and lombard rates is, over the longer term, the cornerstone of interest rate policy'. However, lombard and discount rates were not systematically changed in parallel. Indeed, it was felt that, in this unrestricted setting, more subtle signals could be given with regard to the future monetary policy stance. Still, the 'natural' level of the spread between the two rates was perceived for a long time to be 100 basis points, although it temporarily went as high as 300 basis points (Deutsche Bundesbank 1994b: 102).

---

facility provided a ceiling only to the extent it can be accessed without limit. In fact, this was not always the case. For instance, from 12 August 1970 to 30 May 1973 the Bundesbank restricted lombard borrowing to normally 20% of individual rediscount quotas, on average over the calendar month. From 1 June 1973 to July 1974, it suspended lombard lending altogether (Deutsche Bundesbank 1983). Again, temporary restrictions to lombard lending were imposed in September 1979 and for the last time in February 1981.

4.5.3 The Eurosystem

The Eurosystem has offered a borrowing facility ('marginal lending facility') and a deposit facility from the start of its operations in January 1999. Access to both facilities is unlimited; the borrowing facility requires collateral, of which eligibility criteria are the same as for open market operations (ECB 2001*a*; see also Chapter 5). The maturity of both facilities is overnight. Access is normally possible throughout the day until 6.30 p.m., that is, until thirty minutes *after* the closing of payment systems. An overdraft at the end of day is automatically considered as a request for recourse to the borrowing facility. As shown in Chapter 2, recourse to standing facilities has never been structural in the euro area, and normally recourse to both facilities is on average of similar size. Reflecting this, market rates and open market operations rates are normally close to the middle of the corridor set by standing facilities. The width of the corridor has been 200 basis points with the exception of the first four months of 1999.[17] Interest rates of standing facilities have always been changed since April 1999 in parallel with the rates of the open market operations, suggesting that they effectively had no independent role in signalling the stance of monetary policy.

4.5.4 A few other central banks and the optimal width of the corridor

Exceptionally, we should look here briefly at today's practice of other central banks, namely, of the central banks of Australia, Canada, and New Zealand, all of which use a symmetric corridor approach with a narrow corridor of $+/-25$ basis points. Although not imposing reserve requirements with averaging, all of them achieve a remarkable stability of short-term interest rates, and Woodford (2003) seems to advocate this system as particularly simple and effective. Why do these three central banks impose such a narrow corridor, while the Bank of England and the Eurosystem chose one four times wider? In the case of the Eurosystem, an argument against a narrow corridor (which was at least valid until reforms of its framework were implemented in March 2004) is that the corridor should always be so wide that *changes of target interest rates within the reserve maintenance period can never go beyond the standing*

---

[17] During the first two weeks of the euro, the corridor was narrowed to 50 basis points to reduce the costs to banks as long as the euro inter-bank market was not functioning smoothly. Indeed, recourse to both standing facilities during the first days of 1999 was substantial. Then, over three months, the corridor was 250 basis points wide.

facility rates at the beginning of the period. Consider the following example of what could otherwise happen. Suppose the corridor were +/−25 basis points, and the market expected that tomorrow, within the same one-month reserve maintenance period, the ECB would shift upwards the corridor including the target rate by 50 basis points. Then, it would pay the banks to immediately have such massive recourse to the borrowing facility that they could fulfil their entire reserve requirements within one day. Thus, by choosing a width of the corridor of +/−100 basis points, the ECB revealed the assessment that normally interest rate changes within one month would not go beyond 100 basis points, which seems realistic. In the case of the Bank of England, in contrast, a somewhat narrower corridor could probably have worked as well, since the Bank of England does not impose reserve requirements with averaging. Allen (2002: 431) reports the following money market-related considerations of the Bank of England regarding the appropriate width of the corridor:

Deciding on the width of the interest rate corridor was difficult. A wide corridor or band would not bind on many days and might not have much effect. A narrower band would have more effect and would have been likely to generate more business with the Bank of England, but it would erode incentives for borrowers and lenders to meet in the commercial market. We did not want our operations to overshadow normal market trading: a key feature of our current money market arrangements is that banks must test their name in commercial credit markets regularly. Related to that, any corridor would need to allow for credit tiering, since widening credit spreads are an important signal of potential financial stress.

Finally, note that a series of central banks achieve the effects of a deposit facility simply by remunerating excess reserves (for example, the People's Bank of China). This allows banks to save the transaction costs of active recourse to the deposit facility. Otherwise, there are indeed no differences between the two approaches.

Table 4.1 summarizes a few features of standing facility systems without aiming at being comprehensive.

4.6   THE REVERSED CAUSATION FALLACY

In chapter 2, it was shown that recourse to standing facilities reflects market friction or aggregate imbalances based on the central bank's balance sheet identity. In chapter 3, it was argued that the aggregate imbalances determine the spread between standing facility rates and market rates.

Table 4.1   *Main specifications of standing facility systems*

	BoEngland 1914	Reichs- bank 1914	Fed 1920–2002	Fed 2003–4	Eurosystem, BoEngland, 2004	Aust./Can./ NZ 2004
Borrowing facility	Discount and lombard (lombard more expensive, thus normally less important)		Mainly lombard (but in theory also discount, used more in past)		Lombard (BoE in theory also discount)	Lombard
Deposit facility	No	No	No	No	Yes	Yes
Maturity of facilities	Discount depends on paper, lombard often above overnight		Lombard normally overnight	1 day	1 day	1 day
Width and position of corridor	Roughly 1% between discount rate and market rate	Market rate pegged to discount rate	Market rate above discount rate (varying extent)	Target 1% below borrowing facility rate	2% symmetric corridor around target rate	0.5% symmetric corridor around target rate

In contradiction to this, the review of the perception of the discount window revealed that from Governor McDougal in 1921 ('the discount rate policy should be one which should hold those rates as high or slightly higher than the prevailing rates in the commercial centers': Meltzer 2003: 125), via M. Friedman (1960), Friedman and Schwartz (1963: 514),[18] Goldfeld and Kane (1966), Hamdani and Persistani (1991), Persistani (1991), and Pearce (1993), US economists have nearly systematically perceived a causation *from* the spread between the discount rate and the market rate *to* the use of the discount window (see also Keynes 1930: 230). As seen in Section 4.3, views on this causality were also mixed in the UK during the nineteenth century. However, eventually the normal causation was recognized in the UK and motivated the Bank of England's technique of making 'Bank rate effective' through liquidity-absorbing open market operations, which was well established towards the end of that century.

Section 4.5 has already discussed how the perception of a reversed causation re-emerged in the US in the early twentieth century. It appeared that a combination of possibly insufficient study of the Bank of England money market technique, together with Treasury opposition to interest rate hikes and the use of moral suasion, in the first years of

---

[18] M. Friedman (1960: 39) explains that 'The discount rate is the primary means used to influence the amount of discounting' and, applying this to history, Friedman and Schwartz (1963: 514) argue that 'From 1934 on, the discount rate was seldom below short-term open market rates. . . . The result, of course, was negligible use of rediscounting facilities.'

the Fed quickly established a non-transparent system in which the basic economic relationships were no longer visible. In the following decades, reserve position doctrine dominated the minds of monetary economists looking at implementation issues, and suggested that free reserves, not market rates, mattered for monetary policy implementation. This thinking became dominant and persistent. However, it needs to be noted that one US author, Board of Governors staff member Riefler, explicitly discussed at an early stage two alternative theories of 'the relation between reserve bank operations and money rates' which are close to the two causations (1930: 19):

It is at this point that theories as to the relation between reserve bank operations and money rates diverge. The most obvious theory is that member banks, on the whole, borrow at the reserve banks when it is profitable to do so. . . . The cost of borrowing at the reserve banks, accordingly, is held to be the determining factor in the relation of reserve bank operations to money rates and the discount rate policy adopted by the reserve banks to be the most important factor in making reserve bank credit policy effective in the money market. At the other extreme, there is the theory that member banks borrow at the reserve banks only in case of necessity and endeavor to repay their borrowing as soon as possible. According to this theory . . . the necessity imposed by circumstances on member banks for resorting to the resources of the reserve banks . . . is a more important factor . . . than the discount rate.

After a long discussion, Riefler (1930: 27) leaned towards the latter theory, which is the normal causation approach, by concluding that 'under present conditions, the volume of member bank indebtedness at the reserve banks at any given time is one of the most important single factors in the rate outlook' and 'that the predominant use of the discount facilities of the reserve banks falls under the second of the two theories outlined above'. He furthermore argued that, in practice, the Fed was very well aware of this fact and based its money market management on the normal causation: 'Induced through open market operations, changes in the volume of member bank indebtedness have been used since 1922 both to tighten and to ease the money markets, independently of changes in discount rates' (1930: 28). Unfortunately, subsequent academic writers did not pay attention to Riefler's analysis.

The importance of the reversed causation fallacy for monetary policy implementation can hardly be overestimated, since it goes along with the assumption that short-term market rates are exogenous. Specifically, it is assumed that it is *not* the central bank that controls short-term market rates through its open market operations and the specification of standing facilities rates. Therefore, the reversed causation fallacy is directly linked to the rejection, over decades, of short-term interest rates as the operational target of monetary policy.

The confusion about the relevant causality between the spread and the recourse to the borrowing facility may in fact be largely explained by the failure to distinguish between '*individual*' and '*aggregate*' recourse to standing facilities, concepts introduced in Section 2.6. Individual banks' recourse was defined as that due to payment shocks at the level of individual banks late in the day, while aggregate recourse was understood as that, even in the case of a perfectly efficient banking system, which reflected aggregate imbalances at the end of the reserve maintenance period. Assume a sequence of events as shown by Fig. 3.3. Under perfect markets, there is no individual recourse to standing facilities, and the recourse to standing facilities is mechanically determined through the balance sheet by open market operations and autonomous factors: $\overline{B} - \overline{D} = \overline{M} - \overline{A}$. The recourse to standing facilities then also determines the level of market rates. In the deterministic case: $\overline{B} > 0 \Rightarrow i = i_B$; $\overline{D} > 0 \Rightarrow i = i_D$, and in the probabilistic case according to the fundamental equation (3.2).

Consider now the case in which inter-bank markets are not perfect, and banks are hit, as described in Section 3.2.2, by individual shocks. In this case, one may indeed construct a kind of reverse causality. Assume the perfectly symmetric case in which banks are hit by an individual autonomous factor shock after the closure of the market session and before recourse to standing facility is taken. Assume N identical banks, that $RR = 0$, $XSR = 0$, $M = 0$, $s_j \approx N(0, \sigma_s^2)$ with $j = 1 \ldots N$ being the individual shocks. Each bank will hold exactly zero reserves after the market session, such that recourse to any of the facilities has the same probability. The market rate will obviously be in the mid-point of the corridor set by the two standing facilities. Define the function $\Gamma(x)$ with $\Gamma(x) = x$ if $x \geq 0$ and $\Gamma(x) = 0$ if $x < 0$. Total recourse to the borrowing facility will be:

$$B = \sum_{j=1}^{N} \Gamma(s_j) \tag{4.1}$$

Note that the recourse to the borrowing facility is still independent of the spread between the market rate and the borrowing facility rate: that is, incorporating individual recourse to standing facilities is not in itself sufficient to justify the reversed causation.

Suppose now that banks are able, by investing in their infrastructure and by employing more staff in their front and back offices, to reduce σ_s^2. Assume that $\sigma_s^2 = f(w)$, with w being the value of the resources invested, and that $f(w)$ is decreasing and convex with $\lim_{w \to \infty} f(w) = 0$. Then banks will invest into reducing the variance of individual shocks until the marginal cost of doing so is equal to the marginal benefit. If $E(b) = E(B/N)$ is the expected borrowing volume of a single representative bank, then the expected cost of recourse to standing facilities will be $2E(b)(i_B - i_D)/2 = E(b)/(i_B - i_D)$.[19] The marginal condition for the investment in a reduction of the variance of individual shocks (that is, in higher efficiency of the inter-bank market) will thus be:

$$\frac{\partial E(b)}{\partial \sigma_s^2} \frac{\partial f(w)}{\partial w} = (i_B - i_D) \tag{4.2}$$

The left-hand side of this equation is monotonously falling with w, such that there is a unique optimum. The equation suggests that the higher the spread between the two standing facility rates (which is double the spread between the market interest rate and each of the standing facility rates), the higher will be investment in the efficiency of the inter-bank market and thus the lower will be the expected recourse to the standing facilities. To that extent a reverse causation appears, although it is not clear whether this effect can be easily measured in practice. Eurosystem experience since 1999 seems to suggest that the incentives provided by interest rates to reduce transaction costs were not relevant. For instance, excess reserves, which in the event that a deposit facility is available reflect transactions costs, did not increase when the ECB reduced step by step the level of the deposit facility rate from 4 per cent to 1 per cent.

In any case, the described causation from the spread to the recourse to standing facilities should have little relevance for monetary policy implementation, and in particular it does not support the monetary policy interpretation given to the reversed causation by US authors, such as, for example, Friedman and Schwartz (1963: 514–15) quoted in the previous section.

Finally, it may be useful to mention a *second, more macroeconomic channel for a reversed causation*, which has already been mentioned in connection with the Bank of England's experience of 'following the market' in the period 1844–7. The logic, transmitted to a modern paper standard, is as follows: if the target interest rate and the borrowing rate are at a high level that reduces the inflation rate, and are kept at such a high level even when inflation becomes deflation, then the amount of banknotes in circulation and reserve requirements (the monetary base) will

---

[19] The cost of having to borrow or of having to deposit one unit of account is, relative to the cost of securing funds in the market session, equal to the spread between the market rate and the standing facilities rate. Since everything is symmetric, the expected cost of going to the deposit facility is identical to that of going to the borrowing facility.

decline, and hence, *ceteris paribus*, the refinancing needs of banks towards the central bank and thus, again *ceteris paribus*, the need to come to the borrowing facility will also decline (once the need to go to the borrowing facility is zero, the 'Bank rate' will no longer be effective and market rates will drop to zero). If, in contrast, the target and borrowing rates are too low at the outset, such that inflation emerges, then the monetary base and *ceteris paribus* refinancing needs and use of the borrowing facility increase more and more, resulting in hyperinflation. To that extent, one could conclude that a high borrowing rate will decrease borrowing in the medium and long term, and a low borrowing rate will increase it. However, in practice, such a reversed causation will not be relevant, since central banks should never aim at an interest rate policy which would lead to such extreme macroeconomic fluctuations.

4.7   CONCLUSIONS

In the question 'how to make Bank rate effective?', the relationships among standing facility rates, market rates, and quantities, which remain a key topic of monetary policy implementation to the present day, emerged for the first time in the UK in the early nineteenth century. In the early twentieth century, the Bank of England had a logically consistent and efficient borrowing facility, in which a positive spread between market rates and the borrowing rate was achieved through open market operations, and hence recourse to the borrowing facility remained limited. The Bank of England's approach to the discount facility around 1900 actually appeared to be rather close to today's practice but for the maturity of borrowing, which is today standardized to overnight. The Reichsbank's system, which also seems to have worked well, was built on substantial, permanent use of the discount facility and hence a quasi-pegging of market rates at the discount rate.

The US Fed's discount window was, until end 2002, not regulated by the price mechanism alone, its access conditions were non-transparent, and the implied relationship between borrowing and the spread between market and the discount rate was opaque. A key factor explaining the persistence of this specification seems to be the perception, in particular by US authors, of what was called here 'reversed causation' regarding the relationship between, on the one hand, recourse to standing facilities and, on the other hand, the spread between market rates and the borrowing facility rate. According to reversed causation, market rates are exogenous, and recourse to the facilities is a result of the spread. Others too, like the German central banks, seem to have temporarily lost clarity in their specification of standing facilities over the twentieth century: the discount facility that was so key to liquidity provision in Germany over most of the second half of the century was based later on an administrative rationing system. The rationing, however, in the 1970s allowed the discount rate to be transformed into a *floor* for the market rate, and thus to define rather early a *corridor* for the short-term market rate set by two standing facilities.

Among others, the Bank of England and the Eurosystem apply today a corridor system in which the borrowing facility is complemented by a deposit facility *of the same maturity*, which has the advantage of considerably simplifying the calibration of open market operations (see Chapter 3). The modern view of an appropriate use of standing facilities, as practised today by the Eurosystem and the Bank of England, and to a large extent by the US Fed, may be summarized as follows:

(a) Open market operations should ensure that the recourse to standing facilities is not structural, but covers only non-anticipated probabilistic needs.

(b) The recourse should not be restricted; that is, the only restriction should be achieved via the price mechanism—the borrowing rate should be, for example, one percentage point above the target rate (this is at least the spread chosen by the three central banks).

(c) The list of eligible collateral should be determined only by the aim to limit the credit risk exposure of the central bank and by efficiency considerations.

(d) Borrowing facilities should be specified as *lombard* (advance), not discount, facilities.

5

Open Market Operations

In reviewing the second of the three main instruments of monetary policy implementation, this chapter will proceed as follows. Section 5.1 summarizes views on when and how open market operations were discovered. Section 5.2 and 5.3 each discuss one of the two main historical justifications of open market operations. Section 5.4 sets out today's justification of open market operations and gives an overview of the dimensions on which open market operations need to be specified. Section 5.5 describes today's outright and reverse operations of the three selected central banks. Section 5.6 discusses the respective advantages and disadvantages of fixed and variable-rate tenders. Section 5.7 develops further the main disadvantage of fixed-rate tenders, namely, that they potentially create 'over-bidding' and 'under-bidding'. Section 5.8 analyses the issue of the optimal maturity and frequency of open market operations. Section 5.9 concludes.

5.1   THE FIRST OPEN MARKET OPERATION

In Section 2.1, open market operations are defined as monetary policy operations conducted at the discretion of the central bank. The ideal open market operation is therefore *non-regular* in the sense that its launch cannot be anticipated by the market. Originally, the expression meant that the central bank operates in the inter-bank market (the 'open market') as a normal, possibly anonymous participant, for instance by buying Treasury paper in the secondary market. Also, the original expression was limited to outright (as opposed to reverse) operations.

Open market operations appeared as a monetary policy instrument after standing facilities. Different views can be found in the literature on what was the first open market operation in history.

1. According to King (1936: 87–8), the Bank of England conducted the first open market operation for liquidity management purposes in 1834: 'In 1834, when large special deposits were received from the East India Company, the Bank, having agreed to allow interest on the money, actually

went out of its way to find employment for it. It approached the bill brokers . . . and offered them special advances at what it believed to be the market rate.' Accordingly, the first open market operation would have been conducted in reaction to an autonomous liquidity factor fluctuation—rather like most day-to-day open market operations conducted in the present. Of course, one may also argue that the operation described was more a kind of investment. It seems nevertheless plausible to assume that the fact that the operation would also neutralize the liquidity effect of the deposit by the East India Company was noted. Wood (1939: 80–9) also discusses security operations of the Bank of England before 1844, and calls them 'open market operations'.

2. Clapham (1944: 290–7) also judges that the first open market operations of the Bank of England took place in the 1830s, and sees 'very large scale' liquidity-absorbing operations to make bank rate effective in the 1860s.

3. Bloomfield (1959: 45) sees only 'two clear-cut cases . . . of open market operations by a central bank between 1880 and 1914 as a deliberate instrument of monetary policy':

The main device used by the Bank of England during this period to make its (discount) rate effective, when such was necessary, was that of 'borrowing in the market' from the commercial banks . . . Closely related to this, although apparently of much less importance, were occasional open market sales of consols. On a number of occasions, the Reichsbank similarly sold ('rediscounted') Treasury bills in the market in order to withdraw funds and to force market rates up.

4. For Mishkin (2004: 420), it is the US Fed which invented the instrument:

In the early 1920s, a particularly important event occurred: The Fed accidentally discovered open market operations . . . After the 1920–21 recession, the volume of discount loans shrank dramatically, and the Fed was pressed for income. It solved this problem by purchasing income earning securities. In doing so, the Fed noticed that reserves in the banking system grew and there was a multiple expansion of bank loans and deposits . . . A new monetary policy tool was born, and by the end of the 1920s, it was the most important weapon in the Fed's arsenal.

In sum, it appears that the first monetary policy function assigned to open market operations was '*making Bank rate effective*', that is, driving the market rate to the discount rate through the absorption of funds. This is actually close to today's idea that open market operations are used to keep the market rate at a certain spread relative to standing facility rates.

5.2 OPEN MARKET OPERATIONS WITHIN RESERVE POSITION DOCTRINE

Beyond making Bank rate effective, economists have been aware of and fascinated by the potential of open market operations as a monetary policy tool since the 1920s. Indeed, open market operations are the key monetary policy tool according to reserve position doctrine (see Chapter 1). An early clear statement of the presumed supremacy of open market operations is from Paul M. Warburg in 1923 (Warburg 1930: ii. 851), as quoted in Section 1.3.2. Keynes argued on similar lines but saw a need to discuss the issue of interest rate effects of open market operations:

The first and direct effect of an increase in the Bank of England's investments is to cause an increase in the reserves of the joint stock banks and a corresponding increase in their loans and advances on the basis of this. This may react on market rates of discount and bring the latter a little lower than they would otherwise have been. But it will often, though not always, be possible for the joint stock banks to increase their loans and advances without a material weakening in the rates of interest charged. (Keynes 1930: 226)

Today one would argue—and it should have been valid also in the 1920s—that money market rates obviously always react faster than the loan and investment policy of the commercial bank. It is strange to assume that 'the first and direct effect' of excess reserves is additional loans. Perhaps perceiving the weakness of his argument, Keynes (1930: 227) continued:

I fancy that a considerable part of the value of open market operations delicately handled by the central bank may lie in its tacit influence on the member banks to move in step in the desired direction. For example, at any given moment a particular bank may find itself with a small surplus reserve on the basis of which it would in the ordinary course purchase some additional assets, which purchase would have the effect of slightly improving the reserve positions of the other central banks, and so on. If at this moment the central bank snips off the small surplus by selling some asset in the open market, the member bank will not obstinately persist in its proposed additional purchase by recalling funds from the money market for the purpose; it will just not make the purchase. . . . In this way a progressive series of small deflationary open-market sales by the central bank can induce the banks progressively to diminish little by little the scale of their operations. . . . In this way, much can be achieved without changing the bank rate. A member of the public, who, as a result of the credit restriction, is unable to borrow from his bank, generally has no facilities—at least in England—for obtaining the funds he requires by bidding up the price of loans in the open market, even though he is quite willing to pay more than the market price.

But again, the assumptions taken may appear to be too arbitrary and to lack microeconomic foundation. What one finds least convincing today is that the whole argument seems to rely on a lack of willingness of the banks to arbitrage, which is not even well explained. In fact, Keynes himself recognized that his enthusiasm for open market operations went beyond that of many central bankers of the 1920s. For instance Burgess (1927) admitted that 'increases or decreases in holdings of government securities purchased outright (voluntarily) have been accompanied by almost corresponding changes in bills discounted, bankers acceptance held, etc. (involuntarily)', which reflects the balance sheet logic presented in Chapter 2 (see also Burgess 1964). As well, according to Keynes (1930: 230) the Governor of the Fed New York, Benjamin Strong, 'underestimates' the role of open market operations by assigning only a smoothing role to them:

The operations in the open market are designed, I should say, to prepare the way for a change in rates. Unfortunately, it has always seemed to me that the country has given exaggerated importance to changes of the discount rate sentimentally. The danger is that an advance of rate will operate as a sort of sledge-hammer blow to the feeling of confidence and security of the country as to credit, and the reaction has been somewhat modified by these open market operations ... If considerations move the Reserve Banks to tighten up a bit on the use of their credit, it is a more effective programme we find by actual experience, to begin to sell our Government securities ... The effect is less dramatic and less alarming to the country.

Even this argument in favour of open market operations from Governor Strong is not obvious, since the signalling effect of changes to standing facility rates depends on the size of each step and on the observed time-series properties of changes: that is, it is determined by the central bank. If the central bank prefers to adjust rates by many small consecutive steps, the effect on longer-term interest rates of any *change of direction* of changes of standing facilities will be very large. If instead innovations to the standing facility rates appear as white noise, then changes imply only corresponding parallel shifts to the yield curve.

An advocate of open market operations as prominent as Keynes was M. Friedman (1960), who suggested that open market operations alone are a sufficient and efficient tool for monetary policy. Generations of monetary economists followed Keynes and Friedman, often not even raising again the question of why exactly open market operations should make a fundamental difference relative to liquidity provision through standing facilities. In particular, the textbook literature (for example, Mishkin 2004) has basically accepted to the present day Keynes's (1930) argument that open market operations work directly through the money multiplier, and that interest rates do not need to be affected or at least are secondary. The Fed itself has argued similarly at least since the 1950s. For instance, the Board of Governors (1954: 38–9) explained (as it was to do in the subsequent three decades):

If the Federal Reserve decides to buy, say, 25 million dollars of Government securities, it places an order with a dealer in such securities. . . . The result is that the Reserve Bank has added 25 million dollars to its holdings of United States Government securities, and the same amount has been added to the reserve accounts of some member banks. . . . These member banks are now in a position to expand their loans and investments and deposits. In so doing the banks will lose funds to other banks which in turn may expand. . . . The reserves, the loans and investments, and the deposits of the banking system as a whole will be increased— the loans and investments and the deposits by several times the amount of the added reserves.

5.3 OPEN MARKET OPERATIONS TO INFLUENCE DIRECTLY LONGER-TERM RATES

One more argument in favour of open market operations, which was especially popular from the 1930s to the 1950s, was that they *make it possible, through an adequate choice of the maturity of the paper bought/sold outright, to influence directly longer-term interest rates* and, even more ambitiously, the overall shape of the yield curve.

5.3.1 *The Bank of England*

According to Sayers (1953), controlling the yield curve and in particular longer-term rates through open market operations had already been a topic in monetary policy implementation (that is, not only in fiscal policy) in the early 1930s. At least members of the Macmillan Committee had insisted on the point. However, the Bank of England apparently remained unconvinced at that stage. It was only after the Second World War that the Bank of England eventually seems to have adopted such an approach (Sayers 1953: 394):

After the war came the Dalton episode, with the official attempt to get the long-term rate down to a $2^{1}/_{2}$ per cent basis. Whether the bank itself, as well as Government Departments, joined in the heavy buying of medium and long-term bonds, in this ultra-cheap money drive, has never been satisfactorily established. In any case, the period was short-lived and there has not since the beginning of

1947 been any suspicion of sustained operations by the Bank in the long-term market.

Despite this rapid discontinuation, astonishingly, the UK's Radcliffe Report (Radcliffe et al. 1959: 125–6, 135) still placed emphasis on controlling the yield curve for monetary policy purposes, which, as it argued, would be equivalent to controlling the 'liquidity' of the private sector:

Independently of what is happening to net cash movements, the Bank can alter the maturity distribution of marketable debt held in the private sector. This power gives it a wider influence on the structure of interest rates and so on the liquidity of the private sector. . . . The authorities thus have to regard the structure of interest rates rather than the supply of money as the centre-piece of the monetary mechanism. This does not mean that the supply of money is unimportant, but that its control is incidental to interest rate policy.

5.3.2   *The US Fed*

The US Fed in 1937 bought for the first time long-term paper with the exclusive aim of keeping capital market rates low (Stadermann 1961: 114). For instance, the 1940 annual report of the Board of Governors states simply the purpose of open market operations (p. 3): 'The system's open market policy in 1940, as in 1939, involved the use of a flexible portfolio for the purpose of maintaining orderly conditions in the Government securities market.' Orderly conditions consisted in the pegging of the rate at which it would transact in Treasury bills at three-eighths of 1 per cent, which was maintained until 1947. Since this rate was below the discount rate, these open market operations took over the role of providing the actual borrowing facility. Longer-term rates were also pegged through open market operations, though somewhat less systematically (Meulendyke 1998: 33). This policy, under which open market operations actually no longer aimed at monetary policy implementation, continued until 1951. In the 1950s, inflation reinforced by the Korean War convinced the FOMC that the pegged rates were too low, and in March 1951 an 'accord' was reached with the Treasury that allowed the Fed to return to its monetary policy functions. After 1953, the Fed pursued what became known as a 'bills only' policy—that is, it confined open market operations to short-term paper—which was probably a reaction to the pegging of longer-term rates as well during the previous decade. But in 1961 the bills-only doctrine was abandoned, and some experience in controlling the yield curve was again sought through open market operations. Meulendyke (1998: 35) describes this episode as follows:

The new Kennedy administration was concerned about gold outflows and balance of payment deficits and, at the same time, it wanted to encourage a rapid recovery from the recent recession. Higher rates seemed desirable to limit the gold outflows and help the balance of payments, while lower rates were wanted to speed up economic growth. To deal with these problems simultaneously, the Treasury and the FOMC attempted to encourage lower long-term rates without pushing down short-term rates. . . . The Federal Reserve participated with some reluctance and skepticism, but it did not see any great danger in experimenting with the new procedure. It attempted to flatten the yield curve by purchasing Treasury notes and bonds while selling short-term Treasury securities. . . . The extent to which these actions changed the yield curve or modified investment decisions is a source of dispute, although the predominant view is that the impact on yields was minimal.

Considerations of yield-curve control re-emerged also after the stock exchange bubble burst in 2000, when the Fed, according to some observers, tried to 'talk down' long-term interest rates by suggesting that there was a relevant risk of deflation. In a speech delivered in November 2002, Governor Ben Bernanke even suggested the active use of open market operations for that purpose and explained that he would

personally prefer the Fed to begin announcing explicit ceilings for yields on longer-maturity treasury debt (say bonds maturing within the next two years). The Fed could enforce these interest-rate ceilings by committing to make unlimited purchases of securities up to two years from maturity at prices consistent with the targeted yields. (Bernanke: 2000)

Eventually, the FOMC chose another technique to hold down longer-term interest rates: from August to December 2003, the phrase 'the Committee believes that policy accommodation can be maintained for a considerable period' was added to the FOMC policy statement. The purpose of that phrase was to reduce expectations of future short-term rate increases, and through them to hold down longer-term rates, without the need to intervene systematically in these maturities.

5.3.3 *The German central banks*

The Reichsbank and the Deutsche Bundesbank also had their experience with attempts to control longer-term rates. The Reichsbank obtained the explicit right to conduct open market operations only in 1933 and, until the end of the Second World War, the instrument was used mainly for keeping long-term interest rates artificially low. In 1974, the Deutsche

Bundesbank started again to purchase systematically longer-term government paper in order to keep capital market rates low. In July 1975 the programme was intensified on the recommendation of the government, after which the portfolio of government paper reached a maximum of DM7.5 billion (from only DM6 million as at end 1973). In October 1975, the policy was abandoned as ineffective. Thereafter, with this bad experience in mind, the Bundesbank concentrated on developing a set of instruments to conduct open market operations as *reverse* operations (see von Hagen 1999: 456). The Bundesbank's outright holdings were completely eliminated again in 1996.

In sum, it appears that each of the three central banks temporarily used open market operations for longer-term rate or yield-curve control, but except in wartime such policies were always abandoned quite soon as they were eventually assessed to be ineffective or inappropriate.

5.4   TODAY'S JUSTIFICATIONS AND TYPES OF OPEN MARKET OPERATIONS

Today, in the age of explicit short-term interest rate targeting, most of the historical justifications of open market operations no longer appear relevant. In particular, reserve position doctrine, according to which open market operations directly affect the expansion of credit and money in the banking system, has been rejected. Instead, it is recognized that, before anything else, open market operations will affect money market interest rates and the recourse to standing facilities. Monetary expansion, however, will occur only if a lowering of rates is considered to be *permanent*. Such a lowering is today normally engineered by central banks though a lowering of central bank rates. Central banks have also given up the idea of directly influencing the yield curve beyond its short end. Of course, many central banks continue to invest their resources in outright holdings of longer-term securities to generate *income*, but this is more an argument for *holding* securities than for really *conducting* operations.

Instead, central bankers would today argue that reserves should be provided via open market operations only in order to stabilize market rates without a *structural dependence of the market on a standing facility*, and therefore at a level different from a standing facility rate. Otherwise, according to this view, at the maturity of the borrowing facility the interbank market would to a large extent be substituted by direct operations between the banks and the central bank, which is considered undesirable. Such an argument for open market operations is obviously far less ambitious than those put forward in the past. Also, as will be argued, today's open market operations, compared with those of the 1920s, in fact have many similarities to standing facilities. In particular, they are normally reverse operations and they are conducted regularly. In addition, today's reverse open market operations are often conducted at a pre-announced interest rate, which is also similar to standing facilities. Finally, since they are conducted as tenders, the central bank, by definition, does not enter the market as a normal market participant but plays an idiosyncratic role.

One may specify today's open market operations mainly along the following dimensions:

(a) *tender* procedures (and type of tender) versus *bilateral* operations;
(b) *outright* purchases or sales of securities versus *reverse* operations;
(c) *frequency of operations*: for example, more than daily, daily, or less than daily;
(d) *maturity of operations*: from overnight to normally a maximum of twelve months for reverse operations; and
(e) *direction of liquidity impact*: liquidity-injecting versus liquidity-absorbing.

Table 5.1 summarizes the specification and role of open market operations in the case of the three selected central banks.

The following sections come back to the details of these specifications. Only the direction of the liquidity impact is briefly discussed here. Both outright and reverse operations can be conducted as liquidity-providing and as liquidity-absorbing. An outright purchase of securities injects liquidity, an outright sale absorbs it. Also, the issuance of central bank paper, that is, a 'primary market' outright sale, absorbs liquidity. Reverse

Table 5.1   *Main specifications of open market operations*

	Bank of England	Fed (New York)	Eurosystem
Tender vs bilateral	Tender	Tender	Tender
Tender procedure	Fixed rate	Variable rate	Different procedures across time
Outright operations	For structural purposes	For structural purposes	No
Reverse operations	Yes	Yes	Yes
Frequency	2–3 per day	Several per week	Once a week
Maturity of reverse operations	Up to 2 weeks	Up to 28 days	Mainly 2 weeks, also 3 months
Direction	Liquidity-providing	Liquidity-providing	Liquidity-providing

operations can as well be conducted both ways. The three central banks examined here in more detail have all operated in recent years in a situation, as determined by the net sum of autonomous liquidity factors and reserve requirements, in which the banking system had substantial liquidity needs vis-à-vis the central bank, such that liquidity-absorbing operations were normally not needed (see the balance sheets of the central banks shown in Section 2.3). However, as seen above, this was not the case for the Bundesbank during most of the 1960s and 1970s, when its net foreign assets increased rapidly and injected so much domestic liquidity that open market operations were regularly of a liquidity-absorbing type. Also today, many central banks of smaller countries with an exchange rate target and sustained economic growth experience a similar balance sheet structure and operate on the liability side of their balance sheets. These central banks often issue debt certificates, which create a structural deficit of the banking system in the short term, such that short-term reverse operations of a liquidity-providing type can be conducted to steer day-to-day conditions. One may argue that this constitutes an unnecessary lengthening of the central bank balance sheet, but some central banks seem to feel more comfortable in their day-to-day operations if they *provide* liquidity, that is, if the banking system appears to be dependent on them.

5.5 OUTRIGHT AND REVERSE OPERATIONS OF THE THREE CENTRAL BANKS

5.5.1 *Outright operations of the three central banks*

Outright operations were the dominant way of conducting open market operations until the 1960s. For instance, the Radcliffe Report (Radcliffe et al. 1959: 115) explains the operations of the *Bank of England* in the 1950s as follows:

At the heart of its work as the central bank lie the Bank's open market operations in Government debt, including both operations in Treasury Bills in the course of management of the money market and operations in Government bonds for the purpose of influencing the gilt-edged market. The Bank of England operates almost daily in the money market by buying Treasury Bills from the market (thus putting cash out) or selling Treasury Bills to the market (thus taking cash in), to smooth out shortages and surpluses of funds between one day and another, which arise mainly out of the uneven incidence of payments by and into the Exchequer.

In an outright operation, the type of paper purchased or sold is much more crucial than with a reverse operation, for three reasons: first, the maturity of the security potentially matters for the maturity of the operation; second, the maturity matters since the operations may have an effect on the market interest rate at that maturity (or more generally for the price of the chosen type of paper); finally, the credit and market risk associated with the paper is taken over by the central bank. For instance, outright operations were in the past frequently Trojan horses through which governments made central banks finance their unsustainable deficits. Indeed, both German currency reforms of the twentieth century (in 1923 and 1948) were made necessary after the central bank started to accumulate more and more outright holdings of eventually worthless government paper.

Today, outright holdings of securities still play an important role in the *structural* supply of reserves to the banking system. Indeed, in both the US and the UK, reverse operations are used only for the day-to-day control of reserve conditions, while outright holdings of securities provide the greater share of the total supply of reserves through open market operations (see Chapter 2). The *Fed* has been systematically very transparent with regard to its outright portfolio. According to the Federal Reserve Bank of New York (2002), the domestic 'System Open Market Account' (SOMA), which includes all the domestic securities held on an outright basis, stood at $575 billion at the end of 2001. Normally, changes in the level of the SOMA are used to accommodate *structural* changes in autonomous factors. The SOMA consists almost entirely of Treasury securities. The distribution of securities across maturity and individual issues aims at achieving a liquid portfolio without distorting the yield curve or impairing the liquidity of the market for individual Treasury securities. Typically, any necessary expansion of the portfolio is achieved by making outright purchases of Treasury securities in the secondary market. For primary market purchases, percentage caps have been set that limit the share of the Fed's purchases. For instance, in 2001 secondary market purchases amounted to $68.5 billion. There were no outright sales of securities. The average maturity of the entire portfolio of Treasury securities was 53.5 months at the end of 2001. The share of the Fed's portfolio in all outstanding marketable Treasury securities was 19 per cent.

The *Deutsche Bundesbank's* outright portfolio always remained small, reaching its historical maximum in 1975 with DM7.5 billion (see, for example, Deutsche Bundesbank 1995: 115). The more relevant type of outright operations for the Bundesbank from the 1950s to the 1970s was generally the issuance of some debt paper to absorb excess reserves of the banking system. The *Eurosystem* has no outright portfolio associated with monetary policy implementation. However, it also holds outright securities for investment purposes. According to the Eurosystem balance sheet published by the ECB for 27 December 2002, the Eurosystem held €33 billion of 'securities of euro area residents denominated in euro'. In addition, it held non-marketable government debt amounting to €66 billion.

5.5.2 *Reverse operations of the three central banks*

The use of reverse operations by central banks developed more or less in parallel with the development of this instrument in the inter-bank money market. It has already been noted that central bank reverse operations ('repos') in fact fall somewhere between classic outright open market operations and standing facilities. At the extreme, a daily open market operation with overnight maturity conducted at end day at a fixed rate known in advance and with a 100 per cent allotment of bids is exactly equivalent to a borrowing facility. The ambiguous nature of reverse operations also becomes clear when one considers the US Fed's vocabulary during the twentieth century in which 'borrowed' reserves were defined as recourse to the discount window while 'non-borrowed' reserves were those provided through open market operations. According to the long-prevailing doctrine, the two would be of a fundamentally different nature in terms of monetary policy effects. However, for *reverse* open market operations it seems as well appropriate to use the term 'borrowing', and one should doubt whether it makes a difference whether funds are obtained by a bank through a short-term reverse open market operation or through recourse to unrestricted standing facilities (as long as the interest rate is the same). To that extent, one could say that the triumph of reverse operations in day-to-day monetary policy implementation is also the defeat of the Keynes-Friedman doctrine that open market operations are fundamentally different from standing facilities.

The Bank of England

The Bank of England (2002*a*) steers liquidity conditions by lending to its counterparts mainly in the form of repos, and to a minor extent through purchases of bills (that is, outright operations). In both cases, the repo rate set by the Monetary Policy Committee is applied (in the case of a purchase of bills through discounting). Interestingly, the choice of obtaining liquidity by repo or by outright sale of bills is normally at the counterpart's discretion (Bank of England 2002*a*: 8).[1] Compared with the US Fed's

---

[1] The maximum residual maturity of the bills that the Bank of England is willing to purchase outright is no longer than the maturity of the longest-dated repo for which bids have been invited that day (usually around two weeks). The minimum residual maturity for outright bill purchases is one day (Bank of England 2002*a*: 9).

(and especially with the Eurosystem's) operations, the Bank of England's repo operations have a very high frequency and correspondingly lower average size. This approach is implied mainly by the absence of a reserve requirement system with averaging. The short-term nature of the refinancing provided by the Bank of England ensures that the banking system experiences a net shortage of funds almost every day. The repos usually have a maturity of two weeks. On average, around one-eighth of the lending that makes up the total stock of short-term refinancing matures each day (about £2–£2.5 billion). In this way the Bank of England turns over the short-term assets acquired in its money market operations and has an opportunity to influence the short-term market rate every day. The Bank of England offers two principal daily rounds of operations, at 9.45 a.m. and 2.30 p.m., which are conducted as fixed-rate tenders at the official repo rate set by the Monetary Policy Committee. At the morning round, the Bank of England normally does not relieve all of the forecast shortage since it may need to revise slightly its forecast during the course of the day in the light of updated information. The amount by which the Bank of England seeks to leave the market short of funds after the 9.45 a.m. round is determined mainly by the likely scale of revisions to the forecast shortage. At 2.30 p.m., the Bank of England publishes an update of the day's forecast shortage as well as the residual shortage. If there is still a residual shortage, a further round of bids is invited from the Bank of England's counterparts and the results are once again announced within fifteen minutes. The 2.30 p.m. round is timed so as to enable the Bank of England to make use of a later and more accurate forecast of the market's liquidity needs. By the completion of the 2.30 p.m. round, the Bank of England aims to have supplied the market with enough liquidity to enable all of the settlement banks to maintain positive balances on their operational accounts at the end of the day.

The following *eligible collateral* is accepted by the Bank of England for its repo operations:[2] gilts (including gilt strips); sterling Treasury bills; Bank of England euro bills and euro notes; eligible bank bills; eligible local authority bills; HM government non-sterling marketable debt; sterling-denominated securities issued by European Economic Area (EEA) central governments and central banks and major international institutions; Euro-denominated securities (including strips) issued by EEA central governments and central banks and major international institutions if they are eligible for use in Eurosystem monetary policy operations. The latter securities

---

[2] The range of security that the Bank of England is willing to purchase on an outright basis is narrower and includes only sterling Treasury bills, eligible bank bills, and eligible local authority bills.

may be either those issued directly into Euroclear and Clearstream, Luxembourg, or 'CCBM securities' whereby the central bank in the country in which the relevant securities were issued has agreed to act as the Bank's custodian under the Correspondent Central Banking Model (CCBM; see ECB 2001*a*). The total stock of securities eligible for open market operations is around £2.5 trillion and, normally, only around £15 billion–£20 billion of these will be held by the Bank of England as collateral for open market operations (Bank of England 2002*a*: 9).

The Bank of England (2002*a*: 14) deals in its daily operations with *counterparts*, which need to satisfy a number of functional criteria designed to ensure both that its operations function efficiently and that the liquidity supplied is made available as smoothly as possible to other participants in the sterling money markets. For instance, in May 2002 seventeen counterparts participated to the Bank of England's operations.

The Fed

In the US, reverse operations became the dominant instrument for short-term adjustment of reserve conditions in the 1970s. During the 1980s, there was a daily reverse operation to control non-borrowed and/or borrowed reserves (Meulendyke 1998: 47, 50). The current reverse operations in the US are described, for instance, in Federal Reserve Bank of New York (2002: 14–18). The Fed distinguishes between short-term and long-term repos, the latter being defined as all repos with a maturity of more than fifteen days. During 2001, the New York Fed arranged a repo with a twenty-eight-day maturity on the Monday and/or Thursday of each week. These operations are done in the morning, before final daily reserve estimates are available, as they do not aim at addressing daily volatility in autonomous factors. In other respects, these repos are operationally just like those for short-term maturities. The sizes of the twenty-eight-day repos conducted over the year ranged from $2 billion to $5 billion. Over most of the first half of 2001, their total outstanding value was around $12 billion, peaking at a level of $31 billion in the year-end reserve maintenance period. Short-term temporary operations are the primary tool used to address day-to-day volatility in autonomous factors and in the demand for reserves. Daily volatility in short-term temporary operations outstanding, measured by the average of absolute daily changes in short-term repo agreements out-standing, was around $3.5 billion in 2001 and short-term temporary oper-ations outstanding averaged $10 billion. Volatility in autonomous factors and in demand for Fed balances requires an operation on most days. By far the most common repo maturity in 2001 was overnight, with 133 of such operations having been conducted in 2001.

Interestingly, the US Fed conducts repos normally in the form of three separate simultaneous operations differentiated by *type of collateral eligible*. In the first of these, only Treasury debt is accepted; in the second, direct federal agency obligations (in addition to Treasury debt) are eligible; and in the third, mortgage-backed agency debt is accepted (again in addition to the other two categories of debt). Such a differentiation of collateral is applied neither by the Bank of England nor by the Eurosystem. Also, only the US Fed defines different lists of collateral for open market operations and discount borrowing.[3] The distribution of the allotment amount across the three collateral categories is determined by the relative level of rates in each tranche as compared with current market rates for that class of collateral. The distribution of allotments to the three tranches on outstanding repos tends to be reasonably stable. The differentiation of tranches for different collateral obviously aims at avoiding a situation in which bidders systematically bring only their cheapest collateral to the Fed, that is, that with the lowest value in interbank operations. However, it is not obvious why this should be justified more in the case of the US than in the UK and the euro area. One might argue that the comparison between bid rates and market rates when the allotment decisions are made introduces an element of complexity and possibly even of discretion into the allotment decisions.

For open market operations, the Fed relies on a well-defined set of *counterparts*, called primary dealers, of which there are currently about twenty-five (see Blenck et al. 2001). A primary dealer must be either a commercial bank or a registered securities dealer in good standing with its regulator, and must comply with minimum capital standards. A financial institution that complies with the primary dealer requirements can apply to become a counterpart. Primary dealers are expected to provide satisfactory performance in three areas: making reasonably good markets for the Fed Trading Desk's open market operations, providing meaningful support for the issuance of US Treasury securities (including participation in primary auctions), and communicating valuable market information to the Trading Desk.

The Bundesbank

The Bundesbank conducted repurchase agreements using bills of exchange for the very first time in April 1973. It was, however, only in 1979 that the

---

[3] The range of eligible assets for discount borrowing includes not only public debt instruments but also private debt instruments, both marketable and non-marketable, as well as debt securities of foreign governments and international agencies, denominated also in currencies other than the US dollar (see ECB 2001*a*).

liquidity deficit of the German banking system had increased to the extent that repos in fixed-income securities became a regularly used instrument. Deutsche Bundesbank (1982*a*: 24) explains that they allowed for the use of assets 'which the banks hold in large quantities and wide diversity'. Also, 'the outright purchase and later resale of fixed interest securities would hardly permit liquidity management on such a scale, quite apart from the fact that it would cause unacceptable interest rate movements in the bond market'. Eligible paper consisted of all government and government agency paper, as well as all fixed-interest rate securities that were quoted on a German stock exchange. The maturity of the Bundesbank's operations was at first around one month, but was reduced in 1992 to two weeks. A weekly frequency was established in 1993. Until it adopted the euro in 1999, the Bundesbank conducted weekly operations with two weeks maturity, an approach that would be exported to the entire euro area in 1999. Linzert, Nautz, and Breitung (2003) provide a study of the banks' individual bidding behaviour in the Bundesbank's weekly repos.

The Eurosystem

The Eurosystem adopted the Bundesbank's weekly tenders with two weeks maturity in 1999, but decided in January 2003 to shorten the maturity of its weekly operation in 2004 to one week. From January 1999 to December 2002, the Eurosystem provided through its weekly operations on average €157 billion of reserves to the banking system (that is, €73.5 billion per operation). Fixed-rate tenders were used until June 2000, and variable-rate tenders with minimum bid rate thereafter. The average number of participating bidders during this period was 551, which is more than any other central bank has ever had. However, there was a trend decline in the number of bidders; in 2002, for instance, the average number of participants was only 308. During the variable-rate tender period, the average spread between the minimum bid rate and the marginal rate amounted to 4 basis points, and the spread between the marginal rate and the weighted average rate of successful bids to 2 basis points. The average share of bids allotted amounted to 62 per cent (that is, the average bid-cover ratio was around 1.8).[4]

Besides its main refinancing operations, the Eurosystem has also conducted since January 1999 monthly *longer-term* refinancing operations with three months maturity. These operations were pure variable-rate

---

[4] More detailed overviews of the bidding behaviour of banks in the Eurosystem's main refinancing operations can be found in ECB (2001*b*), Breitung and Nautz (2001), Banque de France (2002), Nyborg and Strebulaev (2001), Nyborg, Bindseil, and Strebulaev (2002), and Scalia and Ordine (2002).

tenders with pre-announced allotment volume. During the first four years of the euro, on average 250 bidders participated in this type of operation for an average allotment amount of €18 billion (see also Linzert, Nautz, and Bindseil 2004). The average spread between the marginal and the weighted average rate was 2.5 basis points. The low average spread between these two rates in the main and longer-term refinancing operations of the Eurosystem provides evidence of bidders' good anticipation of the marginal rate, leading to a high concentration of bids around the expected marginal rate. Both the main and the regular refinancing operations are conducted through so-called standard tenders (see ECB 2002a): the tender is announced on day $T - 1$, bids can be submitted by 9.30 a.m. on the allotment day T, the allotment result is announced at 11.20 a.m. on that day, and settlement occurs on $T + 1$.

For all monetary policy operations of the Eurosystem—that is, standing facilities and open market operations—one list of *eligible collateral* with two tiers applies (see ECB 2002a: ch. 6, 2001a). The collateral eligible for Eurosystem credit operations encompasses a broad spectrum of assets denominated in euros, issued (or guaranteed) by entities established in the European Economic Area. A substantial part of 'tier one' (which comprises debt instruments only) is made up of government bonds, that is, assets issued by central, regional, and local governments. 'Tier one' private-sector securities include asset-backed bonds, uncovered credit institution bonds, and bonds issued by corporates. A substantial share of asset-backed bonds is made up of Pfandbrief-type securities, that is, securities backed by residential mortgages or by public sector debt. Most national central banks of the Eurosystem have proposed assets for inclusion in 'tier two'. The assets range from credit institution bonds to corporate commercial paper, medium-term notes, regional government bonds, and equities. Except for this last category, the liquidity and market depth of tier two assets are generally lower than those of tier one collateral. Many of these assets are not listed or traded on a regulated market, but are traded over the counter. In Spain, the Netherlands, and Portugal, tier two also includes the most liquid shares of non-financial companies listed on the national stock exchanges. Some national central banks have also included non-marketable debt instruments in tier two, including bank loans, trade bills, and mortgage-backed promissory notes.

All credit institutions subject to minimum reserve requirements are, in principle, eligible *counterparts* of the Eurosystem's open market operations and standing facilities, on the assumption that some basic requirements are met. The most important of these are that the credit institutions be financially sound, be subject to harmonized supervision by national authorities, and meet the operational criteria specified by the relevant national central banks (for example, hold a securities settlement account for liquidity-providing operations). Currently, about 7,500 credit institutions are subject to reserve requirements; more than 3,000 of these have access to standing facilities and about 2,500 are eligible for participation in regular open market operations.

5.6   FIXED-RATE VERSUS VARIABLE-RATE TENDERS

In the original sense of the word, an open market operation is conducted like any other transaction in the money or securities market, that is, normally bilaterally. Indeed, in the first open market operation the dealers of the central bank addressed dealers in the market individually in order to frame agreements with them on transactions at market conditions (see for example the Macmillan hearings in 1929: Sayers 1976: iii. 152). Bilateral operations have the advantage that they do not require specific procedures to be set up since the central bank follows normal market convention. Also, bilateral procedures may be preferable in the event that the central bank would prefer to keep the operation secret. The potential disadvantage of bilateral operations lies in the discretionary selection of a single counterpart by the central bank and hence potential preferential treatment. Of course, the central bank can try to rotate its counterparts in these operations or to spread volumes through several bilateral operations conducted in parallel or sequentially. Still, this is unlikely to lead to a totally fair and efficient treatment of all market participants. Therefore, tender procedures have increasingly become the standard tool for open market operations since the late 1970s.

5.6.1   *Fixed-rate tender*

In fixed-rate tenders, the central bank pre-announces the interest rate (or price) applicable to the transaction, and the counterparts submit the amounts they wish to obtain at that rate/price. Two sub-variants have been used. Under the *discretionary allotment variant*, if the total amount bid is above the amount the central bank wishes to provide, it allots pro rata, that is, each bid is satisfied at a certain percentage. This method was applied extensively by, for example, the Bundesbank during the 1980s and 1990s, and also by the Eurosystem from January 1999 to June 2000. Also, the Bank of England systematically applies fixed-rate tenders. The Fed, in contrast, has never applied fixed-rate tenders. Under the *100 per cent allotment variant*, the central bank pre-commits to allot the full amount of bids. This method was applied by the Deutsche Bundesbank in the 1950s and by the Bank of Finland in the years preceding 1999. The disadvantage of 100 per cent allotment relative to pro rata allotment is that the central bank gives away its power to adjust the total allotment to make it correspond to its forecast needs, which is relevant since the sum of the bids of many banks is unlikely to be close to aggregate needs, even if the banks' forecasts of autonomous factors were as accurate as the central bank's.

5.6.2   *Variable-rate tender*

Under variable-rate tenders, bidders submit rate/quantity pairs such that the central bank, after aggregating all bids, is confronted with a standard downward-sloping demand curve. The central bank's allotment decision then consists of choosing one point on this curve. Above the selected rate, called the marginal rate, all bids are fully allotted. Bids below the marginal rate are disregarded. Bids exactly at the marginal rate are allotted pro rata, the central bank choosing the allotment ratio. Several sub-variants may be distinguished in the case of the variable-rate tender. The pure variable-rate tender *with discretionary allotment amount* is the usual tender procedure in the US. Under the variable-rate tender *with pre-announced allotment amount*, the allotment decision by the central bank is automatic, since the intersection of the demand curve with the vertical pre-announced supply curve determines the marginal rate. Its advantage is that it avoids a situation in which the market assigns any signalling content to the allotment decision and the resulting marginal rate. The ECB applies such a procedure to its monthly 'longer-term refinancing operations', in which since 1999 it has pre-announced allotment amounts of either €15 billion or €20 billion. Under the variable-rate tender *with a one-sided restriction to bid rates*, like for example a minimum bid rate, the central bank announces beforehand that it will disregard bids below a certain minimum level. If the minimum bid rate is clearly below the level of market rates, then one effectively has again a pure variable-rate tender; if in contrast the minimum bid rate tends to be at or above the market rate, then one has again a fixed-rate tender (since no bank will bid above the minimum bid rate).

Finally, all variable-rate tenders can generally be specified either as an *American* auction (or 'multiple price auction', in which each successful bidder pays the price he bid for) or as a *Dutch* auction (or 'uniform price auction', in which each successful bidder pays the marginal rate). Today, American auctions are generally preferred since they are said to provide more incentives to bid realistically. According to the Deutsche Bundesbank (1982*a*: 26), which for a long time used the Dutch tender procedure, this latter procedure has the advantage that it helps smaller bidders who may be less able to bid in a competitive way.[5]

5.6.3 *Advantages and disadvantages of the two tender procedures*

Central bankers normally cite four main advantages of fixed-rate tenders.

(1) They can send a strong signal on the central bank's monetary policy stance. Indeed, they constitute an implicit pre-commitment by the central bank to steer the corresponding short-term market rates to levels around the tender rate (otherwise, over-bidding or under-bidding will occur—see the next section). Of course, the central bank could alternatively announce explicitly a target market interest rate, such as the Fed does, but some central banks prefer to avoid such an explicit commitment.

(2) Under the variable-rate tender, the public could attribute signalling content to the marginal rates, which sometimes unavoidably leads to misunderstandings. However, the policy content of marginal rates in variable-rate tenders should depend on the central bank's allotment policy. For instance, the Bundesbank *aimed* to send signals through the marginal rates in its variable-rate tenders, whereby some noise in this signalling strategy was probably unavoidable.[6] Also, the Fed until 1994 signalled to the market its monetary policy decisions through the market rates at which it would intervene. Today, signalling policy through marginal rates in variable-rate tenders is generally rejected. Since 1995, the Fed has announced the Fed funds target directly after each FOMC meeting, and banks have since then attributed no policy content to marginal tender rates (Federal Reserve Bank of New York 2000: 46). Another technique for preventing policy content being attributed to marginal rates in variable-rate tenders is to pre-announce the allotment volume, such as the ECB does in its three months variable-rate tenders. Therefore, this is probably not a legitimate argument against variable-rate tenders.

(3) Fixed-rate tenders are consistent with interest-rate steering. Today, central banks again explicitly steer short-term interest rates. It therefore

---

[5] Nautz (1997) compares the functioning of the Bundesbank's open market operations conducted as Dutch and American auctions.

[6] Expressed in the words of Deutsche Bundesbank (1983: 26): 'Interest rate tenders, in which banks play a part in determining the rate, may appear to be more in tune with market practices than volume tenders. But they leave open for the Bundesbank as well the question of which repurchase rate will emerge when the amount to be allocated is known ... Volume (i.e. fixed rate) tenders are a surer method for the Bundesbank as far as the amount and the repurchase rate are concerned.'

appears natural to offer reserves at the target rate. In contrast, it may appear counterintuitive to let the rates of central bank operations fluctuate, although they are in a clear arbitrage relationship with the market rates at which the central bank aims.

(4) Fixed-rate tenders may not put less sophisticated bidders (for example, smaller banks) at a disadvantage. Indeed, bidding in fixed-rate tenders appears simpler than in variable-rate tenders, since in the latter case the bank also has to make up its mind on the rates at which to bid.

Variable-rate tenders are supposed to have two main advantages relative to fixed-rate tenders. First, they allow banks to express their relative preferences for central bank funds through the bid price or, more generally, they contain all the efficiency advantages of genuine auctions as an allocation mechanism. Second, they make it possible to avoid the phenomenon of over-bidding and under-bidding, which always potentially impair the efficiency of fixed-rate tenders.

As the problem of over-bidding and under-bidding is key to understanding the mechanics of fixed-rate tenders, the following section is dedicated to a more detailed treatment of it.

It is not clear whether the review of the pros and cons of the different tender procedure helps explain the preference of the Fed for variable-rate tenders, of the Bank of England for fixed-rate tenders, and the more eclectic approach of the Bundesbank and the ECB. Probably not. Instead, the choices seem to reflect mainly historical practice and doctrine: as the Bank of England always remained with short-term interest rates as operational targets, it had no theoretical problems conducting its operations at a fixed rate. In contrast, the Fed's traditional preference for reserve position doctrine and its associated reluctance to take responsibility for short-term interest rates needed to be reflected in a variable-rate specification of open market operations. Finally, in continental Europe, reserve position doctrine was adopted to some intermediate extent, and thus the problem of choosing between the two tender procedures seems to have been handled in an intermediate way as well.

5.7   OVER-BIDDING AND UNDER-BIDDING IN FIXED-RATE TENDERS

Although over-bidding and under-bidding are as old as the use of fixed-rate tenders, it is the Eurosystem that has recently triggered the development of a literature addressing these phenomena.[7]

---

[7] Models of over-bidding and/or under-bidding in the euro area have been provided by, for instance, Nautz and Oechsler (1999), Ayuso and Repullo (2001, 2003), Välimäki (2001, 2002),

On over-bidding, the modelling approaches are relatively homogeneous and debate focuses mainly on the question whether over-bidding in the ECB case was unavoidable (Nautz and Oechsler 2003), due to too tight a liquidity policy (Ayuso and Repullo 2001, 2003), or due to rate hike expectations (Bindseil 2005).

On under-bidding, two models have so far been proposed. Ewerhart et al. (2003) focus on the impact of under-bidding on the size of open market operations and on the reaction of a central bank that cares about both a smooth liquidity supply and interest rate volatility. Bindseil (2005) proposes a model focusing on the interest rate volatility created by under-bidding and on whether the central bank can prevent it through a tight liquidity policy.

In the following, the experience of a series of central banks using fixed-rate tenders with under-bidding and over-bidding is reviewed. Exceptionally, the sample of central banks goes beyond the three selected for the rest of the book. Then, some basic modelling of the bidding behaviour is proposed.

5.7.1   *Survey of central bank experience with over-bidding and under-bidding*

Nearly all central banks have sometimes used fixed-rate tenders and in fact it seems that a slight majority of central banks prefers them to genuine auctions. Here, the focus is on a few of them which applied the procedure frequently in the 1990s, namely, the Swiss National Bank (CH), the Deutsche Bundesbank (D), the Banque de France (F), the Bank of Finland (FI), the Bank of Japan (J), the ECB/Eurosystem (ECB), the South African Reserve Bank (SA), the Swedish Rijksbank (SE), and the Bank of England (UK). D, F, and FI are considered up to 1998, that is, up to the introduction of the euro. Two features in particular of the operational frameworks of these central banks should be highlighted. First, regarding collateralization requirements, one needs to distinguish cases in which only *allotments* at the moment of settlement need to be covered by collateral (J, ECB, SA, SE, CH, UK) from cases in which the *entire amount bid* needs to be covered at the moment of bidding (DE). FR switched during the 1990s from the first approach to the second as a reaction to over-bidding

Ewerhart (2002), Neyer (2002), Ewerhart et al. (2003), and Bindseil (2005). Also, Breitung and Nautz (2001), Nyborg, Bindseil, and Strebulaev (2002), and Scalia and Ordine (2002) study individual bidding behaviour of banks in open market operations, and touch upon over-bidding. Nyborg and Strebulaev (2001) study general issues of strategic bidding behaviour in fixed-rate tenders without special focus on over-bidding or under-bidding.

(see below). Second, while D, ECB, F, J, and SA have a reserve requirement system with averaging and a one-month reserve maintenance period, SE, CH, and UK do not impose relevant reserve requirements (CH has in the meantime moved to an averaging system).

Survey of central bank experience: over-bidding

Over-bidding generally occurs if market interest rates are, for the maturity of the tender operation, above the fixed tender rate, such that banks rush to take advantage of this arbitrage opportunity and hence submit large bids. All central banks in our sample experienced at least sometimes in their fixed-rate tenders bids being considerably above the central bank's intended allotment amounts, leading to low allotment ratios. However, the strength of the phenomenon, the reasons behind it, the factors limiting its extent, and central bank policy towards it all differed considerably. It is probably least relevant in Japan, where an ample liquidity policy and rate cut expectations have prevailed since shortly after the introduction of tender procedures in the early 1990s. It is also of little relevance in SA, where allotment ratios are normally between 60 per cent and 100 per cent with a minimum of around 20 per cent. Apparently, even under rate hike expectations, and even though only allotted funds need to be collateralized, scarcity of collateral is sufficient in SA to deter banks from over-bidding. In SE, CH, and UK, allotment ratios have not dropped below a minimum of 10 per cent and normally they are above 20 per cent. It appears that in these countries, due to the absence of reserve requirements, the central banks can, even under rate hike expectations, easily provide incentives against over-bidding by allotting excess funds such that excess liquidity pushes overnight rates below the tender rate, at least until the potential rate hike. Nevertheless, in case of the UK the central bank judged it necessary to have two further tools in hand against over-bidding: counterparts are not permitted to bid for more than the size of the liquidity shortage (an average daily shortage being in the region of £2 billion); and the central bank reserves the rather discretionary right to 'scale down its allotment of funds to individual counterparts' to ensure that 'access to the liquidity provided by the Bank of England is available as smoothly as possible to a wide range of market participants' (Bank of England 2002*a*: 11). In DE, average allotment ratios declined throughout the 1990s and ended at around 15 per cent in 1998. Incentives to over-bid originated apparently from the fact that, through a somewhat tight allotment policy, in the period February 1996–December 1998 (the last period of permanent use of the fixed-rate tender) market rates were kept on average 11 basis points above the tender rate. However, over-bidding was limited in the Bundesbank's case by the requirement to cover *the entire bid at the moment of bidding* by collateral. Since collateral is always scarce, this limits the scope of over-bidding. The case of FR was somewhat similar, in that the spread between market and tender rates was even higher: 39 basis points on average from 1994 to 1998. However, the spread varied considerably over time during this period, the yearly averages amounting to 27, 140, 13, 9, and 7 basis points, respectively. Before FR introduced in 1994 the same requirement regarding collateral as DE—namely, to cover bids entirely at the time of bidding—this led to a decline in allotment ratios to less than 1 per cent. After the change, allotment ratios stabilized at around 20-30 per cent.

Another country that needed to react to acute over-bidding was FI, which switched in 1996 from pro rata allotments to systematic 100 per cent allotments. It continued with this system until the end of 1998. Finally, the ECB also experienced in the period January 1999–June 2000 intense over-bidding, which pushed allotment ratios below 1 per cent and obliged it to switch to variable-rate tenders. One may conclude that, apparently, central banks with reserve requirements and averaging in a banking system with plenty of collateral are the most vulnerable to over-bidding. Then, sufficient conditions for over-bidding to emerge are either expectations of possible rate hikes within the same reserve maintenance period (ECB) or a tendency on the part of the central bank to steer liquidity conditions in a tight manner such that market rates are driven through this channel above the fixed tender rate (DE and F). The three solutions to over-bidding are then to require *bids* to be covered by collateral (DE and FR), to switch to a 100 per cent allotment rule (FI), or to abandon the fixed-rate tender (ECB).

Survey of central bank experience: under-bidding
Under-bidding refers to an aggregate submission of bids which is insufficient, even under full allotment, to allow the central bank to allot the volume it aimed at. Again, first the experience of central banks is briefly reviewed. Three types of under-bidding may be distinguished.

(a) *Under-bidding related to excess liquidity supply.* This occurred in J in 2001/2, when the central bank aimed at providing substantial excess liquidity to the market practically at a zero rate. Since the value of this excess liquidity was also practically zero, there was not necessarily sufficient incentive to participate in the tenders.

(b) *Under-bidding due to scarcity of eligible collateral.* This has been the case a few times in SA and SE in recent years; in SE it related to special settlement dates of inter-bank operations involving collateral.

(c) *Under-bidding due to rate cut expectations.* This was the most frequent case, occurring at least once for each central bank in the panel.

A relevant parameter for the actual likelihood of under-bidding is the
reaction of central banks to under-bidding: specifically, whether central
banks tended to give banks the chance to catch up in their fulfilment of
reserve requirements, either by offering an additional operation or by
providing correspondingly more liquidity in regular operations before
the end of the reserve maintenance period. While SA and J tended to bail
out the banks systematically in the event that they under-bid, D, CH,
ECB, and UK normally did not, and hence imposed some costs on banks
as a consequence of their under-bidding. CH also tends to solve the issue
by shortening the maturity of operations to one day in circumstances of
acute rate cut expectations, which, without reserve requirements and
averaging, makes rate cut expectations irrelevant for single open market
operations.

From July 2000 the ECB applied variable-rate tenders with minimum
bid rate. As specified by the ECB, they are quasi-equivalent to fixed-rate
tenders when interest-rate cut expectations prevail, since in that case
the minimum bid rate becomes a binding constraint. There were six cases
of under-bidding in open market operations between 1999 and mid
December 2002, each time in an environment of rate cut expectations.
The shortfall of bids relative to the neutral allotment amount varied
between €28 billion (11 April and 7 November 2001) and €4 billion
(4 December 2002). While the ECB rescued the market in November 2001
(at least from an *ex post* perspective), the bail-out was especially limited
in February and April 2001.

A striking feature of under-bidding, at least in the ECB's case, is the
extraordinary *news content* of the announcement of under-bid operations and of the allotment amount of operations that followed the under-
bid tenders within the same reserve maintenance period. The news
content may be defined as the impact of the announcement of the allotment decision at 11.20 a.m. on overnight rate quotations made by money
market brokers, whereby, to estimate this news content the average mid-
point of quotations between 8.00 a.m. and 11.10 a.m. is subtracted from
the same figure for the period 12 noon-6.00 p.m.. The average absolute
value of the news content of under-bid tenders was 18.5 basis points,
coincidentally similar to the news content of subsequent allotment decisions, which was 18.7 basis points. In contrast, the average absolute news
content of the other Eurosystem weekly open market operations in the
period June 2000 to December 2002 has been only 1.7 basis points,

suggesting that, as long as under-bidding did not occur, the allotment decisions of the ECB were well anticipated. The news content of under-bid tenders suggests that under-bidding always contains a stochastic element, that is, the extent of under-bidding cannot be anticipated precisely. The news content of allotment decisions following under-bid tenders suggests that the market did constantly learn about the ECB's reaction function to under-bidding (that is, its propensity to bail out the market).

As mentioned above, the Eurosystem solved in June 2000 the *over-bidding* problem by moving to a variable-rate tender with minimum bid rate. In January 2003, the Governing Council of the ECB decided to implement two more general measures to solve also the *under-bidding* problem. First, the timing of the reserve maintenance period would be changed so that it would always start on the settlement day of the weekly open market operation following the Governing Council meeting at which the monthly assessment of the monetary policy stance was pre-scheduled. Furthermore, as a rule, the implementation of changes to the standing facility rates would be aligned with the start of the new reserve maintenance period. Second, the maturity of the operations would be shortened from two weeks to one week (ECB press release of 23 January 2003). The combination of the two measures will remove expectations of interest rate changes during any particular maintenance period, given that changes in the ECB's key interest rates will apply, in general, only to the forthcoming reserve maintenance period. Hence, the measures will contribute to stabilizing the conditions in which bidding in the weekly open market operations takes place.

5.7.2 Modelling over-bidding and under-bidding

In the following simple model, the interest rate volatility caused by under-bidding will not be captured for the sake of simplicity (but see Bindseil 2005 for a more comprehensive model). Instead, only the most basic mechanics of over-bidding and under-bidding will be represented. For the sake of simplicity of notation, it is assumed that the spread between the borrowing facility rate and the deposit facility rate is constantly 1 per cent, that is, $i_{B,t} - i_{D,t} = 1\%$ and that the fixed tender rate, ρ_t, is always in the mid-point of the corridor set by the standing facilities, that is $\rho_t = (i_{B,t} + i_{D,t})/2$. With probability P, a rate change of λ occurs $(0.5 > \lambda > 0)$, whereby either a rate hike (λ) or a rate cut $(-\lambda)$ can occur. Also assume that $A_t = a + \eta_t$, $a > 0$ and $\eta_t \approx N(0, \sigma_\eta^2)$, such that $P(A_t) < 0$ is negligible. Denote by B_t the amount of bids submitted to the open market operation on day t.

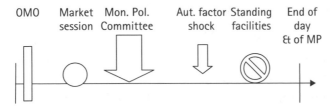

Figure 5.1 *A one-day maintenance period with an interest rate decision after the market session, but before the recourse to standing facility*

The case of only one operation in the reserve maintenance period
This most simple case can be captured in the sequence of events shown in Fig. 5.1, consisting of a one-day reserve maintenance period containing one open market operation, one market session, one monetary policy committee meeting, one autonomous factor shock, and, finally, recourse to standing facilities before the day-end.

Over-bidding Assume that there are rate hike expectations, such that $E(i_{B,t}) = i_{B,t-1} + P\lambda$ (and all other rates being expected to be shifted in parallel) and that the central bank follows an allotment policy $M_t = max(a, B_t)$, that is, it aims at allotting a, but may be restricted by the amount of bids submitted B_t. Then, the market rate will be $i_t = (E(i_{B,t}) + E(i_{D,t}))/2 = \rho_t + P\lambda$. Therefore, participating in the tender will be an arbitrage. With rational expectations and no restriction to bidding, bids will immediately tend to infinity. If a restriction on bidding is introduced, such as the Deutsche Bundesbank and the Banque de France did by requiring banks to cover all bids with collateral, the total bids will correspond to this restriction. For instance, if the amount of available collateral is W (with $W > a$), then the bids will simply be equal to W:

$$B_t = W \qquad (5.1)$$

The allotment ratio will be a/W. If there is a market for collateral, then the market value for borrowing collateral will be $P\lambda a/W$. Therefore, full bidding costs will not be ρ_t but $\rho_t + P\lambda$, such that the arbitrage is eliminated.

Consider now that the central bank switches, as the Central Bank of Finland did, to a 100 per cent allotment rule: $M_t = B_t$. How much will the banks bid in this case? The bid will determine the market rate on day t as follows: $i_t = E(i_{B,t}) - \Phi((B_t - a)/\sigma_\eta)$. The no-arbitrage condition is $i_t = \rho_t = i_{B,t-1} - 0.5$. Finally, rate hike expectations are $E(i_{B,t}) = i_{B,t-1} + P\lambda$. By substitution, one obtains the condition for the equilibrium bid, which can be transformed into:

$$B_t = a + \sigma_\eta \Phi^{-1}(0.5 + P\lambda) \tag{5.2}$$

The function $\Phi^{-1}(\ )$ is the inverted cumulative standard normal distribution. In practice, the problem with the Finnish solution is that collective bidding is always noisy due to the inability of banks to coordinate their bids perfectly, such that also market interest rates will be volatile.

Under-bidding   Assume that there are rate cut expectations, such that $E(i_{B,\,t}) = i_{B,\,t-1} - P\lambda$ and that the central bank follows again an allotment policy $M_t = Max(a,\,B_t)$. If banks were to bid for a or even more, they would lose money in bidding, since the market rate would in that case be $i_t = (E(i_{B,\,t}) - E(i_{D,\,t}))/2 = \rho_t - P\lambda$. They should instead bid such that $i_t = \rho_t$, which is obtained if:

$$B_t = a + \sigma_\eta \Phi^{-1}(0.5 - P\lambda) \tag{5.3}$$

Banks will thus under-bid in equilibrium. In practice, this will again imply interest rate volatility due to the noise in the aggregate bid amount.

The case of a two days reserve maintenance period and two open market operations

The sequence of events in this case is as summarized in Fig. 3.6. What matters relative to the one-day case above is that now there will be a further fixed-rate tender open market operation within the same reserve maintenance period, being conducted at a tender rate $\rho_{t+1} = (i_{B,\,t+1} - i_{D,\,t+1})/2$.

Over-bidding   Assume $E(i_{B,\,t+1}) = i_{B,\,t-1} + P\lambda$ and that the central bank follows an allotment policy, for $M_t = \max(a,\,B_t)$, $M_{t+1} = \max(a,\,B_{t+1})$. Then, one obtains again $i_t = (E(i_{B,\,t+1}) + E(i_{D,\,t+}))/2 = \rho_t + P\lambda$, and defining δ as a dummy variable that takes the value 1 if a rate change occurred, and 0 otherwise $i_{t+1} = \rho_{t+1} = (i_{B,\,t} + i_{D,\,t})/2 + \delta\lambda$. Furthermore, one obtains again over-bidding on day t which can be limited by, for example, the French/German solution of requiring bids to be fully covered by collateral. Thus:[8]

$$B_t = W \tag{5.4a}$$
$$B_{t+1} = a \tag{5.4b}$$

---

[8] To obtain this result, and not the result that the bid on day 2 is indeterminate in $[a,\,W]$, requires that there is a marginal cost associated with submitting bids, such that no more bids than necessary are submitted.

What will happen in the case of the Finnish solution, namely, the 100 per cent allotment rule? In this case, the bids need to satisfy:

$$B_t = 2a + \sigma_\eta \Phi^{-1}(0.5 + P\lambda) \qquad (5.5a)$$
$$B_{t+1} = 0 \qquad (5.5b)$$

Thus, banks will bid exclusively in the first tender, where they will bid even more than the expected liquidity needs over the entire reserve maintenance period. Therefore, the 100 per cent allotment rule leads in the present case to a very uneven path of the fulfilment of reserve requirements, which may be undesirable on its own. Interest rates will be $i_t = \rho_t$; $i_{t+1} = \rho_{t+1} - P\lambda$, that is, second-day interest rates will be below the midpoint of the corridor, independently of whether or not the rate hike occurs. Obviously, the martingale hypothesis is fulfilled, that is, $E(i_{t+1}) = i_t$.

It is interesting to note that, under a discretionary allotment approach, the central bank cannot do anything against strong over-bidding unless it is willing to provide the amount of funds that banks would ask for in the 100 per cent allotment approach. Assume, for instance, $M_t =$ *F*max $(B_t, 2a)$; $M_{t+1} = max(B_{t+1}, a)$. It is easy to show that, in this case, still $i_t = \rho_t + P\lambda$, such that over-bidding will be as intense as if $M_t = a$, i.e. $B_t = W$. In fact, this solution could even be considered worse since it also implies that $B_{t+1} = 0$, such that, again, the path of the fulfilment of required reserves will be extremely uneven.

Under-bidding Assume again $E(i_{B,t+1}) = i_{B,t-1} - P\lambda$ and that the central bank follows an allotment policy $M_t = max(a, B_t)$, $M_{t+1} = max (a, B_{t+1})$. Assume also that $0.5 - \Phi(-a/\sigma_\eta) > P\lambda$ that is, a total reserve deficit corresponding to one day's autonomous factors has a stronger effect on interest rates than the expected value of the rate change. Then, $i_t = \rho_t$; $i_{t+1} = \rho_{t+1} + P\lambda$ and

$$B_t = a + \sigma_\eta \Phi^{-1}(0.5 - P\lambda) \qquad (5.6a)$$
$$B_{t+1} = W \qquad (5.6b)$$

One thus obtains under-bidding on the first day, over-bidding on the second day, and (not reflected in the model) the interest rate volatility associated with under-bidding.

If the central bank instead follows a 100 per cent allotment rule with $M_t = B_t$, $M_{t+1} = B_{t+1}$, which means in particular that it allows banks to get rid of their reserve deficit on the second day, then $i_t = E(\rho_{t+1})$; $i_{t+1} = \rho_{t+1}$ and

$$B_t = 0 \qquad (5.7a)$$
$$B_{t+1} = 2a \qquad (5.7b)$$

This result, which assumes $W > 2a$, looks more reasonable than the outcome under discretionary allotments, but, once again, the interest rate volatility associated to the 100 per cent rule would also need to be taken into account.

5.8   MATURITY AND FREQUENCY OF OPEN MARKET OPERATIONS

In the practice of monetary policy implementation, the frequency and maturity of open market operation needs to be specified. What factors underlie this decision?

First, *banks may have certain preferences* with regard to the maturity structure of their refinancing. For instance, they may want to avoid longer-term liabilities towards the central bank in order to remain flexible, or they may want such longer-term liabilities (for instance, of three months) for the sake of certainty over this period of time. In practice, there will probably be banks of both types, or even single banks may find that it is best if the central bank offers both options of very short-term (overnight) and longer-term (for instance, three months) operations.

Second, the higher the frequency of operations and the longer the maturity, the smaller will be *the average size of a single operation*. If there is only one type of operations with maturity τ days and conducted with a frequency of ω times per day, then $\tau\omega$ operations will always be outstanding and, for a total open market operations volume of M, the size of the single operation will be $M/\tau\omega$. If autonomous factors fluctuate in an unpredictable way, small average volumes make it likely that single operations need to be zero, or even liquidity-absorbing, to achieve a certain path of total reserve supply through open market operations. Also, it may be felt that operations below a certain volume are too insignificant, or create unjustified complexity.

Third, the frequency needs to be such that it *allows the central bank to achieve a sufficient degree of control of its operational target*, that is, the short-term interest rate. This normally requires at the very least that one open market operation is conducted per reserve maintenance period. Recall the example of Section 3.4. There, autonomous factors were modelled as white noise. In reality, they exhibit some degree of autocorrelation. Suppose, for instance, that $A_t = \alpha + \beta A_{t-1} + \eta_t$ with $\alpha \in \Re, 0 < \beta < 1$, $\eta_t \approx N(0, \sigma_\eta^2)$. Autonomous factors are then stationary and fluctuate around $\alpha/(1 - \beta)$. Consider now the most basic case of a one-day reserve maintenance period, as described in Fig. 3.3. Not conducting an open market operation in period t then means that the expectations of reserve availability at the end of the maintenance period corresponding to day t are already biased by $\beta\eta_{t-1}$, since the shock η_{t-1} could not be taken into account in the operation in $t-1$. Therefore, the market interest rate would not be at the mid-point of the corridor set by standing facilities on day t, but would take a random position within the corridor according to η_{t-1}, namely $i_t = i_D + (i_B - i_D)\Phi(-\beta\eta_{t-1}/\sigma_\eta)$. In the case of a multi-day reserve maintenance period (for example, Fig. 3.5), a similar result is obtained for the days *after* the last open market operation of the reserve maintenance period. However, perfect control of rates is possible in principle by conducting a unique open market operation per reserve maintenance period on the last day of the mainte-nance period.

The central bank also has to take into account the problem of leverag-ing effects that make the size of open market operations diverge rapidly. Return to the example displayed in Fig. 3.3 (a one-day reserve mainte-nance period), but assume that the maturity of open market operations is three days and $A_t = 10 + 0.5\ A_{t-1} + \eta_t$. The volume of open market operations is determined each day (= each reserve maintenance period) by the aim to keep overnight rates at the mid-point of the corridor set by standing facilities. Assume that $A_{t-1} = 20$, $M_{t-2} = 7$, $M_{t-1} = 6$. Then, one needs $M_t = 7$ to obtain $i_t = (i_B - i_D)/2$. How will M_{t+1} be distributed? The operation $M_{t-2} = 7$ will need to be replaced, and expected autonomous factors on $t+1$ are $E(A_{t+1}) = 10 + 0.5(20 + \eta_t)$. Therefore $M_{t+1} \approx N(7, \sigma_\eta^2/4)$. One can continue to calculate the probability distri-butions of subsequent open market operations in the same way, whereby the variance of the size increases more and more due to the legacy of the uncertainty from the two previous open market operations. One obtains $M_{t+2} \approx N(6, \sigma_\eta^2/2)$, $M_{t+3} \approx N(7, \sigma_\eta^2)$, $M_{t+4} \approx N(7, 1.75\sigma_\eta^2)$. Generally, one obtains the following ever-increasing time series for the variance of open market operations:

$$Var(M_{t+\tau}) = Var(M_{t+\tau-2}) + Var(M_{t+\tau-1}) + \sigma_\eta^2/4 \tag{5.8}$$

When the variance of M_t increases, then the likelihood that it needs to be zero or negative also increases. However, mixing liquidity-providing and liquidity-absorbing open market operations is generally deemed to add complexity and therefore central banks aim to avoid it. Note too that, in the long run, with increasing variance of the single operations, the difference between the operations also grows without limit. Therefore, very large negative and very large positive operations would overlap, which cannot make sense.

If the central bank nevertheless wants to maintain operations with a maturity of more than the length of the maintenance period, as in this case of three days, it can solve this problem by doing both short-term and long-term operations. For instance, assume that the central bank makes both a three-day and a one-day operation each day. It can then avoid long-term divergence of the size of the single long-term operations by adjusting accordingly the one-day operations. In the example $A_t = 10 + 0.5A_{t-1} + \eta_t$, the central bank can solve the problem by, for example, always allotting 3 in each of the three days operations, such that 9 are structurally provided by the three-day operations. Then, from the perspective of the short-term operations, this is as if there were no three-day operations, and the autonomous factor process would be $A_t = 5.5 + 0.5A_{t-1} + \eta_t$. One can easily verify that the probability that a single one-day operation would need to be negative, also in the long run, is negligible for $\sigma_\eta^2 = 1$, for example.

Similar mechanics can be relevant in the case of a three-day reserve maintenance period (Fig. 3.5). Assume that the central bank wants to operate, for the sake of simplicity and transparency, only once per reserve maintenance period, with three days maturity. If it does so on the first day, this has the disadvantage that its control of the interest rate in the rest of the maintenance period is weak. If it operates on the last day, it solves the interest rate control problem, but again encounters a problem of a unit root in the size of the operations, that is, the size of operations over time can more and more diverge from its starting value. This happens even if autonomous factors are a constant plus white noise, for example $A_t = 10 + \eta_t$. Assume that t is the first day of a maintenance period and that $M_{t-1} = 10$. To achieve a perfect steering of interest rates, the volume of the following operation, conducted on the last day of the maintenance period which started in t, will need to be $M_{t+2} = 10 + \eta_t + \eta_{t+1}$, that is, it will need to compensate, *ex post*, the autonomous factor shocks that occurred within this reserve maintenance period. Therefore, $M_{t+2} \approx N(10, 2\sigma_\eta^2)$. As M_{t+2} hangs over for two days into the next maintenance period, one obtains $M_{t+5} \approx N(10, 10\sigma_\eta^2)$. Generally:

$$Var(M_{t+2+3n}) = 2\sigma_\eta^2 + 4Var(M_{t+2+3(n-1)}) \tag{5.9}$$

The variance therefore increases much more rapidly even than in the one maintenance period case. Once again, a central bank which aims at a good control of short-term interest rates will need to mix short- and long-term operations, and will need to conduct more than one operation per reserve maintenance period. For instance, in the case of a three-day period, it may be a good solution to conduct a three-day operation on each first day of the maintenance period, and a one-day operation on each last day.

5.9 CONCLUSIONS

Open market operations have been regarded as the main instrument of monetary policy implementation since the 1920s. Non-central bank economists in particular, such as Keynes (1930) and M. Friedman (1960), were rather enthusiastic about the supposed possibilities of monetary control inherent in open market operations. With the return to interest rate targeting and the dominance of reverse operations (whose difference from standing facilities is less clear-cut), the former arguments in favour of open market operations have vanished. Today, the essential argument advanced for open market operations is that they do not, in contrast to standing facilities offered at market rates, dry up the short-term inter-bank money market.

Day-to-day open market operations consisted until the 1970s mostly of outright operations, after which reverse operations took over the role of main instrument for the steering of money market conditions. While the US and the Bank of England still provide a large share of structural liquidity needs through an outright portfolio of securities, the Eurosystem uses exclusively reverse operations. In terms of frequency of operations, the Bank of England comes first with several operations a day, followed by the Fed with around one operation per day and the Eurosystem with one per week, these differences being determined mainly by the respective reserve requirement systems. The average size of operations is inversely proportional to their frequency. The Bank of England always uses fixed-rate tenders, the Fed variable-rate tenders, and the Eurosystem switched from the first to the second (keeping a minimum bid rate) in June 2000 after experiencing an over-bidding problem. Generally, the potential for over-bidding and under-bidding in fixed-rate tenders is the main disadvantage of this tender procedure relative to variable-rate tenders. Since the likelihood and intensity of both will depend on the specification of the operational framework, such as whether the central bank is willing to publish its target interest rate (like the Fed) and whether it imposes reserve requirements with averaging and considers central bank rate changes *within* the averaging period (like the ECB from 1999 to 2003). In the latter two cases, variable-rate tenders may be the preferable alternative. Similarly, it was shown that the optimal maturity and frequency of open market operations depended on the operational framework as well and especially, again, on the reserve requirement system.

A key issue in monetary policy implementation is the establishment of the list of *collateral* eligible in reverse operations, and central banks devote considerable resources to it. Generally, central banks aim at a wide list of collateral to prevent scarcity of collateral interfering with monetary policy implementation. At the same time, appropriate risk control measures such as margin requirements and haircuts are imposed. As well, central banks want to avoid receiving systematically relatively bad collateral. While the Fed has adopted the approach of defining separate tranches of open market operations for different types of collateral, the Eurosystem and the Bank of England do not discriminate in this way between different types of collateral. In terms of *counterparts* of open market operations, the Eurosystem is distinct from the two other central banks examined as it transacts in each operation with several hundreds of credit institutions, while the Fed (New York) and the Bank of England tend to have fewer than twenty bidders.

6

Reserve Requirements

6.1 FUNCTIONS AND SPECIFICATIONS OF RESERVE REQUIREMENT SYSTEMS

The previous two chapters set out some controversial twentieth-century debates on the functions and appropriate specifications of standing facilities and open market operations. The present chapter shows that the discussion in the domain of reserve requirements was equally peculiar. As many as seven justifications for imposing reserve requirements have been advanced implicitly or explicitly at some time during the twentieth century, not counting sub-variants:

(a) to help ensure banks' individual liquidity, in particular against bank runs;
(b) to help monetary control as a reserve market management tool of the central bank, substituting, for example, open market operations (requiring *changes* of total reserve requirements);
(c) to help monetary control by serving as a built-in stabilizer;
(d) to contribute to generating central bank income;
(e) to influence competition between banks;
(f) to create or enlarge a structural liquidity deficit of the banking system, stabilizing the demand for reserves above working balances;
(g) to provide an averaging facility, such that short-term transitory liquidity shocks are buffered out without a need for open market operations and without related volatility of short-term interest rates.

The functions that reserve requirements theoretically can perform depend on the specification of the reserve requirement system, and the multiplicity of perceived functions thus also partially reflects the multiplicity of specifications. Even the central banks have had to admit the systematic change over time in the arguments put forward; for instance, Board of Governors (1994: 53) claims that 'The rationale for these requirements has changed over time, however, as the country's financial system has evolved and as knowledge about how reserve requirements affect the monetary system has grown'. While the second part of the explanation is plausible, one may doubt whether changes in 'the country's financial system' really justify the observed changes in argumentation. At least, this explanation has never been given substance by more detailed analysis; on the contrary, detailed surveys of the arguments for reserve requirements like Goodfriend and Hargraves (1987), Stevens (1991), Weiner (1992), and Feinman (1993) generally come to the conclusion that most arguments advanced over time in favour of reserve requirements need to be rejected independently of the prevailing environment.

Before the Second World War, reserve requirements imposed by the central bank were a US phenomenon. After 1945, the idea became popular in most countries. Germany introduced reserve requirements in 1948, Japan in 1959, and even the Bank of England made the customary 8 per cent deposit ratio of discount houses compulsory in April 1960 (Tamagna 1963: 98). In the 1980s and 1990s, a trend emerged to reduce once again the level and complexity of reserve requirements. Still, the instrument remains popular today, although normally only in a specification that supports no more than the last two of the arguments in favour of reserve requirements listed above. In the following, the seven arguments will be discussed in turn. Before that, however, it is worth listing the main dimensions of the specification of a reserve requirement system, whereby the link from each of the dimensions to the potential functions of required reserves is made (see also for example Borio 1997: 315):

1. *Definition of the reserve base categories and size of reserve ratio(s).* Normally, reserve requirement systems have in the past distinguished at least between sight, time, and savings deposits of non-banks with banks to define different reserve ratios on those categories of liabilities. The reserve ratios tended to be the higher the more 'money-like' the type of deposit with banks was considered. The differentiation between different reserve base categories during the 1960s and 1970s was actually much more complex than today (see below). Distinguishing between different reserve base categories and imposing different reserve ratios on them should reveal that the perceived functions of reserve requirements include either monetary control or influencing the competition between different banks (see Sections 6.3, 6.4, and 6.6).

2. *Calculation period for the reserve base.* Two issues are relevant in this respect: (*a*) the lag between the period during which the reserve base is calculated and the period of reserve maintenance, and (*b*) the number of days over which the reserve base is calculated. The first issue was

taken very seriously whenever the monetary control function of required reserves was deemed to be relevant (see, for example, Laufenberg 1976; M. Friedman 1982: 110–13). It was felt that, if monetary control was important, the lag should be as short as possible and that the reserve calculation period and reserve maintenance period should even overlap as much as possible. This, of course, makes liquidity management much more difficult for banks, since it implies that they need to start fulfilling reserve requirements before knowing their exact level. Before 1968, reserve requirements in the US were overlapping in this sense ('contemporaneous'). In that year, a lag was introduced to facilitate the life of banks. After strong lobbying for years by monetarists and continued resistance by the Fed (see M. Friedman 1982) contemporaneous reserve accounting was reintroduced in February 1984, ironically just after the short-term monetary control experience had come to an end. The Fed switched back again to lagged reserve accounting only in 1998, arguing once again, in a press release of 26 March, that 'the switch will make it easier for depositories to calculate their required reserve balances for the current maintenance period and will increase the accuracy of information on aggregate required reserve balances, which is needed by the Open Market Trading Desk to carry out its operations'.[1]

The second issue depends on remuneration and hence on circumvention issues. With full remuneration of required reserves and hence no incentives for banks to circumvent them, the number of calculation days does not matter, since banks will not try to manipulate their balance sheet on the calculation days to reduce their reserve base. Hence, for instance, the Eurosystem, which fully remunerates required reserves, defines only one monthly snapshot for the calculation of the reserve base. In contrast, without remuneration, incentives for circumvention emerge and therefore a need arises to define the reserve base according to an average over several days. For instance, the Bundesbank prescribed the calculation of the reserve base as an average over four days' spread over the month (see Sections 6.4 and 6.5 for the treatment of related functions).

3. *Overall size of reserve requirements.* Depending on the reserve base and the reserve ratio(s), an overall size of reserve requirements is obtained. For instance, during 2000 reserve requirements in the US stood at $40 billion on average while they were €130 billion in the euro area. Assessing whether a certain overall size is adequate also depends on the relevant environment and the functions attributed to the reserve requirement. For

---

[1] For an analysis of the effects of contemporaneous reserve accounting on the federal funds rate volatility, see, for example, Lasser (1992).

instance, if reserve requirements are supposed to constitute through averaging a buffer against short-term liquidity shocks, then the size of reserve requirements needs to be measured against the size of these shocks.

4. *Remuneration.* Required reserves may (Eurosystem) or may not (US, UK) be remunerated. Whether remuneration is deemed preferable depends on the perceived relevance of the taxation function and circumvention possibilities (see Section 6.5) but also on the perception of a specific monetary control function of reserve requirements (Section 6.4)

5. *Averaging within a reserve maintenance period of more than one day.* This feature determines whether reserve requirements serve the function of buffering out the effect of transitory liquidity shocks on short-term interest rates (see Section 6.8).

6. *Use of vault cash.* In some countries, banks can or could fulfil reserve requirements at least partially through vault cash. M. Friedman (1960: 49)

Table 6.1   *Main specifications of reserve requirement systems*

	UK	US	Euro area
Reserve base categories	Short-term deposits beyond £400 million	Transactions deposits	Deposits and debt securities with maturity up to two years
Reserve ratios	0.15%	Different marginal levels, max. 10%	2% (but lump sum of €100,000 on requirement)
Calculation period	End of months averages over half a year for following half-year	Average deposits in reserve period starting 30 days before the maintenance period	End of the month preceding the start of the maintenance period
Size of reserve requirements	£1.5bn	$40bn	€130bn
Remuneration	None	None	At rates of Eurosystem's main refinancing operations
Averaging period	None (i.e. one day)	Two weeks starting on a Thursday	From 24th to 23rd of next month (until March 2004)
Level available for averaging	Zero	Required reserves ($40bn) minus vault cash ($36bn) plus clearing balances ($6bn) = $10bn	Equivalent to reserve requirements
Use of vault cash	No	Yes (up to requirement)	No

argues that vault cash should be counted towards the fulfilment of reserve requirements in order to allow for the most stable relationship between the monetary base and broad money; that is, a specification including vault cash would improve the monetary control function. Indeed, the Fed still allows each bank to satisfy its reserve requirements with vault cash (although not in the specification recommended by M. Friedman). Each bank's level of 'applied vault cash' in a reserve maintenance period is calculated as the average value of the vault cash it held during an earlier computation period, up to the level of its reserve requirements, such that the level of applied vault cash is lagged and known prior to the start of each maintenance period. According to Blenck et al. (2001), up to 90 per cent of the average level of required reserves in 2000 could be with vault cash. Other central banks like the Bundesbank and the Eurosystem did not and do not accept vault cash since it is felt not to perform any relevant functions of required reserves while being administratively burdensome.

Table 6.1 summarizes the main features of the reserve requirement systems in the UK, the US, and the euro area as of 2002.

In the following, the more detailed analysis of reserve requirement systems will be structured by their *functions*.

6.2 RESERVE REQUIREMENTS TO SECURE THE BANKS' LIQUIDITY AND FINANCIAL STABILITY

Goodfriend and Hargarves (1983: 35–7) and Feinman (1993: 573) describe in detail this function, which was perceived to play a role in the US from the 1860s to 1931. Reserve requirements on deposits with banks were first imposed in the US on a national level with the National Bank Act of 1863. This act provided a national charter under which banks could be constituted as an alternative to state charters. Banks with the national charter were required to keep a reserve of 25 per cent against both note and deposit liabilities. Goodfriend and Hargraves (1983: 36) interpret this reserve requirement as 'apparently rationalized as being necessary to ensure bank liquidity, that is, the ability of banks to convert deposits into currency'. A series of bank runs and financial panics in the late nineteenth and early twentieth centuries, however, made it clear that reserve requirements were not sufficient to guarantee liquidity of the banking system. What was missing was a mechanism for accommodating temporary variations in the demand for currency, such as an averaging facility or a borrowing facility (Feinman 1993: 573). The Federal Reserve Act of 1913 was hence in large part designed to solve the two main problems of the National Banking Act period: recurrent liquidity crises and seasonal contractions due to a lack of currency. The establishment of the discount window addressed more directly and effectively the issue of individual banks' liquidity. Still, reserve requirements continued to be imposed after 1914 without any new argument in favour of that instrument being advanced. The Fed rearranged to some extent the system and distinguished not only between central reserve city, reserve city, and country banks, but also between demand and time deposits. The latter differentiation could in theory be in line with the liquidity argument, although the annual reports of the Board of Governors of this period are silent on the reasoning behind it. The official end of this rationale in the US can be fixed as 1931, during which a report of the Federal Reserve System Committee on Bank Reserves concluded (Goodfriend and Hargraves 1983: 37):

The committee takes the position that it is no longer the primary function of legal reserve requirements to assure or preserve the liquidity of the individual member bank. . . . Since the establishment of the Federal Reserve System, the liquidity of an individual bank is more adequately safeguarded by the presence of the Federal Reserve banks, which were organized for the purpose, among others, of increasing the liquidity of member banks by providing for the rediscount of their eligible paper, than by the possession of legal reserves.

6.3 MONETARY CONTROL I: CHANGES OF RESERVE REQUIREMENTS AS POLICY TOOL

A predecessor of this argument is found in the older literature justifying reserve requirements, which argued that only reserve requirements would ensure that the creation of deposit money by private banks did not lead to an infinite monetary expansion and thus an undetermined price level (see, for example, Richter 1990: 324–30, for an overview of this older literature). The critical assumption for deriving this result is that currency and deposit money are perfect substitutes. This can be easily illustrated in the framework of the money multiplier (equation 1.4 in Chapter 1): if the ratio of currency to transaction deposits is not well-defined and thus possibly zero (because of the perfect substitutability of both categories of M1), then the M1 money multiplier will be undefined or even infinite (if the voluntary reserve holdings of the banking sector are zero). In this case, a positive minimum reserve requirement ratio r limits the expansion of M1 by setting the money multiplier at $1/r$ and thus is a necessary condition for the existence of a finite price level. In the real world, deposits and currency are *not* perfect substitutes. If money holders have well-defined preferences for the different components of M1, banks will not be able to create an arbitrary quantity of deposit money, as their customers will transform a part of the bank money into currency. One may nevertheless argue that this is no guarantee that innovations in the private money supply will not in the near future introduce greater instability in the money multiplier and, in the medium term, a far-reaching decline in the demand for currency. Fama (1980) advances the argument a long way by looking at the role of minimum reserve requirements in a futuristic, currency-free economy. He argues that if, in such a context, the central bank defines some good as the *numeraire* for which no natural demand exists—namely, central bank money—then reserve requirements would be a necessary condition for having well-defined prices expressed in this *numeraire*. However, Fama argues that the best long-term solution in such a case would be to choose any real good as the *numeraire* for which scarcity is well-defined without the creation of an artificial demand. Although this supposed function of reserve requirements therefore appears to stand on relatively weak ground, the argument still seemed to be maintained more or less explicitly until recently, for instance by the Deutsche Bundesbank (1995: 128).

The more sophisticated variant of this argument says that *changing* the reserve ratio(s) makes it possible, via the money multiplier, to expand or contract credit and monetary aggregates. This argument was first detailed by Keynes (1930: 65–8). He introduced the case with an example from the UK, in which no reserve requirements were imposed at that time (as is practically the case today):

The Midland Bank had . . . maintained for some years past a reserve proportion a good deal higher than those of its competitors. It is not obvious that this had really been worth while from its own point of view. Accordingly, beginning in the latter part of 1926, a gradual downward movement became apparent in the Midland Bank's proportion from about 14.5% in 1926 to about 11.5% in 1929 . . . this . . . in fact enabled the banks as a whole to increase their deposits (and their advances) by about GBP 100 million without any new increase in their aggregate reserves . . . Now, as it happened, this relaxation of credit was in the particular circumstances greatly in the public interest . . .

Nevertheless, such an expansion of the resources of the member banks should not, in any sound modern system, depend on the action of an individual member bank . . . For we ought to be able to assume that the central bank will be at least as intelligent as a member bank and more to be relied on to act in the general interest. I conclude therefore, that the American system of regulating by law the amount of the member bank reserves is preferable to the English system of depending on an ill-defined and somewhat precarious convention.

Keynes (1930: 68) then proposed a concrete specification of a reserve requirement system, to conclude enthusiastically on its power: 'These regulations would greatly strengthen the power of control in the hands of the Bank of England–placing, indeed, in its hands an almost complete control over the total volume of bank money–without in any way hampering the legitimate operations of the joint stock banks.' This argumentation was taken up by central banks, and, for instance, the Board of Governors (1954, 1974) lists the three main instruments of monetary policy implementation as follows: 'Discount operations, Open market operations, *Changes* in reserve requirements' (emphasis added), that is, reserve requirements were a relevant tool especially in so far as they could be changed. Still, it is interesting that the Fed in the 1950s was still somewhat cautious about this instrument (Board of Governors 1954: 50–1), which, however, did not prevent the Fed from using it:

Because changes in reserve requirements affect at the same time and to the same extent all member banks subject to the action, they are a potent instrument . . . The fact that the multiplying power of bank reserves is affected exerts either a dampening or an accelerating influence on the expansion of bank credit and money . . . The authority to change reserve requirements has not been used frequently . . . Numerous administrative and technical problems handicap changes in reserve requirements. Experience has shown that this instrument is not adapted to day-to-day changes in banking and monetary conditions . . . Frequent changes in requirements even by very small percentage amounts would be disturbing to member banks and to the credit market. For these reasons this method is usually employed only when large scale changes in the country's available bank reserves are desired.

M. Friedman (1960) has little sympathy for *changes* in reserve requirements as a monetary policy tool and argues that this tool should be discontinued (he seems to leave it open whether he regards stable reserve requirements as desirable). While the argumentation in Board of Governors (1974) is still rather similar to Board of Governors (1954), the critique has had an effect on Board of Governors (1994): the argumentation has now totally changed and reserve requirements no longer play any role in monetary control.

How seriously central banks took this function of reserve requirements at different points in time can in principle be measured by observing how frequently required reserve ratios were changed. Indeed, all other arguments in favour of imposing reserve requirements should not per se require variations of the reserve ratio. Figure 6.1 plots for the Bundesbank in the period 1948–98 the number of times per year some ratio was changed.

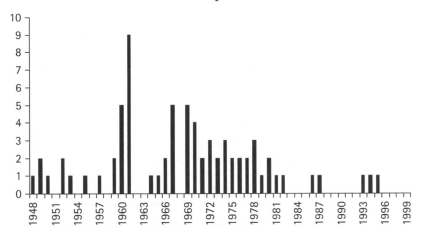

Figure 6.1   *Number of reserve ratio changes per year by the Deutsche Bundesbank*
Sources: Deutsche Bundesbank (1976, 1995).

The high tide of implementing monetary policy through changes in reserve ratios was obviously the 1960s and 1970s. Tamagna (1963: 104) explains that the Bundesbank was indeed using changes of reserve requirements for liquidity management purposes, substituting it for open market operations, for example. According to Tamagna (1963: 115), this reflected the underdevelopment of financial markets in Germany, which implied that no appropriate paper for open market operations would have been available (a counterargument to this explanation is that the Bundesbank could always, and actually did, *issue debt paper*, which had liquidity-absorbing effects like reserve requirements). In any case, this explanation cannot hold for the Fed, which also in the 1950s, 1960s, and 1970s frequently changed reserve ratios for monetary control. The years with very many changes in Germany, such as 1961 and 1967, saw gradual changes in one direction, somewhat similar to gradual changes in official interest rates. Indeed, in both years, both reserve requirements and the discount and lombard rates were gradually lowered, revealing a kind of mixture of quantitative and interest rate instruments.[2] As the last three changes of reserve ratios by the Deutsche Bundesbank (in 1993,

---

[2] In assessments of the effects of changes of reserve ratios on monetary conditions, it should also be taken into account that, beyond the effect of releasing or absorbing free reserves, changes in reserve ratios in a system of non-remunerated reserves constitute also a change in the tax on bank money and has an expansionary or contracting impact through this channel. Estimating in this context the effects of changes in reserve requirements on economic activity, Loungani and Rush (1995: 524) conclude that there are 'statistically significant and quantitatively important' effects.

1994, and 1995) were mere decreases and simplifications of ratios (see Deutsche Bundesbank 1994*a*), one may say that the function of reserve requirements dealt with in the present section has not been considered by the Bundesbank at least since 1987 (for the US, see also Haslag and Hein 1989).

6.4 MONETARY CONTROL II: STABLE RESERVE REQUIREMENTS AS A BUILT-IN MACROECONOMIC STABILIZER

To perform this function, reserve requirements do not need to be *changed* as they need to be for the previous one (at least in its sophisticated version): that is, reserve requirements act as a *built-in stabilizer* which modifies the properties of the macroeconomy such that exogenous shocks become less harmful. This argument won more support from academics than from central banks, which apparently had problems presenting it as an official position. In 1998 the ECB presented its own variant of the built-in stabilizer function, according to which non-remunerated reserve requirements would increase the interest rate elasticity of money demand and would therefore facilitate monetary targeting.

Consider first the academic literature on the topic. For instance, Kaminow (1977), Laufenberg (1979), Santomero and Siegel (1981), Froyen and Kopecky (1983), Van Hoose (1986), and Weiner (1992) analyse the stabilization impact of constant minimum reserves on what they consider to be intermediate targets of monetary policy, such as monetary aggregates or interest rates. The general conclusion of those studies is that the size and remuneration of reserve requirements is relevant for monetary stabilization, which implies that reserve requirements are potentially useful as a built-in stabilizer. However, a general problem with this approach is that it is difficult to motivate focusing on the stabilization of *intermediate* targets and not on the stabilization of final ones. It is assumed implicitly that the two are equivalent; but this is not necessarily true, as, for example, Siegel (1981: 1073) and Baltensperger (1982*a*: 206) argue. It may be shown that cases exist in which the stabilization of monetary aggregates by reserve requirements can end up increasing the volatility of final target variables.

Richter (1968) was the first author to analyse the role of minimum reserves as a general macroeconomic built-in stabilizer in a comparative-static setting. He concludes that the stabilization effect of reserve requirements on economic activity ultimately depends on the coefficients of the model, but that the case in which minimum reserve requirements act as a 'built-in destabilizer' is 'by far the more plausible' (Richter 1968: 288). Siegel (1981) and Baltensperger (1982*a*) argue that the variability of the monetary aggregate is minimized by a 100 per cent reserve ratio. But the reserve ratio minimizing the variability of the price level depends on the coefficients of the model and the correlation structure of the shocks. It can take any value between zero and one. Baltensperger (1982*a*: 214) remains agnostic in his conclusions: 'The fractional reserve system has a flexibility and elasticity that may be a disadvantage in some situations, but that may equally be an advantage in other situations. I conclude that it is difficult and probably not advisable to choose between a low and a high reserve requirement on the basis of this kind of stability considerations.' Siegel (1981) is more courageous and estimates his model for the US with quarterly data from 1952–73. He concludes that the optimal average reserve requirement would have been 7 per cent instead of the actual 11.5 per cent at that time. On the other hand, the difference in the standard deviation of the quarterly price level would have been only minor. For reserve ratios of 7 per cent, 11.5 per cent, and 0 per cent, the standard deviation would have been 0.452 per cent, 0.485 per cent, and about 0.5 per cent respectively, according to Siegel's calculations.

Horrigan (1988) shows in the framework of a macroeconomic model with rational expectations that the size and remuneration of required reserves are irrelevant from the point of view of stabilization of the price level and economic activity, as the impact of reserve requirements can also be effected by an adequate adjustment of the interest-rate elasticity of the supply of central bank money. Horrigan is therefore the first author to explicitly merge the minimum reserve literature such as Baltensperger (1982*a*) with the general stabilization literature based on Poole (1970). In general, however, one should expect that, if the modelling of the economy is sufficiently complex and if enough exogenous shocks are included, it is very unlikely that minimum reserves and the interest rate elasticity of the central bank's money supply would be completely redundant. Yet this does not mean that reserve requirements are indeed a meaningful built-in stabilizer. The model intuition is as follows. Consider again the Poole (1970) model as given in equation (1.5) of Chapter 1. Instead of considering now directly a supply function of the monetary aggregate M ($M = c_1 + c_2 i$), consider a monetary aggregate which is a noisy reflection of the money multiplier and of central bank money, that is $M = d_1(d_2 + c_2 i + \zeta)$, where d_1, $d_2 + c_2 i$ are the money multiplier (as can be determined by the central bank in the domain $[1/c, 1]$ by choosing a reserve requirement ratio between 0 and 1, see equation 1.4) and the monetary base supply function, respectively, and ζ is a further random variable with expected value zero and variance σ_ζ^2. By substituting this into the Poole model (1.5), one obtains the following reduced form for Y:

$$Y = \frac{a_0(b_2 - d_1c_2) + a_1(b_0 - d_1d_2)}{b_2 + a_1b_1 - d_1c_2} + \frac{b_2 - d_1c_2}{b_2 + a_1b_1 - d_1c_2}v$$

$$+ \frac{a_1}{b_2 + a_1b_1 - d_1c_2}\mu + \frac{d_1a_1}{b_2 + a_1b_1 - d_1c_2}\zeta \tag{6.1}$$

Again, one may now find in a first step the optimal policy parameters d_1, c_2 (d_1 implying the minimum reserve ratio) by minimizing the variance of this expression, and then, in a second step, calculate C_2 such as to obtain $E(Y) = Y^*$. It appears that none of the parameters the central bank needs to choose is redundant, so that reserve requirements would be justified as a built-in stabilizer which cannot easily be substituted.

All in all, it nevertheless seems appropriate to conclude by adopting an agnostic position. Although especially high reserve requirements are likely to matter for macroeconomic stability, one knows little or nothing about how and in which direction this really works.

Now, consider briefly another variant of the built-in stabilizer function, according to which non-remunerated reserve requirements would *increase the interest-rate elasticity of money creation* and would hence facilitate monetary targeting. The argument, which cannot as such be traced back clearly to any of the academic papers on the built-in stabilizer hypothesis, is as follows: if reserve requirements are non-remunerated, then they are a tax on the creation of bank money, the tax corresponding to the interest rate times the reserve ratio. Therefore, changes of short-term interest rates by the central bank will have stronger effects on bank money creation whenever non-remunerated reserve requirements are imposed.

The following simplistic model tries to capture the idea. Assume a perfectly efficient banking system in which offering current account services to customers is costless for banks, such that in the competitive equilibrium banks pay the market interest rate on all customer deposits, that is $i_{CD} = i$ (where i_{CD} is the interest rate on customer deposits and i is the market rate), as long as there are no unremunerated reserve requirements. Assume that customers can invest in bank deposits or in Treasury paper, the latter not providing the same transactions services as deposits with banks. If the central bank imposes unremunerated reserve requirements amounting to a ratio r of customer deposits, then the perfectly efficient and competitive banking sector will obviously be able to offer a remuneration rate on customer deposits of only $i_{CD} = (1 - r)i$. This implies that, when the level of market interest rate increases, then the spread between market interest rates and the rate banks pay on customer deposits increases. The demand for deposits with banks, CD, is likely to depend on the difference between the market rate and the remuneration rate of deposits with banks, $i - i_{CD}$, that is $CD = CD(i - i_{CD})$:$[0,i] \rightarrow [CD_{min}, CD_{max}]$ with $\partial CD / \partial(i - i_{CD}) < 0$ and $CD(i) = CD_{min}$ and $CD(0) = CD_{max}$. Thus, when i increases, then $CD(i - i_{CD})$ declines, and thus monetary aggregates also decline. This seems to rationalize interest rate policy by central banks, not in the Thornton–Wicksell–Woodford sense, but as a monetarist tool that is effective only with the help of unremunerated reserve requirements.

The argument is spelled out as the third potential function (after the money market buffer and the structural enlargement functions) of required reserves in the ECB press release of 8 July 1998 outlining the reserve requirement system it would apply from the launch of the euro from 1999 onwards: 'Third, the ESCB's minimum reserve system may also contribute to controlling the expansion of monetary aggregates by increasing the interest rate elasticity of money demand' (ECB 1998). But then the ECB explains that it chose a specification for required reserves which would not support this function, since it did not want to tax banks through reserve requirements and hence wanted to fully remunerate required reserves.

To assess whether monetary control played a role in imposing reserve requirements, one may consider the number of different categories of deposits to which different reserve requirement ratios were applied. Such a differentiation makes sense according to the built-in stabilizer argument (see, for example, Laufenberg 1979), besides the influence on competition argument. The complexity of reserve requirement ratios during most of the twentieth century is indeed impressive. The Bundesbank in 1952 differentiated along the following five dimensions: type of deposit (sight; time; savings); up to six size categories (implying different marginal ratios); whether or not banks were located at major bank places; liabilities towards residents or non-residents; and stocks vs increments of deposits.[3] The simplification of reserve base categories started only in the late 1970s, when the discrimination against non-residents' deposits and increments was eliminated. In the 1980s and early 1990s, the size categories were successively eliminated and the Bundesbank ended with just two different reserve ratios in 1998. The Eurosystem from the beginning of its existence imposed only one positive reserve ratio. Figure 6.2 aims

---

[3] Higher reserve ratios were in these cases imposed on increments. For instance, Poole (1976) argues in favour of a reserve requirement system that discriminates against increments on the grounds that this would stabilize monetary aggregates.

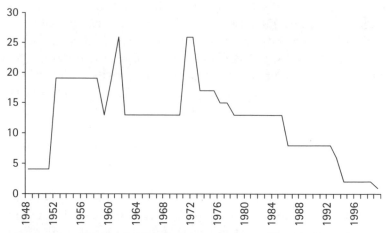

Figure 6.2   *Number of different reserve ratio categories of the Deutsche Bundesbank/Bank Deutscher Länder*

Sources: Deutsche Bundesbank (1976, 1995).

at capturing the number of different reserve ratios during the Bundesbank period.

A broadly similar evolution seems to hold for the US, where twelve different reserve ratios still applied in 1978, but only two remained in 1988. As Hardy (1996: 14) argues, in practice, differentiated reserve requirements are more likely to *complicate* monetary control, especially since the different implicit taxes on different types of deposits will create circumvention and hence instability in the structure of deposits. (For an example of a German academic perception of the 1970s, see Caesar 1976.)

6.5   RESERVE REQUIREMENTS AS A TAX

Unremunerated or only partially remunerated reserve requirements are a tax on the deposits of non-banks with banks, and are hence a source of income for the central bank, and eventually for the government. Already for Keynes (1930: 62), the taxation argument of required reserves comes first:

The custom of requiring banks to hold larger reserves than they strictly require for till money and for clearing purposes is a means of making them contribute to the expenses which the central bank incurs for the maintenance of the currency.

For a given level of deposits of customers with the central bank subject to reserve requirements, *CD*, a reserve ratio *r*, and an interest rate level *i*, the total yearly tax income of reserve requirement will simply be *irCD*. In general, taxes are related to some form of allocative distortion and related welfare losses. However, as long as free public goods need to be provided, such distortions may be unavoidable and the issue is to find the optimal way to distribute the tax burden on different goods or activities. Freeman (1987) and Brock (1989) elaborate on the role of reserve requirements for the total seigniorage and the relevance of inflation to that. A number of papers analyse in a rather abstract form the allocative effects of the taxation component of reserve requirements in the context of models of overlapping generations. For instance, Romer (1985) points out that reserve requirements are not exactly equivalent to a tax on deposits. He derives an optimal combination of public income from monetary expansion, minimum reserve requirements, and debt expansion. Mourmouras and Russel (1992) analyse the conditions under which an unremunerated minimum reserve and a tax on deposits are broadly equivalent. Freeman and Haslag (1995) claim that the distorting effects of reserve requirements are always larger than those of normal taxes. Baltensperger (1982*b*) argues that the taxation effect of reserve requirements compensates for another distortion, namely, that implied by the non-remuneration of currency which is a substitute for deposit money. The non-remuneration of compulsory reserves would accordingly neutralize the distortion by rendering currency relatively more attractive than deposit money.

Ultimately, one has to ask whether the tax effect of non-remunerated reserve requirements represents an optimal tax according to the theory of optimal taxation, which postulates the optimality condition that the marginal welfare costs of different tax incomes should be equal. In the case of open capital markets, the international mobility of at least a part of deposits is high, such that small differences in the tax on deposits (implicit in the reserve requirement) can imply large outflows of the relevant types of deposits. In addition, technical innovations such as so-called 'sweep accounts' in the US have made it possible to circumvent deposits subject to required reserves even without international dislocation. Therefore, the sensitivity of the tax basis to the size of the tax ratio is rather high. In such a context, it should be expected that the marginal welfare cost of income generated by non-remunerated required reserves would be higher than that of other forms of public income and it thus does not seem efficient to keep substantial required reserves unremunerated for the purpose of collecting tax income. According to the survey by Borio (1997: 314), the only central bank in his sample which in 1996 fully remunerated required reserves was de Nederlandsche Bank. Also, the European Central Bank decided in 1998 to fully remunerate the required reserves in the euro area. The UK, in contrast, imposes a rather low non-remunerated reserve requirement amounting currently to 0.15 per cent of sight deposits of banks. The Bank of England explicitly assigns only an income-generation function to this requirement (called 'cash ratio deposits'). Interestingly, although both the UK and the Eurosystem impose some reserve requirements, there is hence *strictly no overlap in the functions they assign to this tool*. According to Borio (1997: 314), in 1996 seigniorage income generated by reserve requirements corresponded both in the UK and the US to 0.01 per cent of GDP, while the highest figure he provides for industrialized countries is for Italy: 0.12 per cent of GDP.

6.6 INFLUENCING COMPETITIVE CONDITIONS BETWEEN BANKS

This argument has not been advanced very explicitly either by central banks or by academics. It is however obvious that it must have played a role since reserve ratios have so often discriminated between different types of banks and different levels of the reserve base. The latter was such that reserve ratios increased progressively with the size of the reserve base, suggesting preferential treatment for small banks or, more generally, support for a polypolistic banking structure. For instance, Board of Governors (1994: 54) explains:[4]

Reserve requirements are structured to bear relatively less heavily on smaller institutions. At every depository, a reserve requirement of 0 percent is applied to a certain amount of liabilities that are subject to reserve requirements (reservable liabilities), and relatively low requirements are applied to such liabilities up to another level. These levels are adjusted annually to reflect growth in the banking system. In 1994, the first $4.0 million of reservable liabilities were made exempt from any requirements, and transaction deposits up to $51.9 million were given a reserve ratio of only 3 percent. Transaction deposits of more than $51.9 million were subject to a 10 percent reserve requirement.

In the US, since before 1914 reserve requirements varied between central reserve city banks, reserve city banks, and country banks. Before

---

[4] From the 1950s the Bundesbank imposed different reserve ratios for different tranches of deposits. For instance, still in the early 1993 the Bundesbank imposed a reserve requirement of 6.6% on sight deposits below DM10 million, of 9.9% on sight deposits between DM10 million and DM100 million, and of 12.1% for sight deposits above that (Deutsche Bundesbank 1995: 123). The Eurosystem no longer differentiates according to the size of the reserve base. The lump-sum allowance of €100,000 for reserve requirements (corresponding to a reserve base of €5 million) has been set for the sake of avoiding the administrative burden of negligible reserve requirements.

1914, these differences were justified by the role of the different types of banks as providers of liquidity but, as M. Friedman (1960: 49) argues, the differentiation could no longer be justified in that way after 1914. Although the differentiation after 1914 was probably not a deliberate instrument of competition policy, the fact that it was not abolished earlier suggests that the Fed did not want to alter the competitive position of the different banks, probably due to pressure from those banks that would have been made relatively worse off. Similar considerations may explain why, until the Monetary Control Act of 1980, only Federal Reserve member banks were subject to reserve requirements.

Membership[5] of the Federal Reserve System was always voluntary for banks with charters issued by the states. Membership was required for federally chartered banks but, before interstate banking was permitted in the 1990s, banks had no pressing reason to hold a Federal charter. Large banks effectively had to be members because they needed access to the clearing and settlement mechanisms that the Federal Reserve provided, and benefited from access to the discount window. Small banks generally hired larger correspondent banks to clear transactions for them, and could look to their correspondent for late day loans if needed. Thus, they did not need to be members of the Federal Reserve System. Banks were dropping membership at a growing rate in the 1970s as rising nominal interest rates lifted the reserve requirement tax. The Federal Reserve could not collect deposit data from non-member banks, so the exodus was also complicating measurement of money and credit. Low reserve requirements on small member banks were justified to encourage them to remain members. The seasonal discount window was also introduced for that reason. After the Monetary Control Act of 1980, non-member banks faced the same requirements as members with regard to holding reserves and reporting data, so there was no longer a reason to give the small banks favourable treatment. Favourable treatment did, however, continue. It had a long history, some of it was written into the law, and small banks have an effective lobby.

6.7 STABILIZING, CREATING, OR ENLARGING A DEMAND FOR RESERVES OF THE BANKING SYSTEM

This argument has two variants. The first depends on the uncertainty that the demand for working balances creates for day-to-day control of the

---

[5] The additional background information in this paragraph was kindly provided by Ann Marie Meulendyke.

overnight rate. The second is independent from this uncertainty. Consider the two in turn.

1. *Stabilizing the demand for reserves by making the demand for working balances irrelevant to short-term market rates.* Most of this book proceeds from the assumption that the 'aggregate liquidity management model' (Section 3.2.1) is more relevant than the 'individual shocks model' (Section 3.2.2). Nevertheless, the latter model is obviously not to be neglected a priori. Accordingly, the central bank would need to forecast the daily demand by banks for individual liquidity buffers. However, since this individual demand for reserves depends on various factors that are unstable and difficult to predict, the control of short-term interest rates is difficult under such circumstances. By making reserve requirements the binding constraint on banks' demand for reserves—that is, by keeping required reserves above the shifting and unpredictable level needed for clearing purposes—the central bank can more accurately determine the banking system's demand for reserves, and eventually exercise better control over short-term interest rates. The Board of Governors (1994: 56) argues exactly in this way (see also Clouse and Elmendorf 1997). To that extent, reserve requirements allow for better control of short-term interest rates, independently of the averaging function.

2. *Increasing the refinancing needs of the banking system vis-à-vis the central bank.* While the first variant refers to an increase in the reserve holdings, the second refers to an increase in refinancing needs, the two being differentiated in terms of the level of autonomous liquidity factors (according to the central bank balance sheet identity of Chapter 2, $M + B = A + R$). Schmid and Asche (1997: 76), for instance, explain this second variant of the function as follows: 'In order to ensure efficiency of monetary policy, i.e. the central bank leadership in the money market, the banking system must be kept sufficiently dependent on central bank refinancing.' Hence, reserve requirements, which increase the level of refinancing needs, would improve the efficiency of monetary policy implementation. The ECB in a press release of 8 July 1998 also refers to this argument as the second amongst the three it cites:

.... such a system will contribute to enlarging the demand for central bank money and thus creating or enlarging a structural liquidity shortage in the market; this is considered helpful in order to improve the ability of the ESCB to operate efficiently as a supplier of liquidity and, in the longer term, to react to new payment technologies such as the development of electronic money.[6]

---

[6] The latter of the ECB arguments justifying reserve requirements—namely, to ensure that the banking system always remains in a liquidity deficit vis-à-vis the central bank—seems to be close to the monetary control variant of the oldest type, that is, reserve requirements being a necessary

It is at least understandable that central banks probably prefer to operate in an environment in which the liquidity position of the banking system does not change its sign easily. Indeed, the switch of open market operations from the asset side to the liability side of the central bank balance sheet requires a review of procedures both for the central bank and for the market, which may be deemed costly. Also, open market operations that are too small, whether on the asset or the liability side of the central bank balance sheet, could be problematic because they probably lead to relatively unstable aggregate bidding behaviour.

Finally, it should be noted that the enlargement function is also regularly considered key by central banks of *small monetary areas*. These central banks often have large foreign exchange reserves such that they would have to *absorb* liquidity through open market operations if they did not impose reserve requirements. These central banks argue that *absorbing* liquidity in day-to-day open market operations makes for less effective monetary policy operations than *providing* liquidity. However, it is plausible to assume that these central banks often also have other arguments in mind, such as raising income and, perhaps, monetary control.

6.8 AVERAGING OUT TRANSITORY AUTONOMOUS FACTOR SHOCKS

Reserve requirements can provide a temporary source of individual banks' and the banking system's aggregate liquidity if they are not enforced on a day-by-day basis. Besides the level of reserve requirements, the length of the reserve maintenance period, that is, of the averaging period, is crucial for this function. Averaging periods in central banking in the twentieth century ranged from half a week to one month. The size of reserve requirements is not necessarily equivalent to the size of the averaging buffer. While this equivalence holds in the euro area, in the US 90 per cent of required reserves were held on average in 2000 as vault cash, which does not qualify for averaging. On the other hand, the US Fed introduced the instrument of 'required clearing balances' to increase the averaging buffer.[7] *Carry-over* provisions are also relevant to

condition for a well-defined demand for central bank money. In view of the unambiguous upwards trend of banknotes in circulation in recent decades (see, for instance, Seitz and Bindseil 2002), the argument appears to focus on the more distant future.

[7] Banks may agree, at their discretion, to hold additional balances at the Fed within each two-week reserve maintenance period to meet a clearing balance requirement. Unlike the balances held to meet reserve requirements, these are de facto remunerated at a market rate. Explicit interest is not paid, but compensation is paid in the form of income credits that can be set against charges for various priced services offered by the Fed. At the end of each two-week period, the Fed

assessing the liquidity buffers provided by the reserve requirement system. Carry-over provisions serve as bridging reserve maintenance periods by allowing banks to shift limited reserve surpluses or deficits into the next reserve maintenance period. This has the advantage of reducing the volatility of overnight interest rates at the end of the reserve maintenance period, which normally cannot be avoided in an averaging system without carry-over. The Fed currently allows for carry-over of 4 per cent of required reserves as a deficit or a surplus into the following reserve maintenance period.

It needs to be recognized that averaging can also be achieved without reserve requirements if banks are allowed to *overdraft* their end-of-day reserve account position. Indeed, such a system has been successfully applied by the Bank of Canada (see, for example, Clinton 1997) and was studied by the Bank of England (Davies 1998). In substance, averaging around zero and a fully remunerated reserve requirement system are rather similar, except for the total refinancing needs of the banking system vis-à-vis the central bank.

To return to the earliest days of reserve requirements, it is noteworthy that, according to Stevens (1991: 12), reserve requirements under the US National Bank Act of 1863 were actually *not* enforced daily. A bank whose reserve fell below the requirement was prohibited both from expanding its liabilities and from paying dividends. When aware of deficiencies, the 'Comptroller of the Currency' was empowered, but not required, to give a bank thirty days' notice to come into compliance. With the establishment of the Fed, rules became *more* rigid, and according to Stevens by 1935 'member banks had little scope to use required reserve deposits even as a short-run source of liquidity'. Still, semi-weekly, weekly, or semi-monthly averaging periods were defined, depending on the bank's size and location. According to Burgess (1927), the *weekly* averaging period was the most relevant in the 1920s. In the mid-1950s, one-week and two-week averaging periods prevailed, and carry-over of limited end-of-maintenance period imbalances into the next reserve maintenance period was allowed. In the period from 1968 to 1984, the averaging period was one week for all sizes of banks. Since 1984, the averaging period has been two weeks for all US banks. The Bundesbank and the Eurosystem always stipulated one-month reserve maintenance periods, but the latter announced in January 2003 that from

---

determines whether a bank has satisfied its clearing balance requirement, based on a bank's average holdings of balances that were not used to meet reserve requirements (for example, Blenck et al. 2001). In 2000, clearing balances contributed on average $6 billion to averaging.

2004 it would adopt a more flexible system in which reserve maintenance periods would be aligned with meetings of the Governing Council of the ECB, after which central bank rates may change (see Section 5.6).

Astonishingly, the implications of averaging and the possibility of deriving from it a rationale for reserve requirements were systematically ignored for a long time, and the first publications which are outspoken on the averaging function appear only in the early 1990s (for example, Stevens, 1991: 12). For the Board of Governors (1994), the Deutsche Bundesbank (1995), and the ECB (2001c), this function is already crucial. Deutsche Bundesbank (1995: 125–6), for example, put it thus:

Minimum reserve requirements, through which central bank balances have to be maintained only on average over a month, rather than daily, act in the money market as a liquidity cushion which absorbs unforeseen fluctuations in liquidity needs, generally with no intervention by the Bundesbank. This contributes to stabilising interest rates and enables the central bank to adopt a 'non-interventionist' stance in the money market.

Models of the working of the averaging function, or in which the averaging function at least played some role, have been provided by Poole (1968), Laufenberg (1979), Baltensperger (1980), Spindt and Tarhan (1984), Angeloni and Prati (1996), Feinman (1993), Hamilton (1996, 1997), Bindseil (2002), Välimäki (1998, 2001, 2002), Perez-Quiros and Rodriguez-Mendizábal (2001), and Würtz (2003). The multiplicity of papers and models suggests that averaging becomes a complex issue as soon as one goes beyond the most basic setting. Such a setting was the one presented in Chapter 3: when inter-bank markets are perfectly efficient and the buffers provided by reserve requirements are always sufficient to cover temporary upwards and downwards movements of autonomous factors, then averaging ensures that the overnight rates on any day will correspond to the weighted expected rates of the two standing facilities at the end of the reserve maintenance period, the weights being the respective probabilities that the market will be short or long at the end of the maintenance period. This also implies the *martingale property* of the overnight interest rate within the reserve maintenance period, that is, the overnight rate on any day corresponds to the expected overnight rates on the following days of the same reserve maintenance period. Otherwise, an arbitrage opportunity emerges and banks can make profits by rearranging their reserve fulfilment path. As aggregate reserves are determined by the central bank balance sheet (except for recourse to standing facilities), the attempt of all the competing banks to rearrange their reserve fulfilment paths will eventually establish the martingale property.

In the practice of monetary policy implementation, averaging implies that any divergence of reserve holdings from reserve requirements in the course of the reserve maintenance period should not affect overnight inter-bank rates as long as money market players expect that it will be reversed before the end of the reserve maintenance period. Therefore, one late open market operation in the reserve maintenance period (for example, on the last day of the reserve maintenance period) in which the central bank is expected to compensate any accumulated excess or deficit of reserves relative to reserve requirements should be enough to fully stabilize overnight interest rates up to the moment of the open market operation. In practice, however, averaging does not work perfectly for a variety of reasons, such as the following:

1. The *aggregate* level of reserve requirements may not be sufficient to provide a sufficient buffer for the (accumulated) aggregate shocks in autonomous factors. For instance, daily shocks of autonomous factors may push aggregate reserve holdings to zero and, since banks cannot overdraft their accounts with the central bank overnight, this would force them immediately to go to the borrowing facility, and inter-bank rates would move upwards to the borrowing facility rate.

2. Not only aggregate liquidity shocks but also *individual* banks' shocks matter, that is, the assumption of perfectly efficient inter-bank markets and payment systems does not need to hold. The idea, as captured in the 'individual shocks' model of Section 3.2.2, is that, after the inter-bank market has closed, banks are subject to payment surprises that drive them below or above their targeted end-of-day reserves (see the individual liquidity shocks model in Chapter 3). As has been shown by Perez-Quiros and Rodriguez-Mendizábal (2001), this again leads to imperfections in averaging and to a preference on the part of banks to back-load their fulfilment of reserve requirements.

3. Hamilton (1996), for instance, proposes a model with transactions costs in the inter-bank market to explain his empirical finding that the martingale property is not fulfilled properly in the US money market. Würtz (2003) reviews some anomalies in the euro area's overnight rate time series, which seem to be related to non-rational behaviour on the part of banks that do not treat the costs of refinancing with the central bank as sunk.

4. Banks' window-dressing at end of months, quarters, and years normally leads to a one-day interest rate spike, since reserve holdings on these days serve not only to fulfil reserve requirements (as they do on other days) but also to beautify the reported balance sheet. Therefore,

demand for them, and *ceteris paribus* their equilibrium price, is higher. See Keynes (1930) for the UK in the early twentieth century, Allen and Saunders (1992) for the US, and Bindseil, Weller, and Würtz (2003) for the euro area.

Although averaging hence does not work perfectly, it is still of major importance for monetary policy implementation. Indeed, it explains why the ECB can achieve a high degree of stability in the overnight rate despite operating only once a week, and why the Bank of England cannot (see Table 3.1), although operating three times a day.

Accepting thus that averaging has some advantages, one may wonder why central banks have never adopted averaging periods of *longer* than one month. The issue is probably that by definition averaging excludes engineering *expected* changes of interest rates within the reserve maintenance period. Indeed, expectations of the central bank interest rates and the liquidity conditions at the end of the maintenance period are relevant to the inter-bank rates at any moment in time, according to the model presented in Chapter 3. Suppose as an extreme case a reserve maintenance of one year. Then, market participants would mainly speculate about what the central bank rates will be at the end of this reserve maintenance period, and the central bank would have difficulty influencing rates independently of this channel. In particular, it could not engineer anticipated changes of inter-bank rates within the course of the year. With fixed-rate tenders, expected rate changes within the maintenance period also cause over-bidding and under-bidding problems, such as described in Section 5.6. If expected rate hikes within the reserve maintenance period year exceed half the width of the corridor set by standing facilities, the banking system could also be tempted to fulfil its reserve requirements for the entire year through one huge recourse to the borrowing facility. Ideally, *averaging therefore takes place only within periods in which changes in central bank rates are not deemed to be necessary.* The ECB has in this respect adopted an innovative approach by announcing that from spring 2004 it would align reserve maintenance periods with meetings of the ECB's Governing Council in which discussions of the monetary policy stance are pre-scheduled.

6.9 CONCLUSIONS

The justifications given for imposing reserve requirements on banks have changed considerably over time. From today's perspective, the biggest question mark hangs over the monetary control function, as assigned to reserve requirements especially from the 1950s to the 1980s. Complex systems with an impressive number of differently treated reserve base categories were created and in some years reserve ratios were changed at a high frequency. Today, these functions of reserve requirements are no longer taken for granted, like most other doctrines of the monetary control era. Instead, there is consensus that the main purpose of reserve requirements is the stabilization of short-term interest rates. If this is indeed the main function of reserve requirements, it matters little how their level is calculated, especially if required reserves are remunerated. For instance, they could also be calculated by applying a certain reserve requirement ratio to some asset-side measure of banks' balance sheets, or to the number of staff members, and so forth.

7

The Practice of Monetary Policy Implementation in the Twentieth Century

This chapter reviews the evolution of the overall practice of monetary policy implementation in the three central banks during the twentieth century. In contrast to the previous three chapters, it focuses as little as possible on *single* instruments but rather on their overall interaction in achieving the operational target. It is argued that, at the end of the century, central banks had at least partially returned to where they stood at its beginning, and that the 1990s in particular witnessed a restoration of older principles of monetary policy implementation. The amplitude of the movement was strongest in the case of the US Fed, and weakest in the case of the Bank of England.

One general point needs to be highlighted for all three central banks: 'direct methods' of monetary control, like regulation of margin requirements and ceilings for interest rates on time deposits, were rather popular everywhere in the post-war period until around the early 1980s (see, for example, M. Friedman 1960, for a critical survey of methods applied in the US, or King 1994: 62–3 for the UK). Such direct methods occasionally appear below when the policy actions of central banks are described, but there is no analysis of the motivation at that time for employing these methods nor any detailed assessment from today's perspective, since it is no longer a matter of debate whether such methods are useful or not in the case of advanced financial systems (it seems that they are not).

7.1 THE BANK OF ENGLAND

Chapter 4, on standing facilities, reviewed the key topics of the Bank of England's monetary policy implementation until 1914, and Keynes (1930) described the 'old doctrine' of the Bank of England as a kind of control of short-term interest rates at a level below the discount rate, in which open market operations were already used to achieve roughly the desired spread between the two rates. Of course, at least before 1914, the major concern of central banks when choosing their main policy rate, namely, the discount rate, was not 'monetary policy' in today's sense, but above all the maintenance of sufficient gold reserves, since the permanent possibility of gold outflows potentially threatened the convertibility of currency. Also, central banks were subject to some legal restriction regarding the maximum issuance of banknotes relative to metal reserves. In the case of the Bank of England, under Robert Peel's Act of 1844 all notes beyond a certain 'fiduciary issue' had to be backed at 100 per cent in gold and silver.[1] Although the threat of a lack of metal was normally not directly present, central banks had in mind the dynamics which could develop when the economy got out of equilibrium (see, for example, Bloomfield 1959; Sayers 1976; Goodfriend 1988). To that extent, *economic dynamics triggered by wrong monetary policy*, that is, mainly by a wrong discount rate, were a permanent issue for central banks, and thus monetary policy already at that time went beyond the direct aim of ensuring sufficient gold reserves.

The relatively explicit focus of the Bank of England on controlling short-term market rates before 1914 seems in essence to have survived all the fundamental changes in monetary policy doctrine of the first half of the twentieth century (see, for example, Sayers 1976 for a detailed account). How could the Bank of England resist reserve position doctrine (RPD) while the Fed adopted it with little resistance (or even initiative) from 1920 on? Although the UK had gone through as bad an inflation during the war as the US, and both countries went through deflation in the 1920s to restore the gold standard at its pre-war parity, the two central banks in 1920 could not have been more different. The Bank of England had a well-elaborated money market technique in 1920, derived from a century of experience. It had a fair degree of independence from the government, and, unlike the Fed, was not decentralized (see, for example, Sayers 1976). Also, it completely lacked the transparency to which the Fed was committed since its very beginning, implying that it did not need to rationalize anything through theory: that is, it also did not need to rationalize failure through fallacious theory, as the Fed was

---

[1] Other central banks were subject to similar schemes. In the case of the Reichsbank, one third of notes needed to be covered by metal, and there was a maximum issuance beyond which the Reichsbank needed to pay a 5% yearly tax, which was supposed to be sufficient to deter the Reichsbank from doing so on a regular basis. Federal Reserve banknotes and deposits needed to be covered at 25% by gold.

tempted to do in the early 1920s. In this respect, it is amusing to consider the following excerpt from the Macmillan Committee minutes of 1929, which is also an example for the relationship between Keynes (who was member of this Committee) and the Bank (Sayers 1976: iii. 154–6; Governor Norman had shown so little interest in these hearings that he sent his deputy Harvey to most of them):

Committee member Gregory: 'I should like to ask you, Sir Ernest, whether you have ever considered the possibility of the Bank issuing an Annual Report on the lines of the Annual Report of the Federal Reserve Board, for instance?'

Deputy Governor Harvey: 'I confess I am sometimes nervous at the thought of publication unless it is historical. The question is whether, when it is merely historical it is of any particular value, or whether from the fact that it is issued from the central bank undue importance may be attributed to certain things that are stated, more importance than perhaps they merit.'

Committee member Keynes: 'Arising from Professor Gregory's questions, is it a practice of the Bank of England never to explain what its policy is?'

Harvey: 'Well, I think it has been our practice to leave our actions to explain our policy.'

Keynes: 'Or the reasons for its policy?'

Harvey: 'It is a dangerous thing to start to give reasons.'

Keynes: 'Or to defend itself against criticism?'

Harvey: 'As regards criticism, I am afraid, though the Committee may not all agree, we do not admit there is need for defence; to defend ourselves is somewhat akin to a lady starting to defend her virtue.'

The personality of Governor Montagu Norman (1919–44) was probably also relevant to keeping RPD outside the Bank. Himself an experienced banker and financial markets expert, and the ideal type of the conservative, independent central banker, he had little sympathy for academic ideas like RPD or their intellectual promoters like Keynes. According to Boyle (1967: 160), already in the early 1920s Montagu Norman looked 'askance at Keynes as a clever dilettante with an even greater potential for public mischief...' The attitude of Norman, and thus of the Bank of England, towards ideas such as RPD is probably well illustrated by Norman's famous reference in 1938, during a speech, to the Arab proverb 'dogs may bark, but the caravan moves on', causing renewed criticism of his supposedly arrogant attitude, 'the stereotyped villain of the thirties... the sinister, hard-faced banker' (Boyle 1967: 288–90). After Governor Norman quit in 1944, and the Bank of England was nationalized after the Second World War, it is still hard to find any references to RPD in the few publications of the Bank of England.

Still, Sayers (1953) is rather outspoken and affirmative on interest rate targeting when describing the Bank of England's policy of his time. Similarly, the Radcliffe Report (Radcliffe et al. 1959: 115) generally advocates an interest-rate steering policy. It argues for stable short-term rates, but adopts the perspective of the central bank as the government's bank, which today would be regarded as inappropriate since it contradicts central bank independence:

The Bank of England operates almost daily in the money market . . . The purpose of these operations is that of maintaining an orderly market . . . It is in the Government's interest, as the largest borrower in the money market, that the money market should be an orderly market; and that requires that the short-term rate of interest should not fluctuate wildly from day to day or week to week but should be reasonably stable.

Radcliffe et al. (1959: 121) is also the first to explicitly mention a lucid *probabilistic* concept of the reserve balance as determining the short-term level of interest rates, as quoted in Section 3.2.1.

Things don't seem to have fundamentally changed in the following decades either. The Bank of England (1982: 87) summarizes the practice of its money market operations in the 1960s and 1970s thus:

The Bank of England operated in the bill market at known, predetermined rates, set for a week at a time by a simple formula based on the rates realised at the regular Treasury bill tender the previous week . . . This was consistent with a monetary policy that usually aimed for periods of stability in short term rates, interrupted by discrete adjustments by the authorities . . .

Basically, the Bank of England operated through high-frequency fixed-rate open market operations and thereby steered short-term market rates around the fixed rate, which was the policy rate. Although the operations were open market operations, their difference from standing facilities was not too fundamental. At the beginning of the 1980s, the Bank of England (1982) felt the need to reform its instruments and to introduce the possibility of variable-rate tenders. The Bank of England changed money market procedures in 1980 in line with the implementation of new 'methods of controlling the money stock', that is, it followed at least to some extent the example of the US of October 1979. One measure adopted that differed from the US approach was to reduce reserve requirements (which in any case never included in the UK an averaging facility) to their present, very low, levels. More importantly, the idea was to reduce to some extent control of short-term interest rates, probably on the assumption that, if one aims more at controlling quantities, one cannot continue controlling rates in the same way. The Bank's

aim would be to keep very short-term interest rates within an unpublished band, set by the authorities by reference to the general monetary situation . . . Behind these proposals lay the desire to introduce a system which, while preserving the Bank's ability to influence short-term rates, would generally permit market forces a greater role in determining their structure. To allow such play for market forces, the system of pre-determined dealing rates had to be abandoned. (1982: 89)

But the Bank of England was apparently not willing to follow also the US *in practice*. It admitted that the changes in the money market procedures provided only 'a framework within which it might be possible to operate some form of monetary base control, although it is not currently being used so' (1982: 94). Eventually, the Bank of England (1982: 93–4) again explicitly defended interest rate control (for a detailed account of this episode in the UK, see Goodhart 1989, 2004):

The Bank cannot avoid involvement in money market operations, and so, either explicitly or implicitly in the determination of interest rates. The authorities have in fact chosen to continue to exercise substantial influence over very short-term interest rates as a positive element of economic policy. Nevertheless, the operations may be designed to influence the stock of money indirectly, through their effect on interest rates. Indeed, the desire to retain a fairly direct influence over interest rates rests on the view that these may have a significant effect on, for example, the demand for money, the demand for credit, and the exchange rate, with consequences for the development of the economy more generally.

One may conclude that the Bank of England basically retained its 'old doctrine' of interest rate steering, even when monetary aggregates were considered to be an intermediate target and the monetary base (or some reserves concept) the supposed operational target in many other countries. Goodhart's (1985, 1987) rather sceptical analysis of the option of monetary base control in general and in the case of the UK in particular also illustrates this position. As well, in following years the Bank of England's position apparently changed little, and Governor Leigh-Pemberton (1987: 356) notes that 'in practice, the authorities are largely dependent on a single instrument—the short term interest rate'. In Bank of England (1988: 4), some further smaller reforms are explained, of which the most noteworthy is the introduction of a more explicit borrowing facility, in which, however, 'the terms on which these facilities are available on a particular day are at the discretion of the bank'—which does not appear overly transparent. Again, in Bank of England (1997) changes are introduced that are 'evolutionary in nature'. Finally, Bank of

England (2002*b*) indicates a pragmatic, purely interest-rate oriented approach:

The main instrument of monetary policy is the short-term interest rate. Central banks have a variety of techniques for influencing interest rates but they are all designed, in one way or another, to affect the cost of money to the banking system. In general this is done by keeping the banking system short of money and then lending the banks the money they need at an interest rate which the central bank decides. In this country such influence is exercised through the Bank of England's daily operations in the money markets . . . Interest rates in the whole-sale money market will generally be closely influenced by those at which the Bank conducts its operations. The decision by the MPC on the rate of interest is announced immediately after the monthly meeting and any change will normally be reflected quickly in the money market in general, and in banks' base rates i.e. the rates they use to calculate their customers' rates.

The approach to interest rate targeting explained here–'keeping the banking system short of money and then lending the banks the money they need at an interest rate that the central bank decides'–confirms once more how similar in practice open market operations in the UK are to standing facilities. It is noteworthy that, despite the clear focus on interest rate steering, the Bank of England never explicitly committed to a target *market* rate or made clear at which specific maturity it would be aiming. With regard to the latter, according to Llewellyn and Tew (1988: 32) the Bank of England's main focus was on the one-week rate, since most of its operations would have such a maturity, and the overnight rate would be significantly more volatile. But even for the one-week rate they feel that control is far from perfect (1988: 36), which is in line with official statements (for example, Leigh-Pemberton 1987: 369).

One may conclude that the monetary policy implementation doctrine of the Bank of England was all in all rather constant over the twentieth century and was never too different from the present one, namely, that ultimately the short-term interest rate is the only sensible operational target. The main technique of the Bank of England in recent decades–conducting fixed-rate tenders at a policy rate in short-term paper (outright) or through repos–may be deemed to be not too different from a pure standing facilities approach, the remaining difference being that standing facilities imply 100 per cent allotment of bids and availability until the very end of the day.

The constancy with which the Bank of England remained with interest rate targeting probably results from its long history, rich experience, and thus intellectual maturity. At the same time, it could be remarked that the Bank of England's framework for monetary policy implementation still seems somewhat complex due to the various required operations each day (see Chapter 5). Furthermore, it may appear disappointing that, despite these frequent operations, the achieved degree of stability of short-term rates is somewhat worse than that in the US and the euro area (see Table 3.1). This seems to be the (possibly not too high) price to be paid for not establishing some kind of averaging system. Finally, the overall very positive assessment regarding implementation technique does not mean that the Bank of England was systematically successful in reaching its policy targets. In fact, its overall inflation performance in the second half of the twentieth century was rather poorer than the Fed's, and much poorer than the Bundesbank's.

7.2 THE FEDERAL RESERVE SYSTEM

The overall stability and consistency of the principles of monetary policy implementation applied by the Bank of England throughout the twentieth century cannot be found in the case of the US Fed. In particular, the Fed did not have the easiest start (in 1914), and it was put on a rather specific path in the domain of monetary policy implementation, which would have repercussions until the end of the twentieth century. Also, it tended to absorb and aim to put into practice new academic ideas, which appear, *ex post*, not always to have lived up to their promise. In line with its high standards of transparency, it aimed to present to the outside world a consistent story of its academically inspired theories of monetary policy implementation. It thereby often committed to approaches that from today's perspective appear surprising, and it needed years and even decades to get rid of those ideas while minimizing the associated loss of credibility. The following structure follows Meulendyke (1998).

7.2.1 *Early years (1914–23): failure to hike discount rates during the war and beginning of non-price regulation of access to the discount window*

This[2] episode is treated in more detail in Chapter 4. The discount window was at that time the dominant instrument, with banks borrowing, at least at first, in a structural way. The first government paper was bought by the Fed as early as 1914, but the amounts remained moderate. From 1917 onwards, the Treasury asked the Fed to buy paper as part of the war

---

[2] More details on the earlier history of US monetary policy implementation may be found in Meulendyke (1998) and in Warburg (1930), Chandler (1958), and Meltzer (2003).

financing effort, and Treasury bills also became the main paper discounted with the Fed (also due to a preferential, that is, lower, discount rate). Despite the extensive experience of, for example, the Bank of England, the role of the discount rate was apparently underestimated, and the designers of the Federal Reserve System had not even seen the necessity to make it unambiguously clear that decisions with regard to the discount rate would be taken homogeneously across all Federal Reserve District Banks.

As, for example, Keynes (1930: 210) explained, the Fed felt (and Keynes seemed to agree) that extensive use of the discount window was an important reason for the inflation of 1916–20. Today, we would instead simply conclude that the Federal Reserve System did not hike discount rates aggressively enough, due to excessive government influence and too decentralized decision-making.

In part, the Fed's focus on excessive borrowing may have been, at least at the beginning, more of a (post-)war time lie than a misunderstanding, as the Fed had good reasons in the early 1920s to prefer denying responsibility for the war inflation (triggered by the failure to hike rates) and the post-war deflation (triggered by the tightening of monetary policy from November 1919 onwards). Even Friedman and Schwartz (1963: 250), who are far from favouring short-term interest rates as an operational target of monetary policy, are astonished by the fact that, for instance, in the Board of Governors' *Annual Report* for 1921 explicit discussion of the Fed's aggressive hiking of interest rates after November 1919 and the implied deflation and recession is avoided:

It is hard to escape the conclusion that . . . this . . . is designed to turn aside criticism without either meeting them or making explicit misstatements . . . For example, in the whole nine-page section, neither the words 'discount rate' nor any synonyms occurs . . . As implied by the absence of the words discount rate, nothing at all is said in the discussion of fundamental principles about the criteria for discount rates or about the effect of the level of discount rates on the total level of Federal Reserve Credit . . . It is a natural human tendency to take credit for good outcomes and seek to avoid the blame for bad.

After this denial of previously undisputed monetary policy logic, the Fed for some reason did not manage to return to normality with regard to its operational target for seventy years. In the early 1920s, we find Fed officials more and more rationalizing why interest rates are secondary, and quantities are more relevant as an operational target.

Instead, the Fed started to develop 'a series of gadgets and conventions' (Keynes 1930: 213) to limit discount window borrowing through non-price means. The Fed got rid of these only in January 2003. Although the first open market operations in the early 1920s were still mainly regarded as a source of revenue, it was felt that they affected money market conditions and hence potentially the economy. To coordinate the operations of the Federal Reserve Banks, the Open Market Investment Committee (OMIC), the first predecessor of the FOMC, was established in 1923.

The economic impact of the Fed's excessively loose monetary policy in its first years was substantial: while the wholesale price index increased by 150 per cent from 1914 to 1920, it declined in the following phase of restrictive policy by around 35 per cent within two years, the latter development being associated with a decline in real GDP of more than 20 per cent (see, for example, Metzler 2003).

7.2.2   1924–1933: 'Discovering' open market operations

The OMIC began using open market operations as a monetary policy tool during the recession of 1924. The OMIC gauged whether credit conditions were tight or easy by watching short-term market interest rates and the amount of borrowing from the discount window (Meulendyke 1998: 26). The joint impact of the discount rate and the amount of discount borrowing on short-term market interest rates was perceived, but it was not considered that the money market rate was a sufficient statistic of the monetary policy stance. Quantities and rates were apparently seen as each independently having some relevance, whereas the idea of the money multiplier discovered by Phillips (1920) was already perceived as relevant in the early 1920s. For instance, the New York Fed's Governor Harrison argued in 1928 for a sharp *increase* of the discount rate, tempered by open market *purchases* (Meulendyke 1998: 28). Still, as Riefler (1930: 28) suggested, the staff of the New York Fed had a relatively clear idea that what was done was in some way steering interest rates, through open market operations in the short term and through discount rate changes in the medium term.

In 1930, the OMIC was replaced by the Open Market Policy Conference (OMPC), reflecting the fact that open market operations had definitely become a tool of *policy* rather than *investment*. The discount rate, borrowed reserves, and market rates remained the measure of the monetary policy stance in the 1930s, when reserve position doctrine developed. The Fed lowered the discount rate in several steps until 1931, but at a pace that may have lagged behind the economic and monetary contraction. Still, easing was also achieved through outright purchases of securities, and 'the low level of indebtedness at the reserve banks was an influence in the direction of easier money conditions . . . the (money) rates in the latter part of 1930 were lower than at any other time during the 12-years period covered' (Board of Governors' *Annual Report* for 1930: 3). In April 1932, the Fed bought outright securities for $500 million, following pressure of the Hoover Administration to stimulate the economy. Discount lending went down and excess reserves started to build up.

7.2.3   *1933–1951: Short-term market rates close to zero due to excess reserves and low discount rates*

In 1935 the FOMC replaced the OMPC. Easy policies were pursued, and discount rates cut to 1 per cent. Huge excess reserves were accumulated also due to massive inflows of gold, which the Treasury made liquid by issuing gold certificates to the Fed. The Fed did not reabsorb the reserves created thereby. Due to the implied excess reserves, the discount rate almost always exceeded market rates and recourse to the discount window remained marginal throughout the second half of the 1930s. Variations in excess reserves were permitted to absorb the swings in autonomous factors, that is, open market operations were not used for compensating autonomous factor changes (see, for example, Board of Governors' *Annual Report* for 1935: 2). Towards the end of the 1930s and the outbreak of war in Europe, the focus of policy turned to 'maintaining orderly conditions in the Government securities market' (*Annual Report* for 1940: 3). A steering of reserve market conditions through open market operations was not really required since banks were in any case holding huge excess reserves and market rates for reserves were therefore close to zero (*Annual Report* for 1940: 3):

Bank reserves and bank deposits continued to increase in 1940, again establishing new high records. The principal factor in the increase was the inflow of gold from abroad after the war entered a new, more active phase in the spring of the year . . . By the end of the year the banks had more idle reserves than at any previous time and more than sufficient to meet all probable credit needs . . . they totalled $14 billion of which nearly half was in excess of legal requirements.

The increase of reserves was reported as the result of an autonomous liquidity factor move, and there was no discussion about the absorption of these inflows through open market operations. However, the money multiplier logic and some reserves position doctrine were apparently at the back of the governors' minds since excess reserves were viewed in connection to possible credit needs. As it is still the case today, the 'record of policy action' was subdivided between the Board of Governors (deciding on the discount rate) and the FOMC (deciding on open market operations and today on the federal funds target rate). Since discount rates remained unchanged in the year, little on monetary policy decisions was to be reported on the Board's side. The record of the FOMC policy actions was still very short compared with later annual reports. The following 'resolution' was adopted at the meeting of 20 March 1940:

That the executive committee be directed until otherwise directed by the FOMC to arrange for such transactions for the system open market account . . . as in its judgement from time to time may be necessary for the purpose of exercising an influence towards maintaining orderly market conditions; provided that the aggregate amount of securities held in the account at the close of this date shall not be increased or decreased by more than $500,000,000.

In the 1940s, monetary conditions remained easy, and the pegging of rates of Treasury bills and bonds remained the major direct objective of the Fed (imposed upon it by the Treasury).

7.2.4   *1951–1969: Resumption of active monetary policy and free reserves targeting*

In the 1950s, inflation triggered by the Korean war convinced the FOMC that the pegged rates were too low. In March 1951, an 'Accord' was reached with the Treasury which returned to the Fed its freedom over monetary policy functions. According to Meulendyke (1998: 36), FOMC members at that time believed that interest rates played an important role in the economy, but felt that it would be unwise to establish interest rate targets even for the short end of the money market yield curve, as this could increase the difficulty of making a break with the strict pegging of rates in the 1940s. Short-run policy focused on free reserves (see Chapter 2). At the conclusion of each meeting, the FOMC created a written directive for the trading desk at the New York Fed. It was deliberately non-specific, avoiding any hint that interest rates should be targeted. The Board of Governors' *Annual Report* for 1954, for example, reflects the return of monetary policy. Open market operations, discount window borrowing, and reserve requirement changes were presented as the three pillars of monetary policy implementation which are used in a coordinated way. During most of 1954, the Fed's policy was directed towards 'actively maintaining a condition of ease in the money market'. Discount rates, borrowing needs, and required reserves were reduced in the course of the year (1954: 6–7):

Open market operations. In January and February 1954, the Federal Reserve made open market sales to absorb only in part the redundancy of bank reserves that appears at that season. Receding credit demands in these and early spring months also contributed to easier bank reserve positions . . . Beginning of September, open market operations were geared to the maintenance of an easy member bank reserve position during the fall phase of bank credit and monetary expansion.

Changes in discount rate. During the first half of February, 1954, the discount rate was reduced from 2 to $1^3/_4$ per cent at all Federal Reserve Banks. A second reduction was made by the Reserve Banks during the period April 14–May 21, when this rate was changed to $1^1/_2$ per cent. In both instances, the actions were designed to bring the discount rate into closer alignment with short-term market rates as well as to make it less expensive for individual member banks to make temporary adjustments in their reserve positions by borrowing at the Federal Reserve Banks.

Change in reserve requirements. On June 21, 1954 the Board announced a program to reduce member bank reserve requirements . . . it included a reduction of 1 percentage point on time deposits at all member banks, a reduction of 2 percentage points on net demand deposits at central reserve city banks, and a reduction of 1 percentage point on net demand deposits at reserve city and country banks. The reductions in reserve requirements, which released about 1.6 billion dollars of reserve funds, were made in anticipation of bank reserve needs over the fall. They took into account probable expansion of financing requirements for private activities, including seasonal needs for marketing crops . . .

Noteworthy from today's perspective is the mention of seasonality on several occasions. Today, any seasonality in the needs for refinancing would naturally be accommodated by open market operations such that it would not affect reserve conditions, and it would not even be mentioned in an account of policy. Furthermore, the lowering of the discount rate is once more motivated by the low level of market rates, thus taking the reverse causation perspective (see Chapter 4). This failure to take explicit responsibility for short-term market rates is difficult to understand from today's perspective, especially since, for example, the contemporaneous UK Radcliffe Report (Radcliffe et al. 1959) reveals a more modern understanding on the other side of the Atlantic. Reserve requirements are apparently also used as an instrument contributing to smooth seasonal fluctuations of autonomous factors. This seems, again from today's perspective, inappropriate since changing non-remunerated reserve requirements does more than just change the demand for reserves: it also affects the cost of money creation by banks. As well, the number of different reserve base categories seems to complicate matters. Overall, the impression is that US monetary policy implementation in the mid-1950s was not really lean and parsimonious, but employed more instruments than necessary, with the side-effect of creating complexity and triggering potentially unintended macroeconomic impulses.

The 1954 edition of the *Purposes and Functions* booklet of the Board of Governors reflects the predominance of the idea of the money market multiplier and reserve position doctrine, although there is a short reference to the interest rate side (see Board of Governors 1954: 38–9, quoted in Section 5.2). There is no reference to any kind of expectations theory of interest rates and to the fact that the central bank can influence through short-term money market rates the longer-term rates relevant to key economic decisions in the private sector.

While the level of the discount rate was fixed by the Board of Governors, the money market desk at the New York Fed, as instructed by the FOMC, needed to focus on reserve market conditions only. A high level of free reserves meant an easy policy, facilitating more loans and investments, while low or negative free reserves were expected to mean contraction of money and credit. The separation of decision-making powers between the FOMC, the Board of Governors, and the New York Fed, and the lack of transparency of the discount rate due to the non-price disincentives against its use, may have been two major reasons for the highlighting of quantities and the low profile given to short-term interest rates.

How can one present the idea of 'free reserves targeting' in the simple one-day model of Chapter 3 (Fig. 3.3)? Recall that free reserves were defined in Chapter 2 as the difference between excess reserves (which are themselves equal to the difference between actual reserves and required reserves, that is $XSR = R - RR$) and borrowed reserves, that is $FR = XSR - B$. With the use of the Fed's balance sheet identity $M + B = A + RR + XSR$, free reserves may also be written as $FR = M - A - RR$. The following two cases may be distinguished: $M - A \geq RR \Rightarrow (B = 0, \quad FR = XSR = M - A - RR); \quad M - A < RR \Rightarrow (B = -(M - A) + RR > 0, XSR = 0, FR = -B = M - A - RR)$.

Targeting free reserves thus means, according to the model of Chapter 3, choosing an open market operations volume M such that the following equation holds, in which FR^* is the free reserves target.

$$\int_{-\infty}^{+\infty} (M - x - RR) f_{(A)}(x) dx = FR^* \tag{7.1}$$

For each single realization of A, the target is missed, but one can choose M in a way that, in expected terms and *ex post* on average (for example, over a quarter), the free reserves target is met. If the central bank takes this approach seriously and does not use it only as a smoke-screen, there would be no short-term target interest rate, and the quantitative target would somehow be derived from something not related to interest rates. If in contrast we suspect that using quantitative targets was more a smokescreen, and that in fact central banks always had an interest rate in mind, the specification of the target simply follows from what the interest rate target implies in terms of the free reserves target. Consider how the central bank needs to react to two different exogenous changes (the same exercise was done in Section 3.4 for interest rate targeting in the symmetric corridor world).

1. *Change of the level of the operational target.* If the borrowing facility rate remains unchanged, changes of quantitative targets will imply that market rates will change, but this should not be relevant to a central bank that takes quantitative operational targets seriously. If, alternatively, the central bank does in fact care about short-term interest rates (that is, the smokescreen interpretation of free reserves targeting holds), a change in the target interest rate needs to be reflected in a change in the quantitative target—at least if the borrowing facility rate remains constant. There is also an alternative way to adjust the borrowing facility rate alone so as to implement changes in the target interest rate without changing the quantitative target. For instance, assume that the central bank's internal target interest rate is lowered from 4 per cent to 3.5 per cent, and that the central bank wishes to keep its free reserves target (its smokescreen) unchanged. In this case, it could lower the full price of the borrowing facility rate from, say, 5 per cent to 4.375 per cent, and the new interest rate target is achieved without changing any of the quantities. Since in the US until 2002 the full borrowing price included substantial intangible elements (moral suasion and so forth), the Fed could often achieve a lowering of the effective rate by lowering the *intangible* costs of using the discount window. Then, the central bank could engineer the desired decline in market rates without sending any clear interest rate signal and without changing its free reserves target, and may succeed in convincing the public that 'the market' was responsible for the fall in market rates.

2. *Change of the probability distribution of autonomous factors.* Changes of $E(A)$ have to be offset mechanically by parallel shifts of M. Any change of second- or higher-order moments of the probability distribution of autonomous factors requires an adaptation of M to keep the quantitative target unchanged. Any change of M that keeps the borrowing target constant also keeps interest rates unchanged. To that extent, an observer cannot tell whether a central bank which adjusts its open market operations due to changes of the probability distribution of autonomous factors has a quantitative target or an interest rate target.

The federal funds rate started to attract somewhat more attention once again during the 1960s, although it could not yet gain the status of an operational target. In 1961, the 'bills only' doctrine, according to which open market operations should consist only of outright purchases (and sales) of *short-term* paper, was abandoned after ten years, and some yield curve control experience was sought through outright open market operations in longer maturities. During the 1960s, the Fed played on the entire keyboard of monetary policy instruments, which, again, appeared excessively complex from today's perspective. Also, the importance of measures of *direct* control was striking.[3]

According to Anderson (1969: 69), another Fed staff member, there were in the 1960s as many as eight measures of money market conditions, namely, 'the Treasury bill rate, free reserve of all member banks, the basic reserve deficiency at eight New York money market banks, the basic reserve deficiency at 38 money market banks outside New York, member banks' borrowing from the Federal Reserve, United States government security dealer borrowings, the federal funds rate, and the Federal Reserve discount rate.' Today, one would judge this mixture of various rates and quantities to be redundant and probably resulting in irrelevant and contradictory signals. Instead, one would suggest, in line with the model presented in Chapter 3, concentrating on the overnight interest rate (that is, the federal funds rate), which appears to be a sufficient measure of the monetary policy stance.[4]

Practice changed little until 1970, when policy actions were again, from today's perspective, of a baroque variety, especially with regard to measures of direct control (see, for example, the Board of Governors' *Annual Report* for 1970).

---

[3] For instance, in January–March 1962 the Fed reduced its holdings of securities by $1.6 billion, but still by so little that the use of the discount window dropped from an average of $900 million in December 1961 to $635 million in March 1962. In June it reduced discount rates from 4% to 3.5% 'to reduce the cost of borrowed reserves for member banks and to bring the discount rate closer to market interest rates'. In the domain of direct credit controls, in July it reduced margin requirements on loans for purchasing or carrying listed securities from 90% to 70% of market values for securities 'in recognition of decline in volume of stock market credit outstanding and lessened danger of excessive speculative activity in the market'. In August, it authorized member banks to 'count about $500 million of their vault cash as required reserves' and 'reduced reserve requirements against net demand deposits at central reserve city banks from 18 to $17\frac{1}{2}$ per cent ... thereby releasing about $125 million of reserves', with the aim 'to provide mainly for seasonal needs for reserve funds, and to implement 1959 legislation directed in part toward equalization of reserve requirements of central reserve and reserve city banks' (from the 1962 *Annual Report* of the Board of Governors of the Federal Reserve System).

[4] See also Guttentag (1966) for a detailed discussion of the money market strategy of the Fed in the early 1960s. This article also contains further literature on this period. A critical assessment from the monetarist point of view is Brunner and Meltzer (1964).

7.2.5   1970–1979: Monetary aggregates as intermediate and the federal funds rate as operational target

In 1970, the Fed officially adopted monetary aggregates targeting as its macroeconomic strategy. From 1970 to October 1979, the framework used by the FOMC for guiding the conduct of open market operations generally included setting a monetary objective and making the federal funds rate move gradually up or down if money was exceeding or falling short of the objective. The federal funds rate became the primary guide and a federal funds *target* rate was defined.[5] Meulendyke (1998) argues that it was an increasingly liquid federal funds market that made the federal funds rate indeed a reliable indicator, but doubts arise on whether short-term rates could really not be measured accurately enough in preceding decades. The FOMC selected growth targets mainly for M1, and the staff estimated the federal funds rate that would achieve desired money growth. As Meek and Thunberg (1971: 83) note, 'one is left with the problem of deciding whether the aggregates are departing significantly from their desired path. Then, there is the question of how much money market conditions are to be changed in an effort to nudge the aggregates back in the desired direction'. Decisions to change the funds target rate were revealed through reverse open market operations, for example, by operations changing reserve market conditions when funds were still trading at the previous target rate. The signals were noted immediately, but it sometimes took market participants some days to extract the size of the target rate change. Over time, the Fed apparently became increasingly keen to prevent even minor deviations of the funds rate from the target. It therefore increased the frequency of its reverse operations instead of conducting outright operations which by definition lack a short-term interest rate signal and hence influence short-term interest rates only via liquidity conditions. According to interpretations of the Fed New York's operations published in the *Wall Street Journal* during the 1970s (see Cook and Hahn 1989: 34–50), the Fed set an informal narrow corridor of, for example, 50 basis points for the federal funds rate, and whenever market rates tended to go through the ceiling or the

---

[5] According to Benjamin M. Friedman (2000: 44), who describes in detail the choice of operational targets in the US in the period 1968–2000, the FOMC had already moved to targeting interest rates around 1968. He notes a detour in monetary policy implementation in the last third of the twentieth century: 'When Frank Morris (in 1968) first joined the FOMC, the Federal Reserve, like most central banks at that time, made monetary policy by setting interest rates. The same is once again true today. In retrospect, much of the intervening experience proved to be a historical detour.' In fact, the detour lasted a total of over eighty years, with a smaller detour within the detour in the last third of the century.

floor, repo operations were conducted at these informal corridor rates. This confirms once again the similarity between standing facilities and reverse open market operations.

Between 1972 and 1976, another attempt was actually made with a quantitative measure as an *operational* target complementing the federal funds rate, partially anticipating the 1979–82 experiment. Short-run guidelines with regard to *reserves on private deposits* (a subset of total required reserves) were formulated in 1972. The FOMC set two-month growth rates for reserves on private deposits consistent with the desired M1 growth, and instructed the trading desk to alter reserve provision in such a way as to achieve the targets. However, fearing that this would raise the federal funds volatility, the FOMC also constrained the federal funds rate. In fact, the relatively narrow federal funds rate limits eventually dominated, and the quantitative targets were often missed. In 1973, reserves on private deposits were changed from an operational to an intermediate target, taking its place with M1. It was dropped as an indicator in 1976 (see Meulendyke 1998).

Apart from this episode, during the 1970s the Fed was rather clear in using the federal funds rate as only an *operational* target to achieve monetary growth as an *intermediate* target. The following paragraph from Board of Governors' *Annual Report* for 1975 illustrates this approach (p. 171):

Subsequent to the meeting, on 5 February, the available data suggested that in January M1 had declined sharply and that growth in M2 had been modest. Growth rates for the January–February period appeared to be well below the lower limits of the ranges of tolerance specified by the Committee ... The System Account Manager currently was endeavouring to supply reserves at a rate to be consistent with a Federal funds rate of 6½%, the lower limit of the range of tolerance that had been specified by the Committee. On February 5 a majority of the members concurred in the Chairman's recommendation that, in light of those developments and on the reduction in discount rates effective that day, the lower limit of the funds rate constraint to be reduced to 6¼%.

Interestingly, the switch to short-term interest rates as the operational target around 1970 had no effect on the way the Fed presented its policy in the September 1974 edition of its *Purposes and Functions* brochure (Board of Governors 1974). Indeed, the section on the financial effects of policy action begins little differently from the 1954 edition and again contains concrete multiplier examples of bank 'balance sheet changes induced by open market operations'. It is indeed astonishing that the Fed's 1974 brochure simply did not mention that the Fed was implementing a federal funds rate target in its day-to-day policy.

7.2.6   *1979–1982: Short-term monetary control and
        non-borrowed reserves as operational target*

In October 1979, Paul Volcker became chairman of the Board of
Governors. He believed that inflation, which stood at two-digit levels
during most of the 1970s, needed to be stopped. The Fed concluded that
the time was ripe for taking monetary control seriously in day-to-day
monetary policy implementation by substituting interest-rate targeting
with a more quantitative target, which this time was defined as *non-
borrowed reserves*, that is, reserves held by banks minus the recourse
to the discount window, $R - B$, which, according to the Fed's balance
sheet identity $M + B = A + R$, is equivalent to $M - A$ (see Chapter 2). In
addition to the balance sheet identity the two constraints $B > 0$ and
$R \geq RR$ need to be respected. Now, one may again distinguish two cases:
$M - A \geq RR \Rightarrow (B = 0, \; NBR = R = M - A)$ and $M - A < RR \Rightarrow$
$(B = RR - (M - A), \; NBR = RR - B = M - A)$. Eventually, in both non-
borrowed reserves are equal to the difference between open market operations and autonomous factors. According to the logic of the aggregate
liquidity management model and the one-day maintenance period as specified by Fig. 3.3, targeting non-borrowed reserves thus means choosing in
the following equation the open market operations volume M, such that
the left-hand side corresponds to the non-borrowed reserves target NBR.*

$$\int_{-\infty}^{\infty} (M - x) f_{(A)}(x) dx = NBR^* \tag{7.2}$$

Again, the target will be missed for each single realization of A but,
on average, non-borrowed reserves will converge on the target when the
calculation period expands.

The Fed began to target reserve measures derived from desired three-
month growth rates of M1. For the federal funds rate, a target corridor
of around 5 percentage points was set. In practice, the FOMC first chose
the M1 target for the calendar quarter and asked staff to estimate
consistent levels of total reserves, which was challenging due to the
different reserve ratios on different types of deposits. From the total
reserve target, the trading desk derived the non-borrowed reserve target
by subtracting a level of borrowed reserves that had been indicated by
the FOMC.[6] The Board of Governors staff made estimates of consistent

---

[6] See Axilrod and Lindsey (1981) for a more detailed official motivation for the 1979–82
approach. Goodfriend (1983) and Van Hoose (1986) model the implications of the non-borrowed
reserves targeting procedure on discount window borrowing, without, however, adopting the balance
sheet identity-based approach suggested in Chapter 2. Santomero (1983) interprets the non-
borrowed reserves targeting procedure in the context of Poole (1970).

combinations of borrowed reserves and money growth for the given discount rate. Since lagged reserves accounting prevailed at that time, the reserves could not in fact be controlled immediately. An increase in money above the target meant, with a lag, reserves going beyond target, and, in the event that the Desk was unwilling to provide the non-borrowed reserves, an increase in discount window lending (and hence in the federal funds rate). One could also interpret this as a triumph of *rules over discretion*: instead of allowing the FOMC and the market desk to look at money in different definitions and all kinds of other indicators, and to think for itself about the appropriate conclusions, a clear rule was defined according to which in theory the implementation of operational actions followed automatically from the observation of information variables. For instance, the domestic policy directive formulated by the FOMC and effective on 1 January 1980 specified:

... the FOMC seeks to foster monetary and financial conditions that will resist inflationary pressures while encouraging moderate economic expansion ... The Committee agreed that these objectives would be furthered by growth of M1, M2, and M3 within ranges of $1\frac{1}{2}$ to $4\frac{1}{2}\%$, 5–8%, and 6–9%, respectively ... In the short run, the Committee seeks to restrain expansion of reserve aggregates to a pace consistent with decelerating in growth of M1, M2 and M3 to rates that would hold growth of these monetary aggregates ... within the Committee's longer run ranges, provided that in the period before the next regular meeting the weekly average federal funds rate remains within a range of $1\frac{1}{2}$ to $15\frac{1}{2}\%$.

It is noteworthy that even at that time the Fed felt the need to complement quantitative operational targets with a corridor for the federal funds rate. Furthermore, discretion was never eliminated, and the FOMC often changed the mechanism and gave leeway to the Desk to make adjustments (see also Cook 1989). To reduce over-weighting of weekly developments, the targets were formulated as averages for the inter-meeting periods (the FOMC started to meet eight times a year in 1981), which had the drawback that towards the end of this period very large adjustments were often needed. Again, discretion finally prevailed to avoid the possibility that taking quantitative rules too seriously would create excessive volatility of short-term rates. Market participants, of course, closely observed the behaviour of M1 in order to anticipate future moves of the federal funds rate. Although the procedure was expected to create more interest rate volatility, the actual result was a disappointment, especially since it increased not only federal funds volatility but apparently even that of monetary aggregates. In 1980, the Monetary Control Act, with its changes to the reserve requirement system and subsequent deregulatory measures, triggered further changes in the evolution of M1 and M2, and contributed in 1982/3 to a weakening of the relationship between these monetary aggregates and economic activity and prices. This was taken as a good excuse for again changing operating procedures in 1983.

Also, the transcripts of the FOMC meetings of that period, which can be found on the Board of Governors' website, help to understand why the approach was abandoned after such a relatively short period of time: it was overly complex in its formulation of various operational and intermediate targets. According to Strongin (1995: 475): 'Non-borrowed reserves targeting was the most complicated of the reserves operating procedures that the Federal Reserve has ever used and it lasted the shortest length of time . . . Considerable debate within the Federal Reserve system about how these procedures actually worked is still going on'. For instance, in the transcript of the FOMC meeting of 31 March 1981, which is the oldest one made available on the Board's website, Volcker needs to admit on four occasions that he is 'confused' or 'lost', and FOMC members Solomon, Corrigan, Black, and Ford admit at some stage to being 'confused' about what they are discussing. So remains the reader of these transcripts.

7.2.7   1983–1989: borrowed reserves as operational targets

The short-term monetary control experiment ended with two changes: first, discretion was again restored more officially; second, the non-borrowed reserves target was replaced with a *borrowed* reserves target, that is, a target of the recourse to the discount window *(B)*. One obtains $B > 0$ whenever $M - A < RR$; thus, with a borrowed reserves target of B^*, one needs to choose the open market operations volume M such that:

$$\int_{M-RR}^{+\infty} (x + RR - M) f_{(A)}(x) dx = B^* \tag{7.3}$$

Monetary aggregates were kept as the main information variable, but attempts were no longer made to translate them mechanically into operations. In any case, as the evolution of the domestic policy directive suggests, the move from the 1979–82 procedure, via borrowed reserves targeting, back to pure interest rate targeting was a gradual process, probably as it was thought to be detrimental to the Fed's credibility completely to change procedures from one day to the next after presenting them originally as a breakthrough and defending them against criticism.[7]

---

[7] For instance, the Domestic Policy Directive on 1 January 1985 in effect revealed how important monetary aggregates were still supposed to be also in the short run, and how little change there had been, at least officially, since 1980: 'In the implementation of policy in the short run, the Committee

The volatility of the federal funds rate declined again from the 1979–82 level.[8] Still, policy remained less transparent than it would have been under explicit federal funds targeting. One problem with a borrowed reserves target in the US context was that the full costs of the use of the discount window changed over time in a non-transparent way. For instance, because of variations in the fragility of the banking system the perceived damage to reputation incurred by having recourse to the discount window varied. Also, because access limits were defined as averages over a certain period of time, substantial collective recourse at any one time influenced restrictions in the future. Therefore, the borrowed reserves target needed to be adjusted regularly if the federal funds rate was supposed to stay within a constant spread to the discount rate. Hence, from 1988 on the FOMC again gave primary importance to the federal funds rate, without, however, asking the Desk to manage it as closely as in the 1970s (see also Cosimo and Sheehan 1994).

Evidence of the dissolution of a systematic relationship between discount window borrowing and the spread is provided by Pearce (1993: 567), who, however, also seems to mainly have a reversed causation in mind. In view of the model presented in Chapter 3, it is in any case not surprising that the relationship between the spread and borrowing is not stable from year to year. Indeed, any change in the probability distribution of autonomous factor shocks is sufficient to destabilize this relationship.

7.2.8   The 1990s: further clarification of federal funds targeting

Federal funds rate targeting again became increasingly explicit and unambiguous during the 1990s. Nevertheless, the official Fed view on monetary policy implementation, as revealed in Board of Governors (1994: 22–3), seemed to reflect still a few residuals from the old view. For

---

seeks to reduce pressures on reserves positions consistent with growth of M1, M2, M3 at annual rates of around 7, 9, and 9% respectively, during the period from November to March ... The Chairman may call for Committee consultation if it appears to the Manager of Domestic Operations that pursuit of the monetary objectives and related reserve paths during the period before the next meeting is likely to be associated with a federal funds rate persistently outside a range of 6 to 10%' (*Annual Report* for 1985).

[8] See also, for instance, D. Thornton (1986, 1988). His model, however, proceeds from the reversed causality assumption (from the spread between market and discount rates to the use of the discount window). See also, for example, Cosimo and Sheehan (1994), for which the same applies. Dotsey (1989) also examines the borrowed reserves targeting procedure, and emphasizes that it would not necessarily be equivalent to interest rate targeting. He argues that a borrowed reserves targeting procedure could be more efficient than interest rate targeting, but that total reserve targeting would be even better.

instance, the idea from the 1979–82 period that an increase in monetary aggregates and hence in required reserves can set self-correcting pressures in motion is repeated.[9] On the other hand, the description of the starting point of the transmission mechanism already suggests that the new view is coming to the forefront: 'As the preceding discussion illustrates, monetary policy works through the market for reserves and involves the federal funds rate. A change in the reserves market will trigger a chain of events that affect other short-term interest rates, foreign exchange rates, long-term interest rates, the amount of money and credit in the economy, and levels of employment, output, and prices.' In contrast, there was no willingness on the part of the Fed to accept that the 1979–82 episode was discontinued on the grounds of disappointing results. Instead, as the following paragraph reveals, the Fed argued that optimal operating procedures depended on macroeconomic circumstances and strategies, as well as on financial market structures (Board of Governors 1994: 35):

In general, no one approach to implementing monetary policy is likely to be satisfactory under all economic and financial circumstances. The actual approach has been adapted at various times in light of different considerations, such as the need to combat inflation, the desire to encourage sustainable economic growth, uncertainties related to institutional change, and evident shifts in the public's attitudes toward the use of money. When economic and financial conditions warrant close control of a monetary aggregate, more emphasis may be placed on guiding open market operations by a fairly strict targeting of reserves. In other circumstances, a more flexible approach to managing reserves may be required.

From 1994/5 on, the federal funds target rate was announced immediately via press release after FOMC meetings to avoid interest rate intentions having to be inferred from operations, as was the case in the 1970s (also see the signal extraction model in Chapter 3). Still, once again things moved only gradually to become fully consistent with the new approach. For instance, in 1997 the Domestic Policy Directive to the Market Desk of the Fed New York still was not outspoken on the federal funds target and, following tradition, did not systematically separate

[9] 'Equilibrium exists in the reserves market when the demand for required and excess reserves equals the supply of borrowed plus non-borrowed reserves. Should the demand for reserves rise—say, because of a rise in checking account deposits—a disequilibrium will occur, and upward pressure on the federal funds rate will emerge. Equilibrium may be restored by open market operations to supply the added reserves, in which case the federal funds rate will be unchanged. It may also be restored as the supply of reserves increases through greater borrowing from the discount window; in this case, interest rates would tend to rise, and over time the demand for reserves would contract as reserve market pressures are translated, through the actions of banks and their depositors, into lower deposit levels and smaller required reserves' (Board of Governors 1994: 23).

elements of macroeconomic analysis, intermediate targets, and operational targets.[10] It was only in 2000 that the Domestic Policy Directive became explicit on the federal funds target rate and that the macroeconomic analysis was systematically presented *before* the conclusions on the appropriate federal funds rate.

Three more very recent developments reveal how much the Fed has now effectively abandoned most of the doctrines that so complicated its monetary policy implementation from the 1920s until nearly the end of the century. First, it again abandoned *contemporaneous* reserve accounting in 1998. Second, since July 1999 it has systematically aligned its federal funds target rate and its discount rate, maintaining a stable spread of 50 basis points (the discount rate being 50 basis points below the federal funds target; already since February 1994, the spread had never been other than 25, 50, or 75 basis points). This reveals that, eventually, only the federal funds target rate matters in terms of monetary policy stance, and that the spread to the discount rate is more a technical matter, such that there is no reason to change it when the stance changes. Third, the Fed fundamentally modernized its discount window at the end of 2002, as described in Chapter 4. One may note that all key changes implemented by the Fed to modernize its operational framework took place during the era of Alan Greenspan, who became Chairman of the Federal Reserve in 1987.

The main difference between today's Fed system and the symmetric corridor approach used by, for instance, the Bank of England, the ECB, and a number of other central banks is the absence of a deposit facility, and thus the *asymmetry* of the corridor with which the Fed operates. What does that mean in practice? Now, equation (3.2) takes, in the case of the simple one-period model presented in Fig. 3.3, the following form if one normalizes the spread $i_B - i^*$ to one (as it is the case since January 2003 in the US):

$$i = i_B P(\text{'short'}) = (i^* + 1)P(\text{'short'}) = (i^* + 1)\int_{-\infty}^{0} f_{(M-A)}(x)dx \qquad (7.4)$$

Hence, $P(\text{'short'}) = i^*/(1 + i^*)$. If, for instance, the target rate is initially 5 per cent, then P('short') needs to be 5/6. Consider now again how the central bank needs to react to two typical exogenous changes.

---

[10] 'In the implementation of policy for the immediate future, the Committee seeks to maintain the existing degree of pressure on reserve positions. In the context of the Committee's long-run objectives for price stability and sustainable economic growth . . . somewhat greater reserve restraint might be acceptable in the inter-meeting period. The contemplated reserve conditions are expected to be consistent with some moderation in the expansion of M2 and M3 over coming months' (Board of Governors' *Annual Report* for 1997: 95).

1. *Change of the target rate.* If the target rate declines, P('short') needs to decrease and eventually needs to reach zero when the target rate reaches zero. This is basically what was observed during the 1930s in the US (and more recently in Japan) when the banks accumulated huge excess reserves and market rates were close to zero. If the target rate and the borrowing facility rate increase, the reverse holds, and if the target rate reaches very high values, P('short') needs to approach 1. Thus, even if the target rate and the borrowing facility rate are moved strictly in parallel, the average recourse to the borrowing facility needs to increase when the interest rate target increases, everything else equal. The implications of the changes of i^* for the appropriate allotment volume M depends in fact on the exact probability distribution of A, since M needs to be chosen

such that $P(\text{'short'}) = \int_{-\infty}^{0} f_{(M-A)}(x)dx = i^*/(1 + i^*)$. For instance, if

$i^* = 5\%$, and, $A \approx N(0,1)$, then the volume of the liquidity-absorbing open market operation needs to be -0.965 (refer to any statistics textbook with a table for quantiles of the normal distribution).

2. *Changes in the probability distribution of A.* Changes in $E(A)$ need once more to be mechanically offset by parallel shifts of M. However, now, even in case of a symmetric density function, changes of higher-order moments need to be counteracted by a change in the open market operations policy. Assume, for instance, that in a given period uncertainty regarding aggregate autonomous factors increases, such that $A \approx N(0,2)$, that is, the variance of A has doubled from 1 to 2. Then, the volume of the liquidity-absorbing open market operation needs to be multiplied by $\sqrt{2}$ to maintain $i = i^* = 5\%$ and hence $P(\text{'short'}) = 5/6$. One may conclude that, generally, changes in the aggregate unpredictability of autonomous factors will require, everything else equal, an adaptation of the liquidity policy. As the degree of unpredictability is indeed far from constant in practice, today's Fed approach requires, even for a stable target rate, constant changes in reserve market conditions, which is not the case for the symmetric corridor approach.

One may conclude that today's interest rate steering approach of the Fed remains slightly more complex than that practised by, for example, the ECB. This is due to the absence of a deposit facility, and the implied asymmetry of interest rate control through open market operations.

7.2.9 *Precision of Fed interest rate control since the 1970s*

Figure 3.7 and Table 3.1 showed that in 2002 the Fed was, of the three selected central banks, the most precise in targeting short-term interest rates. It is worth now briefly looking at how this precision evolved over time, taking into account the different approaches of the Fed described above. The Fed provides on its website a time series for target rates since 1971, showing the ranges for the periods in which no official target rate

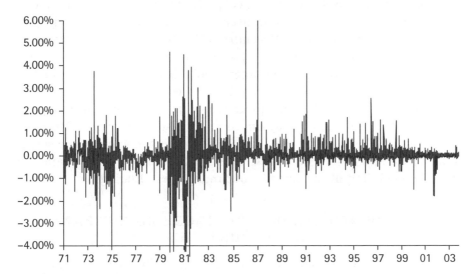

Figure 7.1   *Spread between effective federal funds rate and federal funds target (or mid-point of range), 1971–2003*

Sources: Fed NY and Fed St Louis websites.

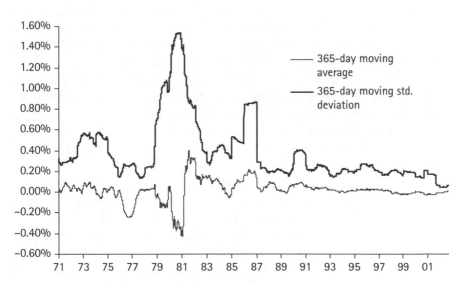

Figure 7.2   *365-day moving average and standard deviation of the spread between the effective federal funds rate and the target rate, 1971–2003*

Sources: Fed NY and Fed St Louis websites.

existed. In these cases, the mid-point of the range is used in the following as a substitute for a target rate. A time series for the effective federal funds rate has been made available by the Fed since July 1954. One can thus compare the variability of the spread between the effective federal funds rate and some kind of target rate since 1971. Figure 7.1 shows this spread.

With regard to the 1970s, one needs to distinguish the period up to around November 1975 from December 1975–September 1979, since the latter was a phase of much more precise interest rate control than the former. After the 1979–82 experiment, volatility seemed to decline for a few years, before stabilizing at a relatively constant level from around 1988 to around 1999. Then, the precision of interest rate control appears to have been improved once again, to reach historical lows in 2002 and 2003. Figure 7.2 shows the moving 365-days average value of the spread (that is, the bias of the effective rate relative to the spread) and the standard deviation of the spread, confirming these findings.

7.3   THE REICHSBANK, DEUTSCHE BUNDESBANK, AND EUROSYSTEM

In contrast to the Fed and the Bank of England with their continuity across the twentieth century, the German central banks twice needed to restart after a quasi-total loss of value of money, and the beginnings of the Bank Deutscher Länder and the Bundesbank are furthermore over-shadowed by the general break in German history in 1945. We saw in Chapter 4 that until 1914 the Reichsbank's system consisted basically of pure rediscounting, with the banking system permanently using the borrowing facility. Short-term market rates therefore followed the discount rate, which was changed by the Reichsbank whenever the stance of monetary policy needed to be changed. Although such a system did not reflect the Bank of England's (and today's central banks') doctrine that there should be a spread between the market rate and the borrowing facility rate, there is little evidence that the system was not functioning well.

Consider what the Reichsbank approach meant in practice, using again the simple one-period model defined by Figure 3.3. The zero spread $i^* = i_B$ is, according to equation 3.2, ensured if $P(\text{'short'}) = 1$, that is, if the variance of the autonomous factor shocks becomes negligible relative to the expected need of the banking sector to go to the borrowing facility. For instance, if $A \approx N(0,1)$, then an expected recourse to the borrowing facility of 4 ensures that the likelihood of excess liquidity is smaller than 0.01 per cent. The remaining deviations of the market rate from the rate of the borrowing facility (which is equal to the target rate) should then be so small that they are never relevant to monetary policy.

Now consider again two typical exogenous changes. First, *if the target rate changes*, the central bank just needs to shift accordingly its borrowing rate, while keeping constant the structural liquidity situation of the banking system, that is, its quasi-deterministic need to go to the borrowing facility. Second, *if the probability distribution of A changes*: when the expected value of A changes, no need for an adjustment appears as long as the expected recourse to the borrowing facility remains large enough. The same holds for changes of higher-order moments of the density function of A: as long as the likelihood of excess liquidity remains negligible, there is no need for the central bank to act. Even an asymmetric density function of A does not matter.

In sum, it appears that this approach is the simplest of all since, whatever happens, the reserve market policy does not need to be changed. It is even somewhat simpler than the symmetric corridor approach, since even changes in the *expected value* of autonomous factors and an asymmetric probability distribution normally do not matter.

Between 1914 and 1924, the gold-convertibility of the mark was suspended, and huge direct financing of government deficits by the Reichsbank, especially after 1919, led to the hyperinflation, which reached its climax in 1923. In 1924, a new Reichsbank law was designed which made the Reichsbank more independent from the government and restored broadly similar operational principles to those prevailing before 1914 (see Gestrich 1941: 329). The relatively good functioning of the system broke down again with the banking crisis in 1931: the gold reserves of the Reichsbank fell dramatically, which increased the liquidity deficit of the banking system vis-à-vis the Reichsbank, while at the same time the volume of eligible trade bills shrank due to the economic downturn. Money market rates were correspondingly above discount rates until 1933, and inter-bank market liquidity was miserable. The revitalization of the German money market was achieved, according to Gestrich (1941: 331), in 1933, with the *Arbeitsbeschaffungswechsel* ('employment creation bills') issued by the Nazi government, which were eligible for rediscounting with the Reichsbank. These were followed by the *Mefo-Wechsel* (already treated in Chapter 4) and eventually the *Reichswechsel*, all in fact some kind of government paper eligible for discounting with the central bank and thus implying direct financing of government expenditure by the central bank. Since these 'trade bills' could in fact eventually be discounted *only* with the Reichsbank, their increased issuance led after in 1937 to excess reserves, with market rates falling towards zero (the discount rate was kept at 4 per cent during those years). Therefore, in 1937, so-called *Sola-Wechsel* were issued by the Gold-Diskontbank, a special central bank institution created in 1924 to overcome the hyperinflation. In fact, this was economically equivalent to the Reichsbank issuing some debt paper to mop up excess liquidity (Gestrich 1941: 334).

If we leave aside the years remaining until 1949, the first document describing monetary policy implementation of the Bank Deutscher Länder (the German central bank between 1948 and 1959) under relatively normal conditions seems to be its *Annual Report* of 1951. This report described again a banking system which systematically rediscounts trade bills as the main instrument to obtain central bank reserves. In 1948, with its establishment, the Bank Deutscher Länder had introduced relatively high reserve requirements with a one-month averaging period. During the 1950s, discount quotas were established and the main pillar of money market management until the early 1990s was set up: this was to guide the market in a kind of corridor set by the discount rate and the lombard rate, the width of which was 100 basis points between 1948 and 1967.[11] As Deutsche Bundesbank (1982b: 48) explains, the 'linchpin' of the Bundesbank's interest rate policy consisted in the fact that, with structural use of the discount facility, market interest rates should not fall below the discount facility's rate and, when discount quotas were exhausted, which they normally were, inter-bank rates should move upwards to the lombard rate but not above it, as long as sufficient collateral was available and the Bundesbank did not introduce further restrictions on its use. The Bundesbank thus achieved an interest rate corridor through two different borrowing facilities, of which the cheaper was, however, quantitatively limited. To that extent, the Bundesbank had over decades a much clearer interest rate target than the Fed, for example, although it never had an *explicit* single target rate. Changes in the monetary policy stance were mainly reflected in changes in the discount and lombard rate. To keep reserve market conditions such that market rates indeed remained normally in the corridor set by the two facilities, the Bundesbank used mainly (*a*) changes in reserve requirements (see Fig. 6.1), (*b*) changes in rediscount quotas, and (*c*) open market operations, which until the 1970s, however, rather resembled additional standing facilities. From the 1950s to the 1970s, that is, during the Bretton Woods period, the inflows of foreign exchange and how to absorb the implied liquidity injection were recurring challenges.

---

[11] The corridor was not really symmetric since the maturity of lombard lending was overnight, while discount lending had an average maturity of close to three months. Therefore, transitory movements of short-term market rates below the discount rate were not excluded. Furthermore, the discount rate was not a binding floor during the first decades since discount quotas were not fully used.

Little can be found in the Bundesbank's publications until the 1970s arguing in favour of the perception of a direct 'open market operations channel' working through excess reserves and the money multiplier, such as was present in the Fed's publications after the 1950s. Even Deutsche Bundesbank (1982*a*, *b*), published during the climax of short-term monetary control, clearly separates monetary policy instruments from the control of the money stock. Still, the Bundesbank did not fully resist US ideas and indeed adopted a kind of monetary base growth reference value from 1975 to 1988. For instance, for 1980 it defined a target range of 5–8 per cent for the growth of this magnitude. However, in day-to-day practice the Bundesbank continued to steer interest rates and, for instance, the section on 'monetary measures' in the *Annual Report* of 1980 is dominated by interest rate considerations. As well, written comments by Bundesbank officials of that time like, for example, Bockelman (1980) suggest a full awareness that monetary policy implementation is about steering short-term interest rates. Bockelman (1980: 347) is also very emphatic that the *overnight* rate is the rate the central bank should focus on, and that it can never deny having full responsibility for its level. Issing (1994) emphasizes that the Bundesbank's refinancing policy is still to a fairly large extent an inheritance from the time of the Reichsbank.

This, of course, also made it easier for the Bundesbank in 1988 to drop once again the monetary base as a kind of intermediate target, and the 1990 *Annual Report* reveals again a clear separation between macroeconomic analysis focusing on broad monetary aggregates and implementation focusing on the control of short-term interest rates. A further trend in the Bundesbank's monetary policy implementation since the 1980s is the increasing use of reverse open market operations, also substituting more and more for discount lending. Deutsche Bundesbank (1994*b*: 60) summarizes its monetary policy implementation approach, which would remain unchanged until 1998, as follows:

Since the mid eighties, a basically unchanged and proven method of money market management has been available to the Bundesbank. In engages in active liquidity management, with securities repurchase agreements being the principal instrument for providing central bank money, and minimum reserves constituting the main structural element of the demand for such money. On the one hand, the Bundesbank bears in mind the banks' interest in the steady provision of liquidity for complying with the minimum reserve requirements; this facilitates a virtually stable trend in the day to day money market. On the other hand, the money market acts as a lever for the monetary transmission mechanism, from which monetary stimuli work through to the supply and demand conditions in the credit, deposits and capital markets and then are also reflected in the intermediate monetary target M3. By accelerating or delaying the provision of liquidity within a month, the Bundesbank can prepare the ground for interest rate changes without any, or any prior, unequivocal signals being given by varying 'official' rates. In the context of this indirect money market management, the day-to-day money market rate is for the Bundesbank the key variable, which it influences direct by means of interest rate policy measures. As the sole supplier of central bank money, the Bundesbank controls pricing at the short end of the money market.

What is somewhat disturbing from today's perspective is the idea of feeding unannounced changes in official interest rates into the market through liquidity management. This should make things much more complex than they need to be, since it implies that market participants scrutinize monetary policy implementation for signals about the stance of monetary policy. This is exactly what the Fed wanted to get rid of when it introduced in 1994/5 the direct publication of the federal funds target rate after FOMC meetings.

The ECB's approach to monetary policy implementation has some similarity to that of the Bundesbank in the 1990s to the extent that *weekly* reverse open market operations dominate reserve provision and that extensive reserve requirements with averaging make it possible to limit open market operations to this low frequency while at the same time achieving a high degree of stability in short-term interest rates. The ECB has never officially declared having any single operational target. However, in ECB (2002b: 52) it concludes with a positive self-assessment that 'finally, but perhaps most importantly, the small and fairly stable spread between the ECB's MRO [main refinancing operation] rate and the short-term money market rates confirms the precision of the ECB's steering of short-term interest rates', suggesting that the ECB's day-to-day aim is to keep short-term inter-bank rates close to the minimum bid rate in its key open market operations. Also, Issing et al. (2001: 112) confirm 'the principle that the implementation of monetary policy in the euro area would be based on the control of a (suitably defined) short term interest rate (or set of rates)'. To that extent, the ECB, like the Bank of England, would follow a relatively similar policy to that of the US Fed, the sole difference being that its target interest rate is not explicit and that, therefore, there is somewhat less precommitment on the part of the ECB to indeed always act in such a way as to achieve the best possible control of short-term interest rates at the target level.

7.4 CONCLUSION

Among the three central banks considered, the Bank of England most consistently followed the approach throughout the twentieth century of focusing on short-term interest rates in monetary policy implementation. On the other hand, today's Bank of England's monetary policy implementation, with its several open market operations each day, may appear somewhat more complex than one may consider necessary. The US was the central bank most 'vulnerable' to ideas coming from academia, such as reserve position doctrine supported by popular economists like Keynes and Friedman, according to which open market operations affect money directly via the multiplier. The Fed sympathized with these ideas especially in periods of very tight monetary policy, such as in 1920-1 and 1979-82, since they allow for denying responsibility for short-term interest rates and the effects of their high levels. The derived techniques of free-, borrowed-, and non-borrowed-reserve targeting were again discontinued after a while; today the Fed is perhaps the most transparent of all in terms of interest rate steering, since it defines explicitly an overnight interest rate target. Still, full remuneration of required reserves, an extension of the reserve base, and the discontinuation of the eligibility of vault cash for fulfilment of requirements might allow for some further simplification of the Fed's management of reserve market conditions and reduce distortions arising from the tax component of reserve requirements. Finally, the Bundesbank (and before it the Reichsbank, while it operated under normal conditions) seems to have generally practised short-term interest rate targeting in its monetary policy implementation. In the 1990s, its approach to monetary policy implementation was apparently deemed to be so well-designed that the Eurosystem largely imitated it, although it fully remunerates reserve requirements to avoid distortions. The Eurosystem had the good fortune to be established at a time when modern views had already prevailed for a few years, and it was, therefore, never tempted to formulate an operational target in quantitative terms.

8

From the Old View to the New

Chapters 4–6 described how the instruments of monetary policy changed fundamentally in the course of the twentieth century. *Standing facilities* played a key role at the beginning of the century but then became, in inverse proportion to the rise of open market operations, less popular, mainly under the influence of US experience and literature. Today, their key role is again recognized. *Open market operations* were, although not so explicitly, already applied in the nineteenth century, at least by the Bank of England, in order to keep Bank rate 'effective', that is, to keep the spread between the Bank rate and the market rate limited. Today, they are systematically used to achieve operational target interest rates (relative to some standing facility rates) and they are conducted mainly through reverse operations. They are thus no longer so fundamentally different from standing facilities. From around 1925 to 1985 they were regarded, especially in the US, as a key instrument of monetary control, making it possible to affect directly the monetary base (or some reserves concept) and hence, via the money multiplier, the broad monetary aggregates. Finally, *reserve requirements*, which played no role as a monetary policy instrument at the beginning of the twentieth century, are today widely used to smooth liquidity conditions in the money market and to define a stable demand for reserves, both in order to contribute to the stability of short-term interest rates. Temporarily, they were in addition regarded as another sophisticated tool for monetary control.

Chapter 7 revealed that the overall strategy of monetary policy implementation also changed fundamentally in the course of the twentieth century, especially in the US, but that towards the end of the century a rather homogeneous 'new view' on monetary policy implementation emerged. This new view was not really new in all of its elements, since it partially reflected principles of central banking which were well-established at the beginning of the twentieth century and which were only temporarily forgotten. Still, it appears that the 1990s witnessed the appearance of an approach which is new in its clarity, theoretical foundation, and acceptance by almost all central banks, such as to justify the label 'new view'.

Section 8.1 recapitulates what exactly was wrong with (mainly US) theory and practice of monetary policy implementation before the 1990s. Section 8.2 inquires why positions considered today to be misleading could be so widely accepted for decades. Section 8.3 assesses the costs of the old view. Section 8.4 summarizes the new view as a consistent overall approach. Finally, Section 8.5 speculates briefly about the future of monetary policy implementation.

8.1 WHAT WAS WRONG WITH THE 'OLD VIEW'?

Only twenty-odd years ago, Milton Friedman (1982: 101) summarized what he regarded as the predominant opinion on monetary policy implementation at that time:

Experience has demonstrated that it is simply not feasible for the monetary authority to use interest rates as either a target or as an effective instrument ... Hence, there is now wide agreement that the appropriate short-run tactics are to express a target in terms of monetary aggregates, and to use control of the base, or components of the base, as an instrument to achieve the target.

If one wanted to describe under the heading of 'old view' an antipode to the current view on appropriate monetary policy implementation, Friedman's statement would capture large parts (but not all) of it.[1] Consider in the following the five key elements of the old view, the first four of which are somehow contained in Friedman's summary.

8.1.1 *Quantitative operational targets*

In Chapter 2, the *monetary base* was defined as the sum of two central bank balance sheet items, namely, banknotes in circulation and current account holdings of banks with the central bank. The proposal to select

---

[1] Beyond claiming such consensus, Friedman (1982) contains some proposals on monetary policy implementation that are particularly surprising from today's perspective. For instance, he proposed to 'make the discount rate a penalty rate and to tie it to a market rate so it automatically moves', which would make interest rates indeterminate or infinite in the event of an anticipated borrowing need. At the same time, he proposes to predetermine the volume of open market operations conducted outright for at least three months, and to 'eliminate all repurchase agreements and similar short-term transactions' (1982: 117), such that random changes of government deposits or of banknotes held abroad would have a huge impact on interest rates.

the monetary base as an operational target was advanced on the basis of the money multiplier idea of Phillips (1920) by, for instance, M. Friedman (1960) and has ever since been repeated in monetary policy textbooks. Central banks were more reluctant to follow. As a comprehensive Bank for International Settlements conference volume on 'The monetary base approach to monetary control' (BIS 1980) reveals, only the central banks of Switzerland and Spain seriously claimed at that time to have selected the monetary base as their *operational* target. Both have abandoned the idea in the meantime. The BIS conference volume is full of explanations by other central bankers why such a concept would not work, at least, in their respective countries. Consider the following issues.

1. *The monetary base cannot reasonably be controlled in the short run.* By definition (see Chapter 1), an operational target variable should be a variable that *can* be controlled in the very short run by the central bank and for which a concrete figure is set by the decision-making committee for the inter-meeting period to (*a*) tell the central bank's implementation experts what to do, and (*b*) indicate the stance of monetary policy to the public. However, this obviously does not make sense for the monetary base. Its normally biggest component, banknotes in circulation, is in the short term purely demand-driven, with innovations to demand rarely linked to macroeconomic developments. Its second component, current account holdings, is mainly determined by reserve requirements. Under a lagged reserve-requirement system, required reserves are given. This is practically the case also under a contemporaneous reserve requirement system, since banks cannot easily change their lending and deposit taking in the very short run such as to correct their reserve requirements. In practice, open market operations, which push reserves on average for the reserve maintenance period below reserve requirements, will create a corresponding recourse to the borrowing facility, and hence will not even affect the monetary base. If there is no borrowing facility, banks will probably need to pay a penalty for not fulfilling reserve requirements, but (*a*) it may seem inappropriate or even legally questionable that the central bank should use its power to squeeze the market in a way that makes it impossible for the banks to comply with requirements, and (*b*) it makes little economic difference whether banks have to pay a direct penalty or a penalty in the form of a borrowing facility rate, provided the levels of the two are identical.

2. *The monetary base should not be controlled in the short run.* First, the monetary base is a heterogeneous product since it is composed of banknotes and reserves (which are themselves subdivided into *required*

and *excess* reserves). Why should changes in these three completely different components be equivalent? *Second,* there are doubts about the predictability and stability of the money multiplier, especially in the event that one wishes to base policy actions on it. In particular, the multiplier is unlikely to remain stable when interest rates move towards zero, since banks then no longer care about holding excess reserves. To that extent, when monetary growth is deemed insufficient and excess reserves are injected to make the banks expand credit, the result will be first that, in an efficient market, short-term inter-bank interest rates drop to zero (if there is no deposit facility). The fact that interest rates have dropped to zero is, of course, relevant and, if judged to be permanent for a longer period of time, medium- and longer-term rates also will drop and economic decisions will be affected. However, once inter-bank rates have fallen to zero and the central bank continues to increase excess reserves through open market operations at zero interest rates, not much more should happen: that is, the money multiplier should fall with every further reserves injection. It is to that extent difficult to really construct a story where an injection of reserves by the central bank through open market operations sets in motion monetary expansion independently from the interest rate channel. *Third,* any attempt to control in the short run the monetary base leads to extreme volatility of interest rates since the market will, due to stochastic and seasonal fluctuations in the demand for base money, permanently either be short or long of reserves, as already observed by Bagehot (1873). One of the core ideas of central banking is to provide an 'elastic currency', that is, one in which the important transitory fluctuations in base money demand no longer need to disturb economic conditions via interest rate effects. What matters for the key economic decisions, namely, to save or consume, to borrow or invest, is interest rates mainly of medium and longer maturity. With extreme volatility of short-term rates, the volatility of longer-term rates will also increase. Such volatility will create noise in economic decisions, and hence lead the economy away from equilibrium.

3. *Alternative quantitative concepts as operational targets.* The Fed and academics, confronted with the conceptual problems of monetary base targeting while still aiming at a framework in which monetary policy transmission could be defined only in terms of quantities from the very start, soon developed alternative quantitative targets. Alternative quantitative concepts applied temporarily as operational target in the US were free, non-borrowed, and borrowed reserves, and M. Friedman (1982) even seems to be proposing an open market operations volume target. In

addition, total reserves targeting was also discussed in the literature (see Meigs 1962). By focusing on reserves, these approaches eliminated the defect of monetary base targeting, which was to put three fundamentally different things, namely, banknotes, required reserves, and excess reserves, into one basket. Also, controlling these quantities in the very short run was clearly easier than controlling the monetary base. However, these approaches were correspondingly less directly linked to the money multiplier story, and therefore needed additional, more complex theoretical justification. Although some justifications were given, today they are judged to be inadequate. The non-borrowed reserves target applied from 1979 to 1982 was not only complex to derive but also created volatility in both longer-term interest rates and monetary aggregates. The free and borrowed reserves targets, in contrast, seem to be rather close to an interest rate target: their theoretical justification, apart from that of being substitutes for short-term rates, appear so weak, and their use was in practice so lacking in transparency, that it seems that they were always smokescreens for short-term interest rate targeting (see for example Goodfriend 2003 and Mishkin 2004). It was argued in Chapter 7 that the derived quantitative operational targets contain instabilities that require a frequent redefinition of targets independently of macroeconomic events, which weakens the concepts considerably. This is underlined by the fact that the Fed never published concrete figures for its supposed quantitative targets. This contrasts with short-term interest rates as operational targets, which can be specified unambiguously and published for the periods between the meetings of the decision-making committee.

A key assumption for making sense of most of the alternative quantitative concepts seems to be that it matters for a bank whether or not reserves are obtained through the borrowing facility. However, this assumption ignores the fact that there is (and has been at least since the time of Bagehot) a highly efficient inter-bank market for reserves. When lending and borrowing, whether towards other banks or the central bank, banks behave as optimizing agents focusing normally on cost, opportunity cost, and return—that is, on interest rates (see also Moore 1988 on this point). It is hard for economists to justify ignoring the optimization behaviour of banks in this market and the resulting price formation. Furthermore, today's systematic use of *reverse* open market operations makes it less convincing to base monetary policy implementation on a distinction between 'borrowed' and 'non-borrowed' reserves.

8.1.2 *Assumption that making the monetary aggregates more stable is desirable on its own, and that monetary policy instruments should contribute to that aim*

Even if one were to assume that the central bank could control the monetary base on a day-by-day basis, and that the monetary multiplier were stable, the desirability of monetary base control would still depend on the desirability of the control of monetary aggregates. Since central banks have in the meantime abandoned the control of monetary aggregates as a target on its own (although many still use them as important *indicator* variables), this precondition for making quantitative operational targets useful is also no longer applicable.

8.1.3 *Assumption that short-term interest rates are not an important indicator variable of the stance of monetary policy*

A key idea underlying quantitative operational targets is that short-term interest rates would not be a very relevant variable to the transmission of monetary policy, nor an indicator of the monetary policy stance. In, for example, M. Friedman (1960), interest rates are indeed rarely mentioned. However, two key arguments speak in favour of short-term interest rates as an operational target.

First, as already argued by, for example, H. Thornton (1802), Bagehot (1873), and Wicksell (1936), and as exemplified by the simple arbitrage diagram in Chapter 1, price stability in equilibrium unambiguously determines a money interest rate, and ignoring interest rates when one speaks about monetary policy to achieve price stability is therefore likely to ignore something of relevance.

Second, as known at least since Bagehot, the market for central bank deposits tends to be very unstable if left alone, due to various demand and supply shocks (which do not relate to macroeconomic developments). Therefore, if a central bank did not steer money market rates through some instrument, interest rates would permanently be either at very low or at very high levels. Depending on expectations building, medium- and longer-term rates, which are key to economic decisions, would also fluctuate heavily, which is likely to destabilize not only the 'real' behaviour of economic agents but also financial and monetary magnitudes (as illustrated by the US experience in 1979–82, when rates were still controlled to some extent).

The claim that central banks *cannot* control short-term rates, as apparently argued by M. Friedman (1982), is falsified by the mere nature of the market in question and abundant evidence.

8.1.4 *Lack of micro-foundation: no modelling of inter-bank market and central bank balance sheet identity ignored*

As already noted in Section 8.1.1, the ideas underlying quantitative operational targets lack microeconomic foundation since they ignore the existence of a money market with price formation and the fact that the prices and the expectations of future prices in this market are key to guiding decisions of banks to grant credit. Another deficit of the literature consists in ignoring most of the time the central bank balance sheet identity. The obvious relationship between open market operations and recourse to standing facilities derived in Chapter 2—that, *ceteris paribus*, any change of reserve conditions through open market operations is compensated through recourse to standing facilities—was considered a 'perplexing problem' in the US that would 'cast doubt upon the effectiveness of the discount rate as a central bank instrument' (Meigs 1962: 7). Indeed, from the 1930s until the 1990s the US literature on discount borrowing assumed most of the time a reverse causation *from* the spread between the discount rate and market rates *to* the volume of borrowing, which seems to be a consequence of ignoring the central bank's balance sheet identity.

8.1.5 *Overestimation of knowledge of the economy; instruments and indicators too complex and numerous*

From today's perspective, central banks' approach to monetary policy implementation during most of the twentieth century seems excessively complex. A priori, complexity is not a bad thing in itself and, if relationships are complex, as they undoubtedly are in the domain of money, then appropriate policies are likely to be complex as well. Still, the described complexities observed in monetary policy implementation do not appear to be justifiable in this way. Consider the following examples.

1. According to Anderson (1969), in the 1960s the Fed followed eight distinct money market indicators (see Chapter 7). It is likely that concentrating on short-term rates and ranking all other money market indicators as secondary or complementary would in the 1960s have clarified things a lot without wasting any useful information.

2. In and around the 1979–82 episode, the Fed had corridors both for various quantities (non-borrowed reserves and several monetary aggregates) and for short-term market rates. The signals sent by these various variables were often contradictory; and transcripts of the FOMC meetings

of that time (which can be found on the website of the Board of Governors) reveal that the system was just too complicated to form the basis of coherent discussions and decisions by policy makers.

3. Reserve requirement systems in many countries were overly complex in terms of defining a multitude of reserve base categories to which different reserve ratios were applied. No convincing theoretical justification for this differentiation was given. Probably, it often reflected compromise between, on the one hand, some vague economic idea of how the degree of 'moneyness' of deposits could be relevant in a quantity-oriented monetary policy approach and, on the other, the pecuniary impact of the requirements on different banks and associated lobbying.

4. The rules in the US that determined how much recourse to the discount window was allowed and which administrative procedures were triggered at what time were complex as well, and made the relationship between borrowing and the spread between the discount rate and the federal funds rate opaque and unstable. This again implied complexity and instabilities in the definition of quantitative operational targets.

5. Much of the complexity may have been due to unwillingness to take responsibility for short-term interest rates. Indeed, the free reserves and borrowed reserves targeting procedures may be understood to have been close to interest rate targeting, the Fed preferring, however, not to make this explicit. As a consequence, the Fed was obliged to sustain its quantitative operational target story and to develop some underlying theory.

6. The direct measures of monetary control (for example, deposit rate ceilings), which over decades constituted a considerable part of monetary policy decisions, are rejected today on the basis that they are in contradiction to a free and efficient allocation of resources.

In sum, from today's perspective, most of the complexity observed during those decades does not appear well-justified. Since complexity always means additional resource use, risk of misunderstandings, and a higher likelihood of mistaken decisions, it became itself a problem of monetary policy implementation.

8.2 WHAT WERE THE COSTS OF THE OLD VIEW?

Three main types of cost can be distinguished. *First*, as mentioned, the design and maintenance of complex systems absorb resources both in the central bank and in the affected banking system. If the complexities are not well-justified, this represents a waste of resources. In the case of *scarce* resources in the central bank, the corresponding reduction of resources available in other relevant fields will lead to less accurate analysis and decisions in these fields, such as the understanding of the relevant macroeconomic relationships and the appropriate definition of the monetary policy stance. *Second,* if taken seriously such as in the 1979–82 episode in the US, short-term monetary control can lead to excessive volatility in interest rates (and even of monetary quantities) and thereby probably also to a sub-optimal achievement of the final targets of monetary policy. *Third,* the sub-optimal specification of the different instruments may have led to direct welfare costs. For instance, unremunerated reserve requirements lead to distortions that are unlikely to be justifiable in terms of the theory of optimal taxation. The US specification of the discount window with non-price disincentives also suffered from the usual inefficiencies of non-price mechanisms. The signalling of the monetary policy stance through open market operations created a complex interaction between the central bank and the money market that led to resource spending and short-run volatility.

8.3   EXPLAINING THE QUANTITATIVE DETOUR

As argued throughout this book, monetary policy implementation, especially in the US, has moved in a big circle in the twentieth century: from interest rate-oriented monetary policy implementation at its beginning, it turned towards quantitative operational targets, only to return to interest rates in the 1990s. In the second half of this big circle, there was an additional, smaller one, which marks the temporary reappearance of explicit interest rate targeting in the US during the 1970s, followed by the 1979–82 experiment (on this smaller detour, see especially B. M. Friedman 2000). It was sometimes claimed by central banks that the change of approach was justified by changes in financial structures. But the absence of facts supporting this explanation rather suggests that the circle was simply a long-lasting misunderstanding. It is therefore interesting to raise the question how it could come to a detour of such a length and of such policy relevance. Three main necessary factors may be distinguished.

8.3.1   *A difficult start for the Fed during wartime, with excessive Treasury influence*

Monetary policy considerations would probably have suggested at some time during the First World War strong increases in US Fed discount rates. Instead, under the influence of the Treasury, which had its refinancing costs in mind, and decentralization, which made decision making inefficient,[2] discount rates remained low during the war and also for some time after, such that important inflationary pressures could build up.[3] The idea of quantitative restrictions on the recourse to the discount window, and generally non-price disincentives against its use, was developed during this period to make it possible to avoid rate hikes (which the Treasury would have disliked), while at the same doing something to limit inflationary pressure. Still, in 1920 the moment came when rates were aggressively hiked and, through a violent deflation, the dollar returned to gold convertibility at the pre-war parity. So far, the history of the early Fed was not too different from those of other central banks in wartime. What was different, however, was that, instead of burying again the muddling-through approach which may be an acceptable compromise in wartime, a doctrine emerged from the early years to the effect that the technique of quantitative restriction of discount window borrowing was a sensible part of monetary policy implementation under any condition, that quantitative control was in any case what mattered most, and that interest rates were only of secondary importance. New theories by US academics, summarized in the next subsection, combined with a lack of direct experience from more normal times, were probably necessary complements for making out of a 'wartime lie' a theory that would dominate textbooks and influence practice for eighty years.

8.3.2 *Academic theories favouring a quantity orientation of monetary policy implementation*

As seen in Chapter 1, Irving Fisher revived the quantity theory of money in 1911 and C. A. Phillips provided in 1920 a relationship between a central bank balance sheet quantity and monetary aggregates. Together, these studies seemed to suggest that a quantitative and hence open market operations-oriented approach to monetary policy implementation

---

[2] According to Warburg (1930: ii. 843), which is the reprint of an interview from 1923: 'Two dangers gravely menace the future of the Federal Reserve System. The greater of these dangers is the growing political pressure on the Reserve Board, tending to wrench the Reserve System away from sound banking and economic practice . . . The second is excessive decentralisation, which has produced a serious lack of cohesion in the System . . .'. 'There is nothing more dangerous for the Federal Reserve System and for the country as a whole than to have party administrations claim credit for low discount rates and easy money' (1930: ii. 852).

[3] As again Warburg (1930: ii. 296) puts it: 'In the life and death struggle of war, sound economic precepts have to give way to the dictates of self-preservation.'

would be both simple and effective. In the 1920s and the 1930s, on the basis of a doubtful interpretation of the role of the discount window in the inflation of 1916–20, such a quantitative theory, called 'reserve position doctrine' by Meigs (1962: 7), could develop which provided the story for monetary policy implementation for decades. At the same time, both the central bank tradition of steering interest rates and the Wicksellian theorists had failed to provide a convincing theory of the *dynamics* of interest rates and prices outside equilibrium. From the 1950s until the early 1980s, brilliant spokesmen of the quantity theory like Milton Friedman exerted constant pressure on central banks to go further with a quantitative approach to monetary policy operations, which culminated in the 1979–82 episode. Beyond that, there was until the 1990s (with the exception of Poole 1968), astonishingly little microeconomic work on the reserve market, that is, the market in which the different monetary policy instruments interact.

It may be noteworthy that the quantitative approach to monetary policy implementation was nowhere as popular as in the US, and that the two key authors that paved the way for this approach, Irving Fischer and C. A. Phillips, were also American. The same holds true for Milton Friedman and most other quantity theorists. In contrast, Bagehot and Wicksell, for example, were Europeans (but Keynes does not fit into this geography). The fact that the US was most deeply involved in the quantitative operational target approach can thus also be explained at least partially by the accident of the nationalities of leading economists in the field. In addition, one observes in the US literature a certain tendency to ignore experience in the rest of the world. One is astonished how rarely the early authors in the US referred to the European literature. Meigs (1961: 7) illustrates this:

Although experience of the Bank of England and other central banks could be looked to for precedents and doctrines when the Federal Reserve Banks opened for business, the American system with its thousands of individual member banks was believed to be unique in many ways. Appearing to confirm the uniqueness of the American system, a perplexing problem arose in 1922 when the Federal Reserve Banks attempted to build up their earning assets by purchasing securities in the open market. As the open market purchases were made, the member banks reduced their borrowings from the Reserve Banks by about the amount of the System purchases, leaving total Reserve Bank credit virtually unchanged.

Normally, detailed study of UK and European central banks' experience and of the lengthy nineteenth-century debates on making Bank rate effective through open market operations should have made the observed impact of open market operations on borrowing most natural (as it reflects the central bank's balance sheet identity), and not to appear as a 'perplexing problem'.[4]

Perhaps as importantly, no other central bank was as committed as the US Fed to openness to the academic world. While many European central banks until the 1990s limited their contacts with the academic world, probably deliberately in order to avoid tiring debate with 'intellectuals', the US Fed has a long tradition of hiring staff who come from and return to universities. Also, no other central bank tried to be so publicly transparent and therefore invited so much academic research on its policy.

8.3.3   *Positive theories of central bank behaviour*

Normally, one understands central banks' policies as those of a benevolent agent that tries to understand best how it should act in order to achieve the goals that have been entrusted to it. Therefore, when reviewing the operational approach of central banks and concluding that we would do it differently today, we interpret this either as reflecting changes in the environment, that is of the *optimal* policy, or as a better understanding today of the economic environment and how monetary policy instruments interact with it. There is, however, a third possibility, followed by, for instance, Guttentag (1966), Kane (1980), and M. Friedman (1982), namely, to view central banks as bureaucracies which seek not only the public's welfare but also, for example, prestige, income, growth of responsibilities, or an easy life. Also, central banks may be politically pressured institutions: even if independent, their decision-making bodies are often composed of former politicians who are anchored in the political class.

Guttentag (1966: 30), after explaining what a 'complete' strategy of monetary policy implementation would look like and what its merits would be, tries to convince the Fed that it does not need to be frightened that such a strategy, which would increase its accountability, would expose it to more criticism:

The real barrier to the adoption of a complete strategy is largely psychological. The Federal Reserve would have to relinquish the illusion that it 'takes account of everything', while exposing its real objectives nakedly to public scrutiny. This could be risky. There is much unreasonable hostility to monetary policy to begin with, and it is likely that in some cases further exposure would merely invite more

---

[4] Interestingly, Meltzer (2003) argues that the founders of the Fed would have looked too much to the Bank of England's experience in the second half of the nineteenth century, and would therefore have focused too much on money market techniques. Also Humphrey (2001) argues in this sense. The interpretation given here is rather the opposite.

vigorous attacks. My own view, however, is that this would be more than offset by heightened support and help from other (and particularly academic) quarters.

Thus, according to this theory, the Fed's reluctance to treat interest rates as operational targets could have reflected its fear of becoming too transparent, so losing all the smokescreens which protect it from criticism.

Kane (1980: 210) argues that the Fed 'acts first and foremost as a political animal' and that 'the perennial incompleteness of Fed control strategies and most of the Fed's special bureaucratic features (its independence, its acceptance of impossible policy assignments, and its murky lines of internal authority) serve definite political ends'. In particular, Kane (1980: 199) argues similarly to Guttentag that 'there are strong political forces that constrain the Fed to dampen the size of short-run increases in nominal interest rates'. Political pressures may furthermore explain why the Fed (and other central banks) preferred *to deny full responsibility for short-term interest rates*, and instead present market rates as being largely market-driven. As the Fed never conducted fixed-rate tender operations, and as the cost of discount window borrowing was non-transparent, the Fed indeed established at least during the 1950s and 1960s a system with maximum ambiguity regarding its responsibility for short-term interest rates. The move to quantitative targets in 1979 may also be interpreted along these lines: the Fed probably felt that the strong increase in interest rates that was necessary to bring down inflation rates from 1970s levels to those of the 1980s was easier to implement without taking explicit responsibility for it, that is, by claiming to be steering quantities and letting interest rate developments appear to be market-driven. For instance, Mishkin (2004: 425) interprets the 1979–82 episode in this way. He observes that things 'went wrong' since monetary control in fact deteriorated under the new procedure: both short-term interest rates and monetary aggregates became more volatile. However, he does not explain this failure by reference to the inappropriateness of quantitative operational targets but by the lack of quantitative commitment of the Fed:

Despite Volcker's statements about the need to target monetary aggregates, he was not committed to these targets. Rather, he was far more concerned with using interest rate movements to wring inflation out of the economy . . . This view of Volcker's strategy suggests that the Fed's announced attachment to monetary aggregate targets may have been a smokescreen to keep the Fed from being blamed for the high interest rates that would result from the new policy.

Mishkin's analysis is even more plausible as it can be applied similarly to the birth of reserve position doctrine in 1919–21, that is, during the first of the two phases of strong disinflationary Fed policy during the twentieth century (see Goodfriend 2003).

For M. Friedman (1982), the main puzzle is why the Fed had still not adopted his advice of the 1950s to follow strictly a monetary growth rule. His interpretation is that the Fed resists clear monetarist rules because it prefers remaining without a benchmark against which its performance could clearly be measured:

Why the enormous resistance of the Fed to moving to monetary aggregates? Fundamentally, I believe, because monetary aggregates permit far more effective monitoring of performance and accountability for achieving targets than money market conditions. Who of us want to be held responsible for our mistakes? It is not very nice to have a bottom line. If we don't have a bottom line, why should we introduce one? (1982: 115)

Also, according to Friedman, a quantitative rule would radically reduce the required number of staff members, which equally cannot be in the interest of a bureaucracy. Moreover, Friedman argues that the Fed would have an interest in macroeconomic instability as this enhances its importance and the public's interest in monetary policy action. The fact that the Fed only tended to 'pay lip service' to quantitative concepts up until 1979 reveals for Friedman the 'unbelievable strength of bureaucratic inertia in preventing the system from learning from experience'. Friedman's interpretation may appear somewhat unfair especially since no other central bank went so far as the Fed in trying to translate into practice a quantitative approach to monetary policy implementation, such as suggested by Friedman. These attempts eventually seem to have created confusion and macroeconomic instability.[5] Still, Friedman should be praised for having always insisted on the point that a target that is not quantified (that is, for which no concrete figure is given) cannot be a serious target, and leaves in the dark what the central bank is actually aiming at. This includes the operational target, for which the Fed did not want to specify an explicit level after 1920. By insisting that the Fed should concretely quantify its supposed quantitative targets, he eventually contributed to push it into the 1979–82 episode, which then revealed the impracticability of reserve position doctrine. It is all the more astonishing that Friedman remains today an uncompromising supporter of this doctrine.

[5] Friedman's perception of the Fed has recently changed to the positive. In a *Wall Street Journal* article of 20 August 2003, he notes a remarkable improvement in the performance of the Fed since the mid-1980s. This seems to coincide well with the perception, suggested in this book, that the Fed started to effectively modernize monetary policy implementation around that time by moving back, step by step, to short-term interest rate targeting. However, Friedman sees no link between the two, and instead reaffirms the quantitative doctrine of monetary policy implementation.

It seems still plausible that, in the case of the Fed, the complex decentralized structure may indeed have contributed to some 'bureaucratic inertia' and thus has made reform more difficult. In the first two decades of the Fed, it was unclear whether there was a common discount rate policy, that is, whether different Federal Reserve Banks could charge to some extent different discount rates. This also contributed to making more difficult a systematic upwards move of rates during the war, since the Fed's power vis-à-vis Treasury was weakened and perhaps commercial banks lobbied their respective Reserve Banks to be 'dovish', that is, to set relatively low discount rates. Since it was not in the interest of the Reserve Banks to hand over power to the Board, it may have been a compromise to agree that all Reserve Banks would at least make an effort to restrict *administratively* recourse to the discount window. Even when it had been clarified that the power to set the discount rate lay with the Board of Governors, decision-making structures remained complex in so far as another body, namely, the FOMC (and its predecessors), was responsible for framing open market operations policies. Specifying the discount window as a rational tool of monetary policy implementation raises the question of uniting the power to decide on both the target rate and the discount rate more directly (although the reform of the US discount window in 2002 was done without a reordering of decision-making powers). In addition, governors of the Federal Reserve Banks may have continued to have special preferences for a burdensome discount window, since execution of such a facility and the associated discretion creates responsibility and staffing needs. In sum, it does not seem implausible that a more centralized system would have taken much earlier steps towards reform of the discount window and hence to a generally more rational approach to monetary policy implementation.

It is impressive how the US Fed freed itself from the doctrines of quantitative operational targets and all related complications after around 1990. It is not obvious what triggered this move at exactly this moment in time. Possibly, the resignation in 1987 of Volcker, who was associated with the 1979–82 experiment, was a necessary condition for breaking with the tradition.

8.4   THE NEW VIEW

This section summarizes the main elements of the new view on monetary policy implementation as it emerged in the last ten to fifteen years. The new view is structured along four main aspects.

8.4.1 *The short-term inter-bank rate should be the one and only operational target of the central bank*

The short-term inter-bank rate and expectations of its future evolution is a sufficient indicator of the stance of the central bank's monetary policy in the sense that it contains all relevant information to describe the stance.[6] From the perspective of the monetary policy stance, it is secondary through which use of the different instruments a certain target interest rate is achieved, since the target rate itself contains all the relevant information. Therefore, the short-term inter-bank rate should be the one and only operational target of the central bank. The short-term interest rate is relevant to achieving the central bank's intermediate and ultimate goals in so far as it determines, depending on the history of the central banks' interest rate decisions, through the expectations hypothesis, the term structure of interest rates. The interest rates of various maturities are key to financial, consumption, savings, and investment decisions, and hence to the intermediate and final targets of monetary policy. Among the short-term interest rates, the most natural choice is the overnight rate, since it is the ultimate starting point of the yield curve and probably most directly controlled by the central bank. Also, expected changes of interest rate targets lead to anomalies at the short end of the yield curve whenever the target is defined for maturities longer than overnight (see Section 3.1). Deviations of overnight interest rates from the target are, however, perceived as a nuisance only if they are transmitted into longer-term rates, that is, into the rates which are most relevant for economic decisions.

The central bank's communication of its stance should be simple, given that it can be summed up in one figure, the target rate. Central banks should publish decisions regarding the target short-term interest rate immediately, to limit uncertainty and to avoid the possibility that banks might try to infer information on monetary policy decisions from the central banks' operations. This implies that central banks do not send signals on their monetary policy intentions through their open market operations (except though a fixed tender rate). This convention simplifies day-to-day monetary policy implementation tremendously since it allows the central bank to concentrate on conducting transparent, simple, and efficient operations to achieve a publicly known interest rate target, instead of worrying permanently about the intended or unintended signals these operations could send.

---

[6] This of course does not mean that a given short-term interest rate, for example '5%', always reflects the same stance. It has to be seen in relation to a 'neutral' stance, also to be expressed in terms of a short-term interest rate, which depends on the real rate of return on capital and the expected inflation.

Finally, according to the new view, the task of day-to-day monetary policy implementation can be fully separated from macroeconomic monetary analysis in the sense that the implementation experts in the central bank do not need to know much about the macroeconomic monetary analysis from which the current stance was derived, and the macroeconomic analysts in the central bank do not need to know how implementation takes place. The monetary policy implementation experts also do not need to know the anticipated future evolution of the interest rate target. If each side indeed knows little about the other and this separation is communicated to the market, it becomes credible that operations do not reveal anything about the monetary policy stance. This already relates to the following subsection.

8.4.2 The choice of the short-term interest rate as the operational target of the central bank is independent of the monetary policy strategy

The new view postulates that the choice of the short-term interest rate as the operational target of the central bank is independent of the monetary policy strategy and hence of the intermediate and ultimate goals of monetary policy. Indeed, interest rate steering was appropriate and practised under the gold standard, it was appropriate under monetary targeting such as practised by the Fed in the 1970s and by the Bundesbank, for example, over decades, and it is appropriate under direct inflation targeting or any of the other present macroeconomic strategies of central banks. Furthermore, operational events and magnitudes normally do not feed back into the operational target, that is, they are not relevant to the monetary policy strategy. Specifically, magnitudes in the central bank balance sheet which play a key role in the central bank's management of reserve market conditions, like banknotes, reserves, the volume of outstanding open market operations, or the use of standing facilities, are not seen to have per se any specific information content for determining the appropriate interest rate target.[7]

8.4.3 The new view on the specification of monetary policy instruments

The new view considers a certain specification of monetary policy instruments as appropriate. Consider the instruments one by one.

---

[7] One exception needs to be mentioned: in the case of strong financial market turmoil or a very underdeveloped financial system, components of the monetary base may be more relevant indicator variables than broad monetary aggregates.

Standing facilities should be provided with unlimited access and have fully transparent prices. Disincentives against their use should not be provided by non-price elements, although credit risk control measures are needed and thus adequate collateral has to be posted. The type of collateral has no monetary policy relevance, and therefore the aim in the definition of the list of eligible collateral should be (*a*) sufficient availability of collateral for monetary policy operations; (*b*) efficiency; (*c*) allowance for sufficient credit risk control. A borrowing facility should take the form of advances (lombard credit) and not of discount. There should be no structural use of standing facilities, as this tends to reduce liquidity in the short-term inter-bank market. Thus, there should be most of the time a positive spread between market rates and standing facility rates. This is achieved through steering the likelihood of the recourse to the facilities appropriately through open market operations and by setting a sufficient distance between the target rate and the standing facilities rates. The maturity of the standing facilities should correspond to the maturity of the target rate, that is, normally overnight.

Open market operations. Reverse open market operations are preferable to pure outright operations as an instrument of day-to-day liquidity management, since they avoid the underlying paper having any effects on the market and thus do not oblige the central bank to think constantly about which paper to buy or sell. Open market operations should be conducted via tender, using competitive allotment methods. Outright operations should be used only for structural liquidity provision. If reverse operations are not conducted as pure variable-rate tenders, but with some restriction in the bidding rates (for example, fixed-rate tenders), these restrictions need to be consistent with the target interest rate to avoid inefficiencies such as over-bidding and under-bidding. In the event of averaging, this includes consistency with the expected interest rate target until the end of the reserve maintenance period. A fixed tender rate should normally be in a stable relationship with the rate of standing facilities. Allotment decisions in open market operations should not be used to signal the current or future monetary policy stance. The drafting of the list of eligible collateral in reverse open market operations should a priori respect the same principles as the list for standing facilities, and an identical list for both may therefore be advantageous.

Reserve requirements. Reserve requirements can play a role as a monetary policy instrument mainly to allow for better control of short-term interest rates through an averaging facility and/or through the stabilization of the demand for reserves. They thereby prevent transitory shocks affecting supply or demand in the reserve market from having an impact on short-term interest rates. In addition, reserve requirements may be justified as a way to enlarge the liquidity needs of the banking system vis-à-vis the central bank. This limitation of the functions of required reserves implies that the reserve ratio should be changed only rarely, that required reserves should be remunerated (at least if they are not very low, that is, higher than in the UK, for example), and that reserve requirements should be calculated with a sufficient time lag such that they are known at the beginning of the reserve maintenance period. Generally, reserve requirement systems should not be more complex than what is clearly justified by the functions assigned to them.

8.4.4   *The implementation of the interest rate target according to the new view*

Starting from the simple model presented in Chapter 3, the simplest system for controlling short-term interest rates is that with a symmetric standing facilities corridor around the target rate (if one disregards the 'Reichsbank' approach of structural dependence on the borrowing facility). In such a framework, changes to the monetary policy stance, that is, of the target short-term interest rate, may be made without any change in reserve market conditions by simply moving the standing facilities corridor in parallel with the target rate. The average recourse to standing facilities and the outstanding open market operations remain *ceteris paribus* unchanged. In an asymmetric system with only a borrowing facility, the spread between the borrowing facility and the target rate should remain constant at, for example, 100 basis points when the target rate is changed, so as to keep signals parsimonious. This implies for the central bank a need to adjust reserve market conditions in the sense of a change of the expected and average recourse to the standing facility through open market operations. However, this change of reserve market conditions has no other significance than to compensate for the increased or decreased asymmetry of the corridor between the zero lower bound and the borrowing facility rate.

8.5   OUTLOOK

The question remains whether what is summarized above as the 'new view' is just the right view, or whether the characteristics of the economy and of financial markets, or our analysis of these, will change such that in a few years or decades another new view will emerge. The analysis in this book suggests that one can be relatively confident that the new view is indeed relatively universal and will thus prevail in the foreseeable future. The danger that quantitative operational targets will return seems limited. The memory of their unsatisfactory performance is fresh, and the focus on interest rates in the new macroeconomic literature gives more backing to a central role of interest rates than the nineteenth-century literature could. The fact that the Bank of England and the Reichsbank, as well as many other central banks, operated around 1900, and thus under rather different circumstances, according to the broad principles of the new view suggests that, indeed, financial market features were never, and are unlikely to be, a good reason for deviating substantially from it. Furthermore, according to Woodford (2001*b*), a standing facility-based approach will be robust in the face of various monetary innovations relating to the 'information economy' that may possibly become relevant in the course of the twenty-first century.

In only one detail may one wonder whether the new view does not reflect simply an inherited doctrine, namely, the fact that the recourse to standing facilities should not be structural in order to preserve an active short-term inter-bank money market. Preserving a market should not be an aim per se, since market transactions cause transaction costs and any change that can eliminate these costs without changing anything else could be beneficial. Indeed, as long as changes in central bank rates cannot take place within one reserve maintenance period (as it has always been the case for the Bank of England and has been the case for the Eurosystem since March 2004), it seems to make only limited, if any, difference from the monetary policy perspective whether banks refinance mainly through reverse open market operations, or whether they cover directly a larger part of their liquidity needs through a standing facility at the target rate.[8] The difference is especially limited if broadly the same set of counterparts accesses both types of operations and if the same collateral can be used for both (as in the case of the Eurosystem and the Bank of England). For instance, the Deutsche Reichsbank, among other continental central banks, seems to have operated successfully with a pure borrowing facility approach between 1876 and 1914, and so did the Oesterreichische Nationalbank even until 1995 (Borio 1997: 325). Such an approach might have the advantage not only of saving some transactions costs in the money market, but also of further simplifying

---

[8] It should be recalled that the Bank of England's doctrine that the market rate should stay around one percentage point below the discount rate related mainly to the problem of 'overdiscounting' in the event of rate hike expectations. This problem is, however, linked to the long maximum maturity of eligible paper at that time (up to three months), and is thus not applicable if the borrowing facility takes the form of an advance facility with overnight maturity.

slightly the operational framework of the central bank by eliminating the need for *two* standing facilities.[9] The drawback of this solution—that it will dry up the inter-bank market at least at the maturity of the standing facility—would, however, need to be studied further. In any case, the benefits of moving to such an approach would not be overwhelming, since the symmetric corridor system has proven its simplicity and effectiveness. On the assumption that the corridor approach eventually prevails, it seems that central banks will have to choose mainly among three interrelated dimensions: whether or not they want a reserve requirement system with averaging, how often they are willing to conduct open market operations, and whether they want a broad or narrow corridor set by standing facilities. The Bank of England has a 200 basis points corridor, no averaging, and daily open market operations. The Eurosystem has the same corridor, but reserve requirements with averaging, and weekly open market operations. Australia, Canada, and New Zealand have a 50 basis points corridor, no averaging, and daily open market operations. While these three were not analysed in detail here, Woodford (2001*b*, 2003) provides evidence that their approach makes it possible to achieve a very precise control of short-term interest rates. For those central banks wishing to move to a corridor system, the main consideration for choosing between the two models would probably be whether they dislike a reserve requirement system with averaging more than daily open market operations (neither of which actually causes problems in practice). With regard to the width of the corridor, it seems that averaging implies a wider corridor (to avoid extreme recourse to facilities in the event of rate change expectations), while a one-day maintenance period seems to be compatible with a narrower one.

Whichever variant of the corridor approach, or of an approach with structural recourse to a standing facility, is chosen, what matters most by far is that the central bank recognizes a short-term interest rate as its operational target and that it uses monetary policy instruments to achieve this target in an unpretentious and effective way. Today, this appears to be the common approach of central banks, and the academic community too seems once again to lean more and more towards this view.

---

[9] A proposal that is relatively close to a Reichsbank approach would be to simply remunerate all reserves of banks (that is, not only required reserves) and to supply excess reserves. Under such an approach, no deposit facility would be needed, and market rates would be pegged to the remuneration rate of reserves (see Goodfriend 2002). Such an approach is in fact currently applied by, for example, the Peoples' Bank of China.

References

Allen, L. and A. Saunders (1992). 'Bank Window Dressing: Theory and Evidence', *Journal of Banking and Finance*, 16: 585-623.

Allen, W. A. (2002). *The Bank of England Open Market Operations: Introduction of a Deposit Facility* (BIS Paper No. 12, Market Functioning and Central Bank Policy). Basle: Bank for International Settlements.

Alvarez, F., R. E. Lucas Jr, and W. W. Weber (2001). 'Interest Rates and Inflation', *American Economic Review, Papers and Proceedings*, 91: 219-25.

Amatayakul, K. (1942). *Die Offenmarktpolitik der Bank von England und der Deutschen Reichsbank*. Zurich: Ernst Lang.

Anderson, L. C. (1965). *Evolution of the Role and Functioning of the Discount Mechanism* (Steering Committee for the Fundamental Reappraisal of the Discount Mechanism). Washington, DC: Board of Governors of the Federal Reserve System.

—— (1969). 'Money Market Conditions as a Guide for Monetary Management', in K. Brunner (ed.), *Targets and Indicators of Monetary Policy*. San Francisco: Chandler Publishing Company.

Angelini, P. (2002). 'Liquidity and Announcement Effects in the Euro Area', *Banca d'Italia Temi di Discussione*, no. 451. Rome: Banca d'Italia.

—— and A. Prati (1996). 'The Identification of Liquidity Effects in the EMS', *Open Economies Review*, 7: 275-93.

Atkinson, T. R. (1970). 'The Discount Proposal from the Standpoint of Commercial Banks', *Journal of Money, Credit and Banking*, 2: 147-50.

Axilrod, S. H. and D. E. Lindsey (1981). 'Federal Reserve System Implementation of Monetary Policy: Analytical Foundations of the New Approach', *American Economic Review*, 71: 246-52.

Ayuso, J., A. G. Haldane, and F. Restoy (1997). 'Volatility Transmission along the Money Market Yield Curve', *Weltwirtschaftliches Archiv*, 133: 56-75.

Ayuso, J. and R. Repullo (2001). 'Why Did Banks Overbid? An Empirical Model of the Fixed Rate Tenders of the European Central Bank', *Journal of International Money and Finance*, 20: 857-70.

—— —— (2003). 'A Model of the Open Market Operations of the European Central Bank', *Economic Journal*, 113: 883-902.

Bagehot, W. (1873/1962). *Lombard Street—A Description of the Money Market*, with a new introduction by F. C. Genovese. Homewood, Illinois: Richard D. Irwin.

Balduzzi, P. G., S. Bertola, S. Foresi, and L. Klapper (1998). 'Interest Rate Targeting and the Dynamics of Short Term Rates', *Journal of Money, Credit and Banking*, 30: 26-50.

Balino, T. J. Y. and L. M. Zamalloa (1997). *Instruments of Monetary Management—Issues and Country Experience*. Washington, DC: IMF.

Baltensperger, E. (1980). 'Alternative Approaches to the Theory of the Banking Firm', *Journal of Monetary Economics*, 6: 1-37.

—— (1982a). 'Reserve Requirements and Economic Stability', *Journal of Money, Credit and Banking*, 14: 205-15.

—— (1982b). 'Reserve Requirements and Optimal Money Balances', *Zeitschrift für Wirtschafts- und Sozialwissenschaften*, 102: 225-36.

Bank of England (1982). 'The Role of the Bank of England in the Money Market', *Bank of England Quarterly Bulletin*, March: 86–94.

—— (1988). *Bank of England Operations in the Sterling Money Market*. London: Bank of England.

—— (1997). *Reform of the Bank of England's Operations in the Sterling Money Markets*. London: Bank of England.

—— (2002a). *The Bank of England's Operations in the Sterling Money Markets*. London: Bank of England.

—— (2002b). *Monetary Policy Fact Sheet* (on the Bank of England's website).

Banque de France (2002). 'Les comportements individuels de soumission aux appels d'offres à taux variable', *Bulletin de la Banque de France*, No. 104/August: 69–83.

Barro, R. J. (1989). 'Interest-rate Targeting', *Journal of Monetary Economics*, 23: 3–30.

Bartolini, L., G. Bertola, and A. Prati (2001a). 'Banks' Reserve Management, Transaction Costs, and the Timing of Federal Reserve Interventions', *Journal of Banking and Finance*, 25: 1287–317.

—— —— (2001b). *The Overnight Interbank Market: Evidence from the G7 and the Euro Zone* (Staff Reports No. 135). New York: Federal Reserve Bank of New York.

—— —— (2002). 'Day-to-day Implementation of Monetary Policy and the Volatility of the Federal Funds Rate', *Journal of Money, Credit and Banking*, 34: 137–59.

Batten, D., M. Blackwell, I. Kim, S. Nocera, and Y. Ozeki (1989). *The Instruments and Operating Procedures for Conducting Monetary Policy in the Group of Five Countries* (IMF Working Paper, WP/89/57). Washington, DC: IMF.

Beek, D. C. (1981). 'Excess Reserves and Reserve Targeting', *Federal Reserve Bank of New York Quarterly Review*, Autumn: 15–22.

Bernanke, B. (2002). 'Deflation: Making Sure it Doesn't Happen Here', remarks made in the National Economists Club, Washington, DC, 21 November.

Bindseil, U. (2001). *Central Bank Forecasts of Autonomous Factors: Quality, Publication, and the Control of the Overnight Rate* (ECB Working Paper Series No. 70). Frankfurt am Main: ECB.

—— (2002). 'Central Bank Forecasts of Liquidity Factors and the Control of Short-Term Interest Rates', *Banca Nationale del Lavoro Quarterly Review*, 220: 13–37.

—— (2005). 'Over- and Underbidding in Central Bank Open Market Operations Conducted as Fixed Rate Tender', *German Economic Review*.

—— and F. Seitz (2001). *The Supply and Demand for Eurosystem Deposits—The First 18 Months* (ECB Working Paper Series No. 44). Frankfurt am Main: ECB.

—— G. Camba-Mendez, A. Hirsch, and B. Weller (2004). 'Excess Reserves of Banks with the Central Bank and the Liquidity Management Framework of the Euro Area'. (ECB Working Paper Series No. 361). Frankfurt am Main: ECB.

—— B. Weller, and F. Würtz (2003). 'Central Bank and Commercial Banks' Liquidity Management—What is the Relationship?', *Economic Notes*, 32: 37–66.

BIS (Bank for International Settlements) (1980). *The Monetary Base Approach to Monetary Control*. Basle: BIS.

—— (1997). 'Implementation and Tactics of Monetary Policy', in BIS, *Monetary Policy Operating Procedures in Industrial Countries* (BIS Conference Papers iii). Basle: BIS.

Bisignano, J. (1996). *Varieties of Monetary Policy Operating Procedures: Balancing Monetary Objectives with Market Efficiency* (BIS Working Paper No. 35, July). Basle: BIS.

Blanchard, O. J. and S. Fischer (1989). *Lectures on Macroeconomics*. Cambridge, MA: MIT Press.

Blenck, D., H. Hasko, S. Hilton, and K. Masaki (2001). 'The Main Features of the Monetary Policy Frameworks of the Bank of Japan, the Federal Reserve and the Eurosystem', in

BIS (ed.), *Comparing Monetary Policy Operating Procedures Across the United States, Japan, and the Euro Area* (BIS Paper New Series No. 9). Basle: BIS.

Bloomfield, A. I. (1959). *Monetary Policy under the Gold Standard: 1880–1914*. New York: Federal Reserve Bank of New York.

Board of Governors (1954/1974/1994). *The Federal Reserve System: Purposes and Functions*. Washington, DC: Board of Governors of the Federal Reserve System.

—— (2002a). 'Extension of Credit by Federal Reserve Banks' (announcement made on 17 May), website of the Board of Governors of the Federal Reserve System.

—— (2002b). *Alternative Instruments for Open Market and Discount Window Operations*. Washington, DC: Board of Governors of the Federal Reserve System.

Bockelman, H. (1980). 'Die Zinsbildung am Geldmarkt', *Kredit und Kapital*, 13: 339–48.

Bofinger, P. (2001). *Monetary Policy. Goals, Institutions, Strategies and Instruments*. Oxford: Oxford University Press.

Bomhoff, E. J. (1977). 'Predicting the Money Multiplier', *Journal of Monetary Economics*, 3: 325–45.

Bopp, K. (1954). 'Die Tätigkeit der Reichsbank 1876–1914', *Weltwirtschaftliches Archiv*, 90: 34–56.

Borio, C. E. V. (1997). 'Monetary Policy Operating Procedures in Industrial Countries', in BIS, *Monetary Policy Operating Procedures in Industrial Countries* (BIS Conference Papers iii). Basle: BIS.

Boyle, A. (1967). *Montagu Norman*. London: Cassel.

Breitung J. and D. Nautz (2001): 'The Empirical Performance of the ECB's Repo Auctions: Evidence from Aggregated and Individual Bidding Data', *Journal of International Money and Finance*, 20: 839–56.

Brock, P. L. (1989). 'Reserve Requirements and the Inflation Tax', *Journal of Money, Credit and Banking*, 21: 106–21.

Brunner, K. (1970). 'The Federal Reserve Discount Policy', *Journal of Money, Credit and Banking*, 2: 135–7.

—— and A. Meltzer (1964). *The Federal Reserve's Attachment to the Free Reserves Concept*. Washington, DC: House Committee on Banking and Currency. Reprinted in K. Brunner and A. Meltzer (eds.) (1989), *Monetary Economics*. Oxford: Blackwell.

Burgess, W. R. (1927). *The Reserve Banks and the Money Market*. New York and London: Harper and Brothers.

—— (1964). 'Reflections on the Early Developments of Open Market Policy', *Federal Reserve Bank of New York Monthly Review*, 46/November: 219–26.

Butler, S. and R. Clews (1997). 'Money Market Operations in the United Kingdom', in BIS, *Monetary Policy Operating Procedures in Industrial Countries* (BIS Conference Papers iii). Basle: BIS.

Cabrero, A., G. Camba-Mendez, A. Hirsch, and F. Nieto (2002). *Modelling the Daily Banknotes in Circulation in the Context of the Liquidity Management of the European Central Bank* (ECB Working Paper Series No. 142). Frankfurt am Main: ECB.

Caesar, R. (1976). 'Die Rolle der Mindestreserve im Rahmen der Geldbasiskonzeption der Deutschen Bundesbank', *Jahrbücher für Nationalökonomie und Statistik*, 191: 229–50.

Campbell, J. Y. (1987). 'Money Announcements, the Demand for Bank Reserves, and the Behavior of the Federal Funds Rate Within the Statement Week', *Journal of Money, Credit and Banking*, 19: 56–67.

Cancelo, J. R. and A. Espasa (1987). 'Un nuevo modelo diario para la prediccion de la circulacion fiduciaria', *Banco de Espana, Servicio de Estudios*, 1987/73. Madrid: Banco de Espana.

Carr, H. C. (1959). 'Why and How to Read the Federal Reserve Statement', *Journal of Finance*, 14: 504–19.

Cassel, G. (1928). 'The Rate of Interest, the Bank Rate, and the Stabilisation of Prices', *Quarterly Journal of Economics*, 42: 511–29.

Cassola, N. and C. Morana (2003). *Volatility of Interest Rates in the Euro Area: Evidence from High Frequency Data* (ECB Working Paper Series No. 235). Frankfurt am Main: ECB.

Chandler, L. (1958). *Benjamin Strong, Central Banker*. Washington, DC: Brookings Institution.

Christiano, L. J., M. Eichenbaum, and C. Evans (1996). 'The Effects of Monetary Policy Shocks: Some Evidence from the Flow of Funds', *Review of Economics and Statistics*, 87: 16–34.

Clapham, J. (1944). *The Bank of England* (two vols.). Cambridge: Cambridge University Press.

Clarida, R., J. Gali, and M. Gertler (1998). 'Monetary Policy Rules in Practice: Some International Evidence', *European Economic Review*, 42: 1033–67.

Clinton, K. (1997). *Implementation of Monetary Policy in a Regime with Zero Reserve Requirements* (Bank of Canada Working Paper No. 97/8). Ottawa: Bank of Canada.

Clouse, J. A. (1994). 'Recent Developments in Discount Window Policy', *Federal Reserve Bulletin*, 80: 966–77.

—— and J. P. Dow (1999). 'Fixed Costs and the Behavior of the Federal Funds Rate', *Journal of Banking and Finance*, 23: 1015–29.

—— —— (2002). 'A Computational Model of Banks' Optimal Reserve Management Policy', *Journal of Economic Dynamics and Control*, 26: 1787–814.

—— and D. W. Elmendorf (1997). 'Declining Required Reserves and the Volatility of the Federal Funds Rate' (working paper). Washington, DC: Board of Governors of the Federal Reserve System.

Cook, T. C. (1989). 'Determinants of the Federal Funds Rate: 1979–1982', *Economic Review*, Federal Reserve Bank of Richmond, 75, Jan/Feb: 3–18.

—— and T. Hahn (1989). 'The Effect of Changes in the Federal Funds Rate Target on Market Interest Rate in the 1970s', *Journal of Monetary Economics*, 24: 331–51.

Cosimo, T. F. and R. G. Sheehan (1994). 'The Federal Reserve Operating Procedures, 1984–1990: An Empirical Analysis', *Journal of Macroeconomics*, 16: 573–88.

Cramp, A. B. (1987). 'Bank Rate', in *The New Palgrave: A Dictionary of Economics*. New York and London: Macmillan.

Curie, L. (1935). *The Supply and Control of Money in the United States*. Cambridge, MA: Harvard University Press.

Davies, H. (1998). *Averaging in a Framework of Zero Reserve Requirements: Implications for the Operation of Monetary Policy* (Bank of England Working Paper Series No. 84). London: Bank of England.

Deutsche Bundesbank (1976). *Geld- und Bankwesen in Zahlen, 1876–1975*. Frankfurt am Main: Deutsche Bundesbank.

—— (1982a). 'Central Bank Money Requirements of Banks and Liquidity Policy Measures of the Bundesbank'. *Monthly Report of the Deutsche Bundesbank*, 34/4: 20–5.

—— (1982b). *The Deutsche Bundesbank. Its Monetary Policy Instruments and Functions*. Frankfurt am Main: Deutsche Bundesbank.

—— (1983). 'The Bundesbank's Transactions in Securities Under Repurchase Agreements', *Monthly Report of the Deutsche Bundesbank*, 35/5: 23–30.

—— (1994a). 'The Restructuring and Lowering of the Minimum Reserves', *Monthly Report of the Deutsche Bundesbank*, 46/2: 13–17.

— (1994*b*). 'Money Market Management by the Deutsche Bundesbank', *Monthly Report of the Deutsche Bundesbank*, 46/5: 59–74.

— (1995). *The Monetary Policy of the Deutsche Bundesbank*. Frankfurt am Main: Deutsche Bundesbank.

Dewald, W. G. (1963). 'Free Reserves, Total Reserves, and Monetary Control', *Journal of Political Economy*, 71: 141–53.

Dotsey, M. (1989). 'Monetary Control Under Alternative Operating Procedures', *Journal of Money, Credit and Banking*, 21: 273–90.

Dow, J. P. (2001). 'The Demand for Excess Reserves', *Southern Economic Journal*, 67: 685–700.

ECB (European Central Bank) (1998). 'The Use of a Minimum Reserve System by the European System of Central Banks in Stage Three' (press release, 8 July). Frankfurt am Main: ECB.

— (2000). 'The Switch to Variable Rate Tenders in the Main Refinancing Operations', *Monthly Bulletin*, July: 31–6.

— (2001*a*). 'The Collateral Framework of the Eurosystem', *Monthly Bulletin*, April: 49–62.

— (2001*b*). 'Bidding Behaviour of Counterparties in the Eurosystem's Regular Open Market Operations', *Monthly Bulletin*, October: 51–64.

— (2001*c*). *The Monetary Policy of the ECB*. Frankfurt am Main: ECB.

— (2002*a*). *The Single Monetary Policy in the Euro Area: General Documentation on Eurosystem Monetary Policy Instruments and Procedures*. Frankfurt am Main: ECB.

— (2002*b*). 'The Liquidity Management of the ECB', *Monthly Bulletin*, May: 41–53.

— (2003). 'Measures to Improve the Efficiency of the Framework for Monetary Policy' (press release, 23 January). Frankfurt am Main: ECB.

Edgeworth, F. Y (1888). 'The Mathematical Theory of Banking', *Journal of the Royal Statistical Society*, 51: 113–27.

Ejerskov, S., C. M. Moss, and L. Stracca (2003). *How Does the ECB Allot Liquidity in its Weekly Main Refinancing Operations? A Look at the Empirical Evidence* (ECB Working Paper Series No. 244). Frankfurt am Main: ECB.

Escriva, J.-L. and G. Fagan (1996). *Empirical Assessment of Monetary Policy Instruments and Procedures in EU Countries*, European Monetary Institute Staff Papers, No. 2, Frankfurt am Main: European Monetary Institute.

Ewerhart, C. (2002). *A Model of the Eurosystem's Operational Framework for Monetary Policy Implementation* (Working Paper Series No. 197). Frankfurt am Main: ECB.

— N. Cassola, S. Ejerskov, and N. Valla (2003). 'Optimal Allotment Policy in the Eurosystem's Main Refinancing Operations' (Working Paper Series No. 295). Frankfurt am Main: ECB.

Fama, E. F. (1980). 'Banking in the Theory of Finance', *Journal of Monetary Economics*, 6: 39–57.

Federal Reserve Bank of New York (2000). *Understanding Open Market Operations*. New York: Federal Reserve Bank of New York.

— (2002). *Domestic Open Market Operations During 2001*. New York: Federal Reserve Bank of New York.

Feinman, J. (1993). 'Reserve Requirements: History, Current Practice, and Potential Reform', *Federal Reserve Bulletin*, 79: 569–89.

Fisher, I. (1911). *The Purchasing Power of Money*. New York: Macmillan.

Fousek, P. G. (1957). *Foreign Central Banking: The Instruments of Monetary Policy*. New York: Federal Reserve Bank of New York.

Freeman, S. (1987). 'Reserve Requirements and Optimal Seigniorage', *Journal of Monetary Economics*, 19: 307–14.

Freeman, S. and J. H. Haslag (1995). 'Should Bank Reserves Earn Interest?', *Federal Reserve Bank of Dallas Economic Review*, 4th quarter: 25–33.

Freixas, X. and J.-C. Rochet (1997). *The Microeconomics of Banking*. Cambridge, MA: MIT Press.

Friedman, B. M. (1990). 'Targets and Instruments of Monetary Policy', in B. Friedman and F. Hahn (eds.), *The Handbook of Monetary Economics*, ii. New York: North-Holland.

—— (2000). 'The Role of Interest Rates in Federal Reserve Policymaking', in R. W. Kopcke and L. E. Browne (eds.), *The Evolution of Monetary Policy and the Federal Reserve System Over the Past Thirty Years* (Conference Series No. 45). Boston: Federal Reserve Bank of Boston.

Friedman, M. (1960). *A Program for Monetary Stability*. New York: Fordham University Press.

—— (1982). 'Monetary Policy: Theory and Practice', *Journal of Money, Credit and Banking*, 14: 98–118.

—— and A. Schwartz (1963). *A Monetary History of the United States, 1867–1960*. Princeton: Princeton University Press.

Frost, P. A. (1971). 'Banks' Demand for Excess Reserves', *Journal of Political Economy*, 79: 805–25.

Froyen, R. T. and K. J. Kopecky (1983). 'A Note on Reserve Requirements and Monetary Control with a Flexible Deposit Rate', *Journal of Banking and Finance*, 7: 101–9.

Furfine, C. H. (2000). 'Interbank Payments and the Daily Federal Funds Rate', *Journal of Monetary Economics*, 46: 535–53.

—— (2003). 'The Fed's New Discount Window and Interbank Borrowing'. Unpublished manuscript. Chicago: Federal Reserve Bank of Chicago.

Galbraith, J. K. (1975). *Money—Whence It Came, Where It Went*. London: Andre Deutsch.

Garfinkel, M. and D. L. Thornton (1991). 'The Multiplier Approach to the Money Supply Process: a Precautionary Note', *Review of the Federal Reserve Bank of St Louis*, July/August: 47–64.

Gaspar, V., G. Perez-Quiros, and H. Rodriguez-Mendizábal (2004). 'Interest Rate Determination in the Interbank Money Market'. (ECB Working Paper Series No. 351). Frankfurt am Main. ECB.

Gestrich, H. (1941). 'Aufbau und Dynamik des deutschen Geldmarktes', in *Deutsche Geldpolitik*. Berlin: Duncker & Humblot.

Gilbert R. A. (1985). 'Operating Procedures for Conducting Monetary Policy', *Federal Reserve Bank of St. Louis Review*, 20: 13–21.

Goldenweiser, E. A. (1925). *The Federal Reserve System in Operation*. New York: McGraw-Hill.

Goldfeld, S. M. and E. J. Kane (1966). 'The Determinants of Member Bank Borrowing: An Econometric Study', *Journal of Finance*, 21: 499–514.

Goodfriend, M. (1983). 'Discount Window Borrowing, Monetary Policy, and the Post October 6, 1979 Federal Reserve Operating Procedure', *Journal of Monetary Economics*, 12: 343–56.

—— (1988). 'Central Banking Under the Gold Standard', in K. Brunner and A. Meltzer (eds.), Money, Cycles, Exchange rates: Essays in Honor of Allan H. Meltzer, *Carnegie-Rochester Conference Series on Public Policy*, 29: 85–124.

—— (2002). 'Interest on Reserves and Monetary Policy', *Economic Policy Review*, Federal Reserve Bank of New York, 8/1: 77–84.

—— (2003). 'Review of Allan Meltzer's *A History of the Federal Reserve, Volume 1: 1913–1951*, Federal Reserve Bank of Minneapolis, *The Region*, December.

— and M. Hargraves (1987). 'A Historical Assessment of the Rationales and Functions of Reserve Requirements', in M. Goodfriend, *Monetary Policy in Practice*. Richmond: Federal Reserve Bank of Richmond.

Goodhart, C. A. E. (1985). *Monetary Theory and Practice*. London: Macmillan.

— (1987). 'Monetary Base', in *The New Palgrave: A Dictionary of Economics*, iii. London and New York: Macmillan.

— (1989). 'The Conduct of Monetary Policy', *Economic Journal*, 99: 293–346.

— (2000). 'The Inflation Forecast' (working paper). London: London School of Economics.

— (2001). 'The Endogeneity of Money', in P. Arestis, M. Desai, and S. Dow (eds.), *Money, Macroeconomics and Keynes*, Routledge.

— (2004). 'The Bank of England, 1970–2000', in R. Michie and P. Williamson (eds.), *The British Government and the City of London in the Twentieth Century*, Cambridge University Press, forthcoming.

Görgens, E., K. Rückriegel, S. Schich, and F. Seitz (forthcoming). *European Monetary Policy*. Dordrecht: Kluwer.

Green, R. (1987). 'Real Bills Doctrine', in *The New Palgrave: A Dictionary of Economics*, iv. New York and London: Macmillan.

Gros, D. and F. Schobert (1999). *Excess Foreign Exchange Reserves and Overcapitalisation in the Eurosystem* (CEPS Working Document No 128). Brussels: Centre for European Policy Studies.

Guthrie, G. and J. Wright (2000). 'Open Mouth Operations', *Journal of Monetary Economics*, 46: 489–516.

Guttentag, J. M. (1966). 'The Strategy of Open Market Operations', *Quarterly Journal of Economics*, 80: 1–30.

Haase, H. (1962). *Die Lombardpolitik der Zentralnotenbanken*. Berlin: Duncker & Humblot.

Hagen, J. von (1999). 'A New Approach to Monetary Policy (1971–1978)', in Deutsche Bundesbank (ed.), *Fifty Years of Deutsche Mark*. Oxford: Oxford University Press.

Hakkio, C. S. and G. H. Sellon (2000). 'The Discount Window: Time for Reform?', *Federal Reserve Bank of Kansas City Economic Review*, 87/1: 57–63.

Hamdani, K. and S. Persistani (1991). 'A Disaggregated Analysis of Discount Window Borrowing', *Federal Reserve Bank of New York Quarterly Review*, Summer: 52–62.

Hamilton, J. D. (1996). 'The Daily Market for Federal Funds', *Journal of Political Economy*, 104: 26–56.

— (1997). 'Measuring the Liquidity Effect', *American Economic Review*, 87: 80–97.

— (1998). 'The Demand and Supply for Federal Reserve Deposits', *Carnegie-Rochester Conference Series on Public Policies*, 49: 1–44.

Hanes, C. (1999). 'Open Mouth Operations and the Disappearance of the Borrowing Function'. Unpublished manuscript. University of Mississippi.

Hardy, C. O. (1932). *Credit Policies of the Federal Reserve System*. Washington, DC: Brookings Institution.

Hardy, D. (1996). *Reserve Requirements and Monetary Management: An Introduction* (IMF Working Paper WP/93/35). Washington, DC: IMF.

Harris, S. E. (1933). *Twenty Years of Federal Reserve Policy* (2 vols.). Cambridge, MA: Harvard University Press.

Hartmann, P., M. Manna, and A. Manzanares (2001). 'The Microstructure of the Euro Money Market', *Journal of International Money and Finance*, 20: 895–948.

Haslag, J. H. and S. E. Hein (1989). 'Federal Reserve System Reserve Requirements, 1959–1988', *Journal of Money, Credit and Banking*, 21: 515–23.

Hawtrey, R. G. (1938). *A Century of Bank Rate.* London: Longman.

Hayashi, F. (2001). 'Identifying a Liquidity Effect in the Japanese Interbank Market', *International Economic Review*, 42: 287–315.

Hester, D. D. (1970). 'Reflections on the Discount Window', *Journal of Money, Credit and Banking*, 2: 151–7.

Ho, T. S. Y. and A. Saunders (1985). 'A Micro Model of the Federal Funds Market', *Journal of Finance*, 15: 977–88.

Holland, R. C. (1970). 'The Federal Reserve Discount Mechanism as an Instrument for Dealing with Banking Market Imperfections', *Journal of Money, Credit and Banking*, 2: 138–46.

Horrigan, B. R. (1988). 'Are Reserve Requirements Relevant for Economic Stabilization?', *Journal of Monetary Economics*, 21: 97–105.

Humphrey, T. H. (2001). 'Monetary Policy Frameworks and Indicators for the Federal Reserve in the 1920s', *Federal Reserve Bank of Richmond Economic Quarterly*, 87, Winter: 65–92.

Issing, O. (1994). 'Experience Gained with Monetary Policy Instruments in Germany', in Institut für Bankhistorische Forschung e.V. (ed.), *Monetary Policy Instruments: National Experiences and European Perspectives.* Frankfurt am Main: Fritz Knapp Verlag.

Issing, O., V. Gaspar, I. Angeloni, and O. Tristani (2001). *Monetary Policy in the Euro Area.* Cambridge, MA: Cambridge University Press.

Jarchow, H.-J. (1974). *Theorie und Politik des Geldes, Teil II: Geldmarkt und Geldpolitische Instrumente.* Göttingen: Vandenhoeck.

Johannes, J. M. and R. H. Rasche (1979). "Predicting the Money Multiplier," *Journal of Monetary Economics*, 5: 301–25.

Judd, J. P. and B. Motley (1992). 'Controlling Inflation with an Interest Rate Instrument', *Federal Reserve Bank of San Francisco Economic Review*, Summer: 3–22.

Kaminow, I. (1977). 'Required Reserve Ratios, Policy Instruments, and Money Stock Control', *Journal of Monetary Economics*, 3: 398–408.

Kane, E. (1980). 'Politics and Fed Policymaking: The More Things Change, The More They Remain The Same', *Journal of Monetary Economics*, 6: 199–211.

Käppeli, R. B. (1930). *Der Notenbankausweis in Theorie und Wirklichkeit.* Jena: Gustav Fischer.

Kasman, B. (1993). 'A Comparison of Monetary Policy Operating Procedures in Six Industrial Countries', in M. Goodfriend and D. Small (eds.), *Operating Procedures and the Conduct of Monetary Policy: Conference Proceedings* (Finance and Economics Discussion Series, Working Studies 1, Parts 1 and 2). Washington, DC: Board of Governors of the Federal Reserve System.

Kaufman, H. M. and R. E. Lombra (1980). 'The Demand for Excess Reserves, Liability Management, and the Money Supply Process', *Economic Inquiry*, 18: 555–66.

Keynes, J. M. (1930/1971). *A Treatise on Money*, ii: *The Applied Theory of Money*, The Collected Works of John Maynard Keynes, 6. London: Macmillan/Cambridge University Press.

King, M. (1994). 'Monetary Policy Instruments: The UK Experience', in Institut für Bankhistorische Forschung e.V. (ed.), *Monetary Policy Instruments: National Experiences and European Perspectives.* Frankfurt am Main: Fritz Knapp Verlag.

King, W. T. C. (1936). *History of the London Discount Market.* London: Frank Cass.

Kneeshaw, J. T. and P. Van den Bergh (1989). *Changes in Central Bank Money Market Operating Procedures in the 1980s.* Basel: BIS.

Kopecky, K. J. and A. L. Tucker (1993). 'Interest Rate Smoothness and the Non-Settling-Day Behavior of Banks', *Journal of Economics and Business*, 45: 297–314.

Kuttner, K. J. (2001). 'Monetary Policy Surprises and Interest Rates: Evidence from the Fed Funds Futures Market', *Journal of Monetary Economics*, 47: 523–44.

Lasser, D. J. (1992). 'The Effect of Contemporaneous Reserve Accounting on the Market for Federal Funds', *Journal of Banking and Finance*, 16: 1047–56.

Laufenberg, D. E. (1976). 'Contemporaneous vs. Lagged Reserve Accounting', *Journal of Money, Credit and Banking*, 8: 239–45.

—— (1979). 'Optimal Reserve Requirement Ratios Against Bank Deposits for Short-Run Monetary Control', *Journal of Money, Credit and Banking*, 11: 99–105.

Leigh-Pemberton, R. (1987). 'The Instruments of Monetary Policy', *Bank of England Quarterly Bulletin*, August: 365–70.

Leone, A. M. (1993). *Institutional and Operational Aspects of Central Bank Losses* (IMF Paper on Policy Analysis and Assessment, 93/14). Washington, DC: IMF.

Lindsey, D. E., H. T. Farr, G. P. Gillum, K. J. Kopecky, and R. D. Porter (1984). 'Short-run Monetary Control: Evidence under a Non-Borrowed Reserve Operating Procedures', *Journal of Monetary Economics*, 13: 87–111.

Linzert, T., D. Nautz, and J. Breitung (2003). *Bidder Behavior in Repo Auctions Without Minimum Bid Rate: Evidence from the Bundesbank* (Discussion Paper 13/03). Frankfurt am Main: Deutsche Bundesbank.

Linzert, T., D. Nautz, and U. Bindseil (2004). *The Longer Term Refinancing Operations of the ECB* (Working Paper Series No. 359). Frankfurt am Main: ECB.

Llewellyn, D. and B. Tew (1988). 'The Sterling Money Market and the Determination of Interest Rates', *National Westminster Bank Quarterly Review*, May: 25–37.

Loungani, P. and M. Rush (1995). 'The Effects of Changes in Reserve Requirements on Investment and GNP', *Journal of Money, Credit and Banking*, 27: 511–26.

Luther, H. (1964). *Vor dem Abgrund. Reichsbankpräsident in Krisenzeiten*. Berlin: Propylaeen Verlag.

Lutz, F. (1936). *Das Grundproblem der Geldverfassung*. Stuttgart und Berlin: W. Kohlhammer.

McCallum, B. T. (1981). 'Price Level Determinacy with an Interest Rate Instrument and Rational Expectations', *Journal of Monetary Economics*, 8: 319–29.

—— (1986). 'Some Issues Concerning Interest Rate Pegging, Price Level Determinacy, and the Real Bills Doctrine', *Journal of Monetary Economics*, 17: 135–60.

—— (1990). 'Could a Monetary Base Rule have Prevented the Great Depression?', *Journal of Monetary Economics*, 26: 3–26.

—— (1994). *Monetary Policy and the Term Structure of Interest Rates* (Working Paper No. 4938, November). Cambridge, MA: National Bureau of Economic Research.

Madigan, Brian F. and W. R. Nelson (2002). 'Proposed Revision to the Federal Reserve's Discount Window Lending Programs', *Federal Reserve Bulletin*, 88: 313–19.

Mankiw, N. G. and J. A. Miron (1986). 'The Changing Behavior of the Term Structure of Interest Rates', *Quarterly Journal of Economics*, 101: 211–28.

Meek, P. and R. Thunberg (1971). 'Monetary Aggregates and Federal Reserve Open Market Operations', *Federal Reserve Bank of New York Monthly Review*, 53/April: 80–9.

Meigs, J. A. (1962). *Free Reserves and the Money Supply*. Chicago: University of Chicago Press.

Meltzer, A. H. (2003). *A History of the Federal Reserve*, i. *1913–1951*. Chicago: University of Chicago Press.

Meulendyke, A.-M. (1990). 'Possible Roles for the Monetary Base', in Federal Reserve Bank of New York, *Intermediate Targets and Indicators of Monetary Policy: A Critical Survey*. New York: Federal Reserve Bank of New York.

Meulendyke, A.-M. (1992). 'Reserve Requirements and the Discount Window in Recent Decades', *Federal Reserve Bank of New York Quarterly Review*, Autumn: 25–43.

—— (1998). *US Monetary Policy and Financial Markets*. New York: Federal Reserve Bank of New York.

Mishkin, F. (2004). *The Economics of Money, Banking And Financial Markets* (7th edn.) Reading, MA: Addison-Wesley.

Modigliani, F., R. Rasche, and J. P. Cooper (1970). 'Central Bank Policy, the Money Supply, and the Short-Term Rate of Interest', *Journal of Money, Credit and Banking*, 2: 166–218.

Moore, B. (1988). *Horizontalists and Verticalists: The Macroeconomics of Credit Money*. New York: Cambridge University Press.

Mourmouras, A. and S. Russel (1992). 'Optimal Reserve Requirements, Deposit Taxation, and the Demand for Money', *Journal of Monetary Economics*, 30: 129–42.

Nautz, D. (1997). 'How Auctions Reveal Information: A Case Study on German Repo Rates', *Journal of Money, Credit and Banking*, 29: 17–25.

—— (1998). 'Banks' Demand for Reserves When Future Monetary Policy is Uncertain', *Journal of Monetary Economics*, 42: 161–83.

—— and J. Oechsler (2003). 'The Repo Auctions of the European Central Bank and the Vanishing Quota Puzzle', *Scandinavian Journal of Economics*, 105: 207–20.

Neyer, U. (2002). *Banks' Behaviour in the Inter-Bank Market and the Operational Framework of the Eurosystem* (Volkswirtschaftliche Diskussionsbeiträge Nr. 30, November). Halle: Martin Luther Universität Halle-Wittenberg.

Nyborg, K. and I. Strebulaev (2001). 'Collateral and Short Squeezing of Liquidity in Fixed Rate Tenders', *Journal of International Money and Finance*, 20: 769–92.

—— U. Bindseil, and I. Strebulaev (2002). *Bidder Behaviour and Performance in Repo Auctions: The Case of the Eurosystem* (Working Paper Series No. 157). Frankfurt am Main: ECB.

Orr, D. and W. G. Mellon (1961). 'Stochastic Reserve Losses and Expansion of Bank Credit', *American Economic Review*, 51: 612–23.

Pagan, A. R. and J. C. Robertson (1998). 'Structural Models of the Liquidity Effect', *Review of Economics and Statistics*, 80: 202–17.

Palgrave, R. H. I. (1903). *Bank Rate and the Money Market in England, France, Germany, Holland, and Belgium, 1844–1900*. London: John Murray.

Pearce, D. (1993). 'Discount Window Borrowing and Federal Reserve Operating Regimes', *Economic Inquiry*, 31: 564–79.

Pentzlin, H. (1980). *Hjalmar Schacht*. Berlin: Ullstein.

Perez-Quiros, G. and H.R. Rodriguez-Mendizábal (2001). *The Daily Market for Funds in Europe: Has Something Changed with EMU?* (Working Paper Series No. 67). Frankfurt am Main: ECB.

Persistani, S. (1991). 'The Model Structure of Discount Window Borrowing', *Journal of Money, Credit and Banking*, 23: 13–34.

Phillips, C. A. (1920). *Bank Credit*. New York: Macmillan.

Plenge, J. (1913). *Von der Diskontpolitik zur Herrschaft über den* Geldmarkt. Berlin: Julius Springer Verlag.

Poole, W. (1968). 'Commercial Bank Reserve Management in a Stochastic Model: Implications for Monetary Policy', *Journal of Finance*, 23: 769–91.

—— (1970). 'Optimal Choice of Monetary Policy Instruments in a Simple Stochastic Macro Model', *Quarterly Journal of Economics*, 84: 197–216.

—— (1976). 'A Proposal for Reforming Bank Reserve Requirements in the United States', *Journal of Money, Credit and Banking*, 8: 137–47.

Pösö, M. and L. Stracca (2004). 'Is There a Role for the Monetary Base in Monetary Policy?', *Kredit und Kapital*.

Prion, W. (1907). *Das deutsche Wechseldiskontgeschäft*. Leipzig: Duncker & Humblot.

Radcliffe, G. B. E. et al. (1959). *Report of the Committee on the Working of the Monetary System* ('Radcliffe Report'). London: HMSO.

Reichsbank (1900/1910). *The Reichsbank 1876–1900* (trans. National Monetary Commission). Washington, DC: Government Printing Office.

—— (1925a). *Die Reichsbank 1900–1924*. Berlin: Reichsdruckerei.

—— (1925b). *Vergleichende Notenbakstatistik*. Berlin: Reichsdruckerei.

Richter, R. (1968). 'The Banking System Within Macroeconomic Theory', *German Economic Review*, 6: 273–93.

—— (1990). *Money: Lectures on the Basis of General Equilibrium Theory and the Economics of Institutions*. Berlin et al.: Springer Verlag.

Riefler, W. W. (1930). *Money Rates and Money Markets in the United States*. New York: Harper & Bros.

Romer, D. (1985). 'Financial Intermediation, Reserve Requirements, and Inside Money: A General Equilibrium Approach', *Journal of Monetary Economics*, 16: 175–94.

Roover, R. de (1963). 'The Organization of Trade', in M. M. Postan et al. (eds.), *The Cambridge Economic History of Europe*, iii. Cambridge: Cambridge University Press.

Rudebusch, G. D. (1995). 'Federal Reserve Interest Rate Targeting, Rational Expectations, and the Term Structure of Interest Rates', *Journal of Monetary Economics*, 35: 245–74.

Santomero, A. H. (1983). 'Controlling Monetary Aggregates: The Discount Window', *Journal of Finance*, 38: 827–43.

—— and J. J. Siegel (1981). 'Bank Regulation and Macro-economic Stability', *American Economic Review*, 71: 39–53.

Sargent, T. J. and N. Wallace (1975). '"Rational" Expectations, the Optimal Monetary Instrument, and the Optimal Money Supply Rule', *Journal of Political Economy*, 83: 241–54.

Sayers, R. S. (1953). 'Open Market Operations in English Central Banking', *Schweizerische Zeitschrift für Volkswirtschaftslehre und Statistik*, 89: 389–98.

—— (1976). *The Bank of England, 1891–1944* (3 vols.). Cambridge: Cambridge University Press.

—— (1981). *Bank Rate in Keynes' Century*. London: The British Academy.

Scalia, A. and M. Ordine (2002). 'New Evidence on Money Market Integration in the Euro Area: A Panel Study on Banks' Participation in the Eurosystem's Auctions'. Unpublished manuscript.

Schacht, H. (1955). *My First Seventy-Six Years*. London: Alan Wingate.

Schmid, P. and H. Asche (1997). 'Monetary Policy Instruments and Procedures in Germany: Evolution, Deployment and Effects', in BIS, *Monetary Policy Operating Procedures in Industrial Countries* (BIS Conference Papers iii): Basle: BIS.

Seitz, F. and U. Bindseil (2002). 'Currency in Circulation, the Cash Changeover and the Euro-Dollar Exchange Rate', *Ifo-Studien*, 47: 531–48.

Siegel, J. J. (1981). 'Bank Reserves and Financial Stability', *Journal of Finance*, 34: 1073–84.

Smith, W. L. (1958). 'The Discount Rate as a Credit Control Weapon', *Journal of Political Economy*, 77: 171–7.

Spindt, P. A. and J. R. Hoffmeister (1988). 'The Micromechanics of the Federal Funds Market: Implications for Day-of-the-week Effects in Funds Rate Volatility', *Journal of Financial and Quantitative Analysis*, 23: 401–16.

References

Spindt, P. A. and V. Tarhan (1984). 'Bank Reserve Adjustment Process and the Use of Reserve Carryover as a Reserve Management Tool', *Journal of Banking and Finance*, 8: 5–20.

Sprague, O. M. W. (1921). 'The Discount Policy of the Federal Reserve Banks', *American Economic Review*, 11: 16–29.

Stadermann, B. (1961). *Offenmarktgeschaefte als Instrument der Liquiditaetspolitik.* Frankfurt am Main: Fritz Knapp.

Stella, P. (1997). *Do Central Banks Need Capital?* (IMF Working Paper 97/93). Washington, DC: IMF.

Stevens, E. J. (1991). 'Is There a Rationale for Reserve Requirements?', *Federal Reserve Bank of Cleveland Economic Review*, 27/4: 2–17.

Strongin, Steven (1995). 'The Identification of Monetary Policy Disturbances. Explaining the Liquidity Puzzle', *Journal of Monetary Economics*, 35: 463–97.

Svensson, L. E. O. (2003a). 'What is Wrong with Taylor Rules?', *Journal of Economic Literature*, 41: 426–77.

— (2003b). *Escaping from a Liquidity Trap and Deflation: The Foolproof Way and Others* (Working Paper No. W10195, December). Cambridge, MA: National Bureau of Economic Research.

Tamagna, F. M. (1963). 'Processes and Instruments of Monetary Policy: A Comparative Analysis', in F. M. Tamagna et al. (eds.), *Monetary Management.* Englewood Cliffs, NJ: Prentice-Hall.

Taylor, J. B. (1993). 'Discretion Versus Policy Rules in Practice', *Carnegie-Rochester Conference Series on Public Policy*, 39: 195–214.

Thornton, D. L. (1986). 'The Discount Rate and Market Interest Rates: Theory and Evidence', *Federal Reserve Bank of St. Louis Review*, August/September: 5–21.

— (1988). 'The Borrowed Reserves Operating Procedure: Theory and Evidence', *Federal Reserve Bank of St. Louis Review*, January/February: 30–54.

— (2001). 'The Federal Reserve's Operating Procedure, Non-Borrowed Reserves, Borrowed Reserves, and the Liquidity Effect', *Journal of Banking and Finance*, 25: 1717–39.

Thornton, H. (1802/1962). *An Inquiry into the Nature and Effects of Paper Credit of Great Britain.* New York: Kelley.

Tinbergen, J. (1939). *Business Cycles in the United States of America, 1919–1932.* Geneva: League of Nations.

Turner, R. C. (1938) *Member-Bank Borrowing.* Columbus: Ohio State University Press.

Vaez-Zadeh, R. (1991). 'Implications and Remedies of Central Bank Losses', in Patrick Downes and Reza Vaez-Zadeh (eds.), *The Evolving Role of Central Banks.* Washington, DC: IMF.

Välimäki, T. (1998). *The Overnight Rate of Interest Under Averaged Reserve Requirements* (Bank of Finland Discussion Papers, 7/1998). Helsinki: Bank of Finland.

— (2001). *Fixed Rate Tenders and the Overnight Money Market Equilibrium* (Bank of Finland Discussion Papers, 8/2001). Helsinki: Bank of Finland.

— (2002). 'Bidding in Fixed Rate Tenders: Theory and Experience with the ECB Tenders' (Bank of Finland Discussion Papers, 1/2002). Helsinki: Bank of Finland.

Van Hoose, D. D. (1986). 'A Note on Interest on Required Reserves as an Instrument of Monetary Control', *Journal of Banking and Finance*, 10: 147–56.

— (1987). 'A Note on Discount Rate Policy and the Variability of Discount Rate Borrowing', *Journal of Banking and Finance*, 11: 563–70.

Vocke, W. (1973). *Memoiren, Die Erinnerungen des früheren Bundesbankpräsidenten.* Stuttgart: Deutsche Verlags-Anstalt.

Wallace, R. F. (1956). 'The Use of the Progressive Discount Rate by the Federal Reserve System', *Journal of Political Economy*, 64: 59–68.

Walsh, C. E. (2003). *Monetary Theory and Monetary Policy* (2nd edn.). Cambridge, MA: MIT Press.

Warburg, P. M. (1930). *The Federal Reserve System, its Origins and Growth* (2 vols.). New York: Macmillan.

Warburton, C. (1948). 'Bank Reserves and Business Fluctuations', *Journal of the American Statistical Association*, 18: 547–58.

Weiner, S. E. (1992). 'The Changing Role of Reserve Requirements in Monetary Policy', *Federal Reserve Bank of Kansas City Economic Review*, 4/92: 45–62.

Whitesell, William (2003). 'Tunnels and Reserves in Monetary Policy' (working paper). Washington, DC: Board of Governors of the Federal Reserve System.

Wicksell, K. (1936). *Interest and Prices. A Study of the Causes Regulating the Value of Money*. London: Macmillan. (Translation of Geldzins und Güterpreise, *Eine Studie über die den Tauschwert des Geldes bestimmenden Ursachen*. Jena: Gustav Fischer, 1898.)

Wood, E. (1939). *English Theories of Central Banking Control (1819–1858)*. Cambridge, MA: Harvard University Press.

Woodford, M. (1995). 'Price Level Determinacy Without Control of Monetary Aggregates', *Carnegie-Rochester Conference Series on Public Policy*, 43: 1–46.

— (2001a). 'The Taylor Rule and Optimal Monetary Policy', *American Economic Review*, 91, 232–237.

— (2001b). 'Monetary Policy in the Information Economy'. Paper prepared for the Symposium on Economic Policy for the Information Economy, Federal Reserve Bank of Kansas City, Jackson Hole, Wyoming, 30 August–1 September.

— (2003). *Interest and Prices: Foundations of a Theory of Monetary Policy*. Princeton: Princeton University Press.

Woodworth, W. G. (1972). *The Money Market and Monetary Management* (2nd edn.). New York: Harper & Row.

Würtz, F. R. (2003). 'A Comprehensive Model of the Euro Overnight Rate' (ECB Working Paper Series, no. 207). Frankfurt am Main: ECB.

Young, R. A. (1973). *Instruments of Monetary Policy in the United States: The Role of the Federal Reserve*. Washington, DC: IMF.

Zvoll, J. H. von (1954). *Mindestreserven als Mittel der Geld- und Kreditpolitik* (Finanzwissenschaftliche Forschungsarbeiten, Neue Folge, H. 8). Berlin: Duncker & Humblot.

Index

Index